ASPCA®
Complete Guide to
cats

ASPCA®
Complete Guide to
cats

James R. Richards, D.V.M.

CHRONICLE BOOKS
SAN FRANCISCO

For Jesse and Seth

First published in 1999 by Chronicle Books LLC.

Fifteen percent of the royalty income of this book
goes to the ASPCA for humane programs.

Prepared and produced by
Chanticleer Press, Inc., New York.

Color separations by
Bright Arts, Hong Kong.

Printed and bound in Singapore.

Library of Congress Cataloging-in-Publication Data

Richards, James R., 1948–
    ASPCA complete guide to cats / James R. Richards.
        p.   cm.
    Includes index.
    ISBN 0-8118-1929-9
    1. Cats. 2. Cats—Health. 3. Cats—Diseases.
I. American Society for the Prevention of Cruelty to
Animals. II. Title.
SF447.R53   1999
636.8—dc21   99-12354
                                                          CIP

Distributed in Canada by Raincoast Books
9050 Shaughnessy Street
Vancouver, British Columbia V6P 6E5

10 9 8 7 6 5 4 3

        Chronicle Books LLC
        85 Second Street
        San Francisco, California 94105

        www.chroniclebooks.com

Contents

Foreword

When examining the bookshelves, one is struck by the sheer number of volumes dedicated to this mysterious yet most personable of animals, the cat. Seemingly every nuance of cat behavior, every subtle shade of coat color, every funny or touching story, and every aspect of care has been examined in the greatest detail by countless writers and experts. The choices are bewildering: specialized tomes about feline homeopathy, books on grooming the show cat, primers on how the cat's brain functions. And yet despite the domestic cat's enduring popularity as both pet and literary subject, owners are at a loss to find a single comprehensive volume that fully encompasses the basics of life with their cat.

The *ASPCA Complete Guide to Cats* at last provides all the practical information you'll ever need, clearly and completely explained and conveniently compiled in one book. This guide will help you determine whether a cat is the right pet for you and, if it is, which breed or type. It contains invaluable, easy-to-understand information on the training, care, and enjoyment of your new cat and addresses common feline health and behavior problems, first aid, and times when your cat will require special care.

Felis catus has been enchanting us for thousands of years, ever since the Egyptians first designated this elegant animal as sacred. Today, cats are the most popular house pet in North America. Why do some of us relate to cats and find pleasure in their company? And why do cats seem to find pleasure in ours? What is it about cats that so amuses and comforts us? The *ASPCA Complete Guide to Cats* touches on these and other important aspects of the human–cat relationship, making this book an eminently readable and enticing journey into the history and nature of our furry friends.

Throughout this guide you will be reminded that cats are not idle or casual possessions but faithful companions and valuable members of your family. Contrary to popular belief, cats do not fare well on their own; once you have your partner in hand, her health and happiness rest with you. Your cat will need a great deal of care; the *ASPCA Complete Guide to Cats* outlines your responsibilities and endeavors to help you meet them. Most cats must be spayed or neutered. They need regular veterinary checkups and lifesaving periodic vaccinations. Their diets should be under your control and not hit or miss. They have to be protected from their own curiosity and desire to wander and explore. In short, they have to be loved, cared for, and cared about by you.

Sharing your life with a cat is a wonderful thing. You will be taking on a friend for life. Make it a long, healthy, and happy life for your cat, and your own life is sure to improve in quality and perhaps in longevity as well.

Roger A. Caras, President Emeritus
American Society for the Prevention of Cruelty to Animals

How to
Use This Guide

The joys of owning a cat are many, but many, too, are the accompanying responsibilities. This book will prepare you for those joys and responsibilities
by carefully detailing both your cat's long-term requirements and his everyday needs. The following pages are designed to guide you through the entire process of owning a cat, from making the initial decision to bring a cat
into your life all the way to learning how to care for your pet in his old age.
Cats contribute an abundance of amusement and warmth to the lives of their
owners. This book focuses on the contributions *owners* must make to ensure
their cats' health and happiness, from the first day to the last.

The *ASPCA Complete Guide to Cats* is divided into four sections: How to
Bring a Cat into Your Life, Reference Guide to Cat Breeds, What Makes a
Cat a Cat?, and Taking Care of Your Cat. Together, they will tell you everything you need to know in order to have a successful and rewarding experience as a cat owner.

The first section, How to Bring a Cat into Your Life, begins with the
questions any potential cat owner needs to ask and offers sensible answers
for consideration. Important issues are broken down into segments offering
guidance through the process of deciding to get a pet, choosing the right
cat for your home and family, and preparing your home. This section provides you with vital information about what to expect as a new pet owner.

Section II, the Reference Guide to Cat Breeds, will interest you whether
you choose a purebred cat or a domestic shorthair (that is, a common house

cat). A brief introduction gives an overview of feline features—the common coat colors and patterns found in all cats, and other physical characteristics. A catalog of fifty modern cat breeds follows. Each entry provides information about personality, appearance, grooming and exercise needs, origins, and breed-specific health concerns.

Section III, What Makes a Cat a Cat?, begins with a brief history of the domestic cat, outlining how cats have come into our lives and homes through the millennia. The section continues with How the Cat Works, a primer on cat anatomy and senses that gives you the inside-out information on what makes the cat such an incredible work of natural art. Understanding Your Cat answers intriguing questions about cats: How smart are cats? How do they communicate? Why are some cats aloof and others so friendly? Features on cat courtship, cleanliness, sleep, and play behavior will help you better understand why your cats behave the way they do.

Section IV, Taking Care of Your Cat, is an essential guide to the daily care of your pet. The chapter Everyday Care for Your Cat covers feeding, litter box training, grooming, recognizing and solving behavior problems, and playing and traveling with your pet. Keeping Your Cat Healthy guides you through all the steps of home examinations and includes checklists and questions for visits to a veterinarian. Common Feline Health Problems outlines important ailments as well as possible treatments. Home Nursing follows with instructions for at-home health care. No pet owner ever wants to perform first aid on his cat, but knowing what to do in an emergency can vastly improve your cat's chances for recovery or even survival. The First Aid chapter walks you through procedures every cat owner should know. Last is the chapter The Beginning and End of Life: Times for Special Care, which begins with an overview of feline mating rituals, pregnancy, delivery, and postnatal care. The latter part of the chapter offers advice on caring for an elderly cat and dealing with a cat's death.

The appendices include five sections. The glossary defines cat-related terms used in this book. Important Telephone Numbers gives numbers for poison-control centers, veterinary help lines, and pet-loss hot lines. Breed Registries will help you find a breeder, register your cat with a breed registry, or obtain information on shows. Recommended Reading includes books on subjects beyond the scope of this guide. Finally, Resources lists Web sites and addresses of other organizations that may interest cat owners.

How to Bring a Cat into Your Life

Cats enrich our lives tremendously. They enchant us with their beauty and grace. They entertain us with their acrobatics. They intrigue us with their feline mystique. So well adapted to domestic surroundings and yet so closely resembling their wild relatives, cats bring the natural world right into our living rooms. Perhaps most of all, they give us companionship and comfort—holding a purring cat in your lap is a truly heartwarming sensation. Cats can even improve our health by keeping us calm and returning our love and affection. In exchange for all this, they ask relatively little and may seem to be fairly independent creatures, especially compared to dogs. But cat ownership is an important responsibility that we must take seriously every day of their lives. Not a day goes by that they don't need us to provide fresh food and water, to clean out the litter box, and to give —to even the most aloof feline—human contact and affection.

The cat–human relationship is one that too many people enter into lightly. As a result, many cats do not grow old in their first homes, and each year millions of cats are left to roam the streets or are relinquished to shelters (and too often put to death) because their owners have found them too much trouble or unsuited to their lifestyles. Countless other cats that stay in family settings are ignored or poorly cared for and so do not get to enjoy the benefits of a comfortable home life.

This section of the *ASPCA Complete Guide to Cats* is designed to help you ascertain whether you are ready to handle the responsibility of cat ownership, for it is not a relationship to enter into casually. You will find advice on how to choose a cat that will fit into your living situation and how to welcome that cat into your home as smoothly as possible. As a whole, this section is meant to help you plant the seeds necessary to ensure a happy, healthy, and long-lasting relationship between you and your cat.

Stroking a cat lowers your blood pressure.

Even the most aloof cats need human attention every day.

Cats that have been handled by humans as young kittens are more likely to be people-friendly as adults.

First Things First: Are You Ready for a Cat?

On a day-to-day basis, cats are fairly self-sufficient creatures, requiring little from their owners other than food, shelter, a clean place to eliminate—and, of course, regular stroking and nuzzling. Most cats don't need much grooming or bathing, and unlike dogs, they don't have to be walked several times a day. Cats are better adapted than dogs to spending time alone, which makes them ideal companions for people who work outside the home. Nevertheless, cat ownership is a long-term commitment. Many cats live fifteen to twenty years, and some live even longer. You must consider the impact a cat will have on your daily life. For the next decade or two you will have to change the cat box, vacuum up litter and cat hair, repair scratches in your upholstery, buy litter and food week after week, and pay for regular veterinary care.

Before you go ahead and adopt a cat, read the following questions and consider each one seriously. Involve everyone in your household in the decision-making process. If you have children, read Cats and Kids on page 32.

Is the timing right?

Before you get a cat, think about where your life is headed and how changes in your lifestyle might affect a pet. If you travel often, or if you expect to take a long trip in the near future, you must think about who will care for the cat while you are away. If you plan to move or to have a baby, consider that some cats will not adapt well to such changes. Keep in mind that many landlords do not welcome pets, which limits your housing choices if you move to a rented home.

How many hours do you spend away from home?

Many healthy adult cats can thrive in a busy, working household and are not terribly put out by the occasional weekend on their own, but it's not a good idea to leave any cat alone for twelve hours or more on a daily basis. Leaving a cat for long periods of time day after day can make her difficult to handle, unstable, and, depending on the cat, either excitable or aloof. The less companionship you provide for your cat, the less companionable she will be. Some people choose to adopt two cats to provide social interaction for one another, although owning more than one cat can present its own challenges (described in One Cat or More? on page 30).

When choosing a cat for a working household, keep in mind that kittens under four months of age should never be left alone for more than four hours at a time and that adolescent cats (six to eighteen months) need more attention during the day than adult cats—or else they may be more active at night when you are trying to sleep. If you are

Kittens have a way of getting into just about everything.

thinking about a purebred cat, you may want to stay away from the "oriental" breeds (including members of the Siamese family, as well as Burmese, Burmillas, Havana Browns, and Tonkinese), which tend to demand a lot of attention throughout their lives.

Do you travel often?

Most cats hate to travel, so it is likely you will have to hire a cat sitter when you plan to be away. Healthy, well-adjusted adult cats can usually be left alone with an automatic food-dispenser for a couple of days from time to time, but for extended absences you'll need someone to visit daily or even stay in your home. Cats left alone for long periods can get lonely, and those with fastidious litter box habits may begin to eliminate elsewhere when the box becomes more soiled than usual.

Do you have children?

Most cats get along well with children, especially if they are introduced to them as kittens. Some cats accept only the children in their own household, while other cats are uncomfortable around any child under the age of seven or so. For suggestions on finding a cat that can fit into a home with children and on teaching kids how to behave with cats, see Cats and Kids, page 32. In the Reference Guide to Cat Breeds (Section II, starting on page 65), breeds that are known to get along with children are marked with the Good with Kids icon 🐾. If you are bringing a new baby into a home where a cat already resides, see page 250.

Do you have other pets?

The same cats that do well with children—cats with relatively tolerant, adaptable temperaments—also tend to take relatively well to other pets in the home. If you plan to introduce a purebred cat into a home with other pets, consider the breeds in the Reference Guide to Cat Breeds that are marked with the Good with Kids icon 🐾. Cats that have been exposed to dogs early in life are more likely to accept canine housemates than cats that have never lived with a dog. If you have a resident adult cat, it will be easier to introduce a kitten rather than another adult. Most animal behaviorists advise against bringing an adult male cat into a home with a resident male cat.

Selecting a feline friend for your cat takes some careful consideration.

Smaller pets—guinea pigs, birds, rabbits, mice, fish—must be kept in a safe, enclosed environment if you plan to introduce felines into the mix. Cats are predatory by nature, so if you allow small animals to run free in the house, expect your cat to pursue them. Fish tanks provide an endless source of amusement to cats but must be securely placed and covered.

Can you afford a cat?

Your relationship with your cat may last for twenty years—and you're the one footing the bill. After you acquire the cat, you'll need to purchase basic household equipment, such as grooming tools, litter boxes, a cat carrier, and scratch posts. On a regular basis, you'll have to pay for food, litter, and veterinary care, including neutering (a one-time expense), routine examinations, vaccinations, dental care, and treatment for sickness or injury.

Facing page: Cats and dogs are not natural enemies and can live together quite harmoniously.

Are any members of your household allergic to cats?

Unfortunately, some people just can't live in a home with a cat. It's not fair to the person with allergies—or the cat—to initiate a relationship that will be cut short. You should make every effort before you decide to adopt a cat to be sure that no one in your household is allergic. Everyone should spend time handling the cat you have chosen in the environment in which it has been living.

Cat Allergies

When people with feline allergies are around cats, their eyes itch and swell, they sneeze incessantly, their sinuses become congested, and they may cough and even become asthmatic. Allergy sufferers feel miserable when they are exposed to an allergen, and there is very little that can be done to make them feel better.

It is not a cat's hair that affects most allergy sufferers, but a protein in the cat's saliva. It can take weeks for enough allergens to build up in your home to affect certain people, so all allergies don't make themselves evident right away. Some people with mild allergies can live with a cat by keeping the house very clean and bathing the cat several times a month.

The safest way to predict a problem is to have everyone in your household spend time at the homes of people with different types of cats, as well as at catteries and shelters. It is essential that they also spend time with the cat you have chosen to adopt in its home environment before you bring it home.

All cats lick themselves, so contact with the allergen, protein in the saliva, is inevitable in a house with cats.

Are you prepared for the mess?

If you have a cat, you will have cat hair on your clothes and furniture. Virtually all cats shed to some degree, although the Cornish Rex sheds relatively little and the hairless Sphynx does not shed but can leave oily spots on furniture. Longhaired cats leave more hair about than shorthaired cats. By brushing your cat regularly, you can minimize the amount of hair that winds up around the house—or that your cat spits up in hairballs. Another mess to think about is the litter box. Even the most fastidious cat needs constant human assistance in keeping this area clean. Cats can also cause minor destruction by using furniture to give themselves manicures. You can limit the damage by keeping their nails blunt and providing suitable scratch posts. If you have breakable objects, you might consider putting them out of the way— keeping in mind that cats are adept at getting into out-of-the-way places.

A virtually hairless cat, the Sphynx does not shed, but can leave oily spots on furniture.

There's more to selecting a pet cat than just picking the prettiest coat pattern.

Matchmaking:
Which Cat Is Right for You?

Once you've decided you are ready for a cat, you must consider whether you want a garden-variety house cat or a purebred, a kitten or an adult, a male or a female. Taking the time to find the right feline match is an essential step in becoming a responsible pet owner and the best insurance you can have for a long and happy life with your new companion.

Kitten or Adult?
While a kitten's cuteness is tough to resist, its rambunctious behavior can take a toll on a household. Kittens under four months of age tend to

climb objects rather than jump on them, which can result in shredded curtains and furnishings, not to mention legs. Although kittens are adept at climbing up drapery, they are often unable to get down and will hang on and screech until help arrives. Kittens under twelve weeks of age have a way of running headlong into danger—getting stuck behind or inside furniture and appliances, chewing electrical wires, and so forth. If a kitten or young cat does not have enough stimulation during the day, he is much more likely to be rowdy at night, perhaps when his human companions are sleeping—or trying to sleep. Getting two kittens instead of one usually helps to alleviate the nighttime crazies (see One Cat or More? on page 30).

Kittens often make ideal companions for children over age six or seven. Growing up together creates a strong bond, and a cat that is accustomed to a child's attention is less likely to run away and hide when playtime gets a little noisy.

If you already have adult cats in the home, feline household harmony may be more quickly restored if the new addition is a youngster rather than another mature cat. Another advantage to getting a kitten is that it is much easier to train kittens than adult cats to use a scratch post and to accept such grooming procedures as nail-trimming, tooth-brushing, and bathing.

If you decide on a kitten, plan to adopt one that is between

Healthy kittens naturally have a lot of energy.

Two kittens—littermates, ideally—can keep each other entertained when they've tired out their human companions.

eight and sixteen weeks old. Younger kittens will not have had sufficient time to become properly socialized with their littermates. You should not get a kitten younger than four months of age if you must be away from home during the day for more than four hours at a stretch.

While you cannot be sure how a kitten's personality will turn out, the temperament of an adult cat is already established. When you meet an adult, you can tell whether he is friendly or aloof, placid or active, noisy or quiet, high-strung or calm, short-tempered or tolerant. This makes it much easier to match your requirements to the right cat. If you have children, you can choose a calm, friendly adult cat rather than one that might hide from children or perhaps even strike out during play. Adult cats are usually better able than kittens to tolerate being alone much of the day.

Male or Female?

There is no shortage of cat lovers who vehemently claim that a male cat makes a better pet than a female, while an equal number take the opposing view. In truth, there is much individual variation from cat to cat, and a neutered cat of either sex can make a delightful family companion. Most animal behaviorists do not recommend introducing an adult male cat into a household that already has a resident male cat.

Domestic Shorthair or Purebred?

By far the most popular kind of cat is the basic nonpurebred domestic cat. In this book these cats are referred to as domestic shorthairs for the sake of simplicity, even though the common domestic cat's hair can be short, medium-length, or long. Domestic shorthairs come in a vast array of colors, patterns, hair types, and physical builds, and display an endless range of personalities. They usually have a broad genetic background that makes hereditary problems relatively unlikely. Domestic shorthairs are easy to acquire and are usually inexpensive, or even free. Most of the millions of unwanted cats that are euthanized each year are domestic shorthairs. If you adopt a domestic shorthair from a shelter, you may be saving its life.

Purebred cats are much less common than domestic shorthairs, comprising less than 10 percent of pet cats. There is much variation among individual cats, but purebreds generally are much more predictable in physical appearance and, to some extent, behavior and

A nonpurebred such as the cat on the right makes every bit as good a companion as a cat with a pedigree, such as the Ragdoll on the left.

personality—including such traits as companionability, liveliness, and talkativeness—than domestic shorthairs. Often when you buy a purebred you can see how the cat spent its first weeks and you can investigate its parents' health and temperament.

Certain breeds or lines of purebred cats are prone to hereditary conditions or other disorders associated with years of selective breeding. These can include deformities, such as those seen in the knees of some Devon Rex and Chartreux cats; medical conditions, like the kid-

Purebreds such as the Persian shown here tend to have more predictable personalities than nonpurebred cats.

ney problems that occur in some Persian and Abyssinian lines; or structural problems, such as those suffered by some Persians with extremely shortened faces. Kittens born and reared indoors in multiple-cat households, like the majority of purebred catteries, are more likely to be exposed to certain viruses, such as coronavirus, the cause of the fatal disease feline infectious peritonitis.

The cost of a purebred cat varies; a pet-quality cat can usually be purchased for 300 to 500 dollars, but a show-quality cat can cost double or triple that, and a highly desirable breeding animal can cost several thousand dollars. Peruse the Reference Guide to Cat Breeds to find the breeds that will best fit into your household.

Persians and other longhaired cats tend to need more grooming than shorter-haired cats.

Long Hair or Short?

Longer-haired cats tend to need more grooming from their owners than do breeds with short or medium-length hair. The hair of certain breeds, especially the Persian and Himalayan, mats quickly unless it is brushed daily. Longhaired cats are also particularly prone to forming hairballs (page 297). If you are a fastidious housekeeper and suspect that you'd hate having cat fur all over the place, you should probably stay away from a longhaired cat. Shorthaired cats shed, too, but less copiously than longhaired ones. Breeds that need to be groomed more than once a week are marked with the Special Grooming Needs icon ⌇ ✂ in the Reference Guide to Cat Breeds.

Even shorthaired cats shed and should be groomed at least once a week. Some breeds, including British Shorthairs like the one shown above, have dense coats and require grooming more than once a week.

Talkative or Quiet?

How vocal your cat is may be important to you. The meow of most cats is far from floor-rumbling (though it can be rather piercing in some), but a particularly talkative feline might annoy you or your neighbors. Some of the high-energy breeds (Balinese, Colorpoint, Cornish Rex, Javanese, Ocicat, Oriental, Russian Blue, Siamese, and Tonkinese) are the most vocal, with the Siamese topping

The Siamese is famous for its distinctive voice.

the list. At the other end of the spectrum are the Persians, quiet and calm cats that rarely make a sound. In the Reference Guide to Cat Breeds, very vocal breeds bear the Talkative icon .

High or Low Energy?

There is much variation in temperament among individual cats, especially domestic shorthairs. Purebred cats have somewhat more predictable behavioral tendencies, although breed type is far from the only consideration. Some of the most significant factors in shaping a cat's temperament are early learning experiences and the behavior of the cat's parents and other relatives. Not only do cats that are related share a

Birmans tend to have docile dispositions.

Abyssinians are very energetic and inquisitive—the prototypical curious cats.

common genetic background, but they also may have had similar environmental and socializing influences if they came from the same breeder. The age of a cat is also significant; all kittens and adolescents (cats from six to eighteen months of age) are high-energy felines. The activity levels of adults (three-plus years) tend to vary much more depending on breed and body type.

If you want a cat that is active and inquisitive, you may want to consider one of the breeds marked with the High Energy icon in the Reference Guide to Cat Breeds.

Cats that generally have quiet, calm personalities and prefer resting peacefully to strolling along a mantelpiece include the American Shorthair, Birman, British Shorthair, Exotic Shorthair, Himalayan, Korat, Persian, Ragdoll, and Selkirk Rex.

Other breeds tend to have temperaments somewhere in the middle, neither extremely active nor somnolent. See the Reference Guide to Cat Breeds for overviews of breed personality traits.

Cats brought up together tend to get along well and may bond more closely with one another than with their owner.

One Cat or More?

From the feline perspective, two can be a crowd. According to many animal behaviorists, being a singleton can be a fine situation for a cat. If you don't travel much or work long hours outside the home, you can give your cat all the social interaction and companionship she needs. If you are away a lot, two young cats (ages six to eighteen months) can keep each other entertained and are less likely to engage in destructive or otherwise irksome behavior (such as racing around the house in the wee hours). Experts do not recommend taking on kittens under four months of age if you will be away for more than four hours at a time, as such youngsters need lots of supervision. When adopting two cats, if you cannot get littermates, which is ideal, try at least to obtain kittens of the same age.

Cats raised together are likely to be close companions, get along well, and may not seek as much attention and affection from their owner as a single cat that bonds more tightly with the humans in the household. Generally, if a second cat is added later, the first cat will maintain a close relationship with the humans, while the second cat may be more cat-bonded.

How Many Cats Are Too Many?

How many cats can live comfortably in one household? The answer depends largely on the personalities of the cats involved. Sociable cats are better suited to life in a multiple-cat household than those with more solitary temperaments. Kittens that stayed with their littermates until twelve weeks of age are more likely to be sociable with other cats; orphan kittens are less likely to be cat-friendly.

If you are set on adopting two cats or kittens, it's best to get littermates or two cats that have shared a previous home.

When a household has too many cats, significant problems can arise. Cleanliness is more difficult to maintain, and infectious diseases become harder to control. The cats may become stressed and anxious, and you may see an escalation in behavior problems, such as aggression and urine marking. An overused, unclean litter box repels some cats, and you'll find those cats eliminating elsewhere.

Each cat in a multiple-cat household must have her own "personal space." Cat owners should provide a variety of resting places and observation posts, preferably at different heights, to allow each cat to choose that special place. Some cat owners install window-sill shelves for the cats to rest on or purchase a multi-level "cat condo."

Kittens will nap together, but adult cats need separate resting places.

Cats and Kids

When appropriately matched, cats and children are a joyous sight. When there is a mismatch, however, the situation can become unpleasant and stressful for the cat, the child, and the family. Before bringing a cat into a home with children, carefully review the following guidelines.

Discuss getting a cat with the children in advance, rather than bringing one home as a surprise gift. This way the children have a chance to express their fears and desires, and it is clear from the beginning that the cat will be a family member rather than a possession.

Cats and kids that grow up together often share a special bond.

Talk over the responsibilities (feeding, cleaning the litter box, grooming, playing) that each person in the family will take for the cat. All care given by children should be supervised by an adult who will be prepared to step in if the children do not uphold their responsibilities.

Choosing a Cat with Your Kids

The first thing to do is to decide what type of cat you want. Explain to your children that this must be done thoughtfully and that you may make several trips to animal shelters and breeders before settling on your new family pet.

If you have children under six or seven years of age, it's best to select a cat over six months old. Kittens younger than four months of age are especially fragile and less able to jump out of harm's way.

Cats that have grown up around kids tend to get along with them better than adult cats that haven't lived in a household with children. A kitten with parents that behave well around children is more likely to grow up to be a kid-friendly adult cat.

Since the temperament of an adult cat is already established, you can more reliably select a grown cat with a calm, tolerant personality. If you are set on adopting a kitten, look for one that had littermates and remained with them until at least eight to ten weeks of age, that was exposed to children beginning at about three weeks of age, and that had a healthy, sociable mother.

If you are adopting a cat from a shelter, you may find that little is known about your chosen cat's background. In such cases, look for a cat or kitten that moves toward people, not

Choose a kitten that doesn't mind being cradled on his back.

away from them, and that enjoys being held in all sorts of positions. Avoid cats that resort to using their claws and teeth too readily.

If you want a purebred cat, consider the breeds marked with the Good with Kids icon  in the Reference Guide to Cat Breeds. Certain breeds—including the American Shorthair, Birman, British Shorthair, and Maine Coon—tend to have relatively adaptable, laid-back temperaments and can generally be relied upon to take children in stride, as they do almost everything.

How to Treat a Cat

Teach your children to play gently with all cats. Even the most easygoing cat is likely to retaliate if his hair, tail, or ears are pulled. Instruct children to approach cats slowly. Show them how to pet a cat by stroking gently in the direction in which the fur grows and to avoid petting a cat's stomach, hips, and feet. Teach children how to hold a cat properly (see How to Hold a Cat, page 37), but don't let a child under age six or seven hold a cat unsupervised. Instruct your children to leave cats alone when they are eating, grooming, napping, or pursuing prey—or even thinking about pursuing prey, as when they are studying birds through the window, with tail swishing and body tensed. Encourage children to use toys with the cat rather than playing games with their hands.

For the cat's sake, as well as the child's, do not allow a young child to play with a cat unsupervised. Once a child is old enough to treat a cat gently and compassionately, he can be allowed to spend time alone with the cat.

Cats respond best to quiet, gentle handling.

Inside or Out?

The hazards of the outdoors—automobiles, dogs, rival cats, poisonous plants, infectious diseases, and fleas, to name but a few—are compelling reasons to keep cats exclusively indoors. It is especially important to keep declawed cats indoors, as they are poorly equipped to defend themselves or escape danger by climbing trees. Indoor cats are unquestionably safer and healthier than outdoor cats, and they make better household pets. They don't endanger birds and other wildlife or bring home fleas or dead animals, nor do they need frequent visits to the veterinarian to treat injuries sustained in scraps with rival cats.

Screened-in porches or specially constructed window enclosures allow indoor-only cats to sniff the fresh air, peruse the goings-on outside, and bask in the sun. By regularly changing the indoor environment, you can help keep your cat challenged; strategically situated empty cardboard boxes or plain brown shopping bags (minus the handles) can provide an old space with new interest.

If you want to allow outdoor excursions, let your cat out only in areas where escape is impossible and other animals cannot intrude. Do not let a

Access to windowsills gives indoor cats the pleasure of observing the world outdoors.

cat out in early morning or late afternoon through evening when birds and other small animals are feeding. Midday is safer for your local fauna. Although few cats will accompany their owners in the same way a dog would, with a little patience most young cats can be trained to at least tolerate a harness and go for an occasional stroll.

To turn an outdoor cat into an indoor cat: Confine the cat to one room (a bathroom is fine) with no absorbent surfaces except a litter box. Interact and play with her often. When she is using the box regularly, allow the cat some time out of the room under your supervision. When you are sure she will return to the box, give her more space, eventually allowing her to explore unsupervised. Provide access to sunny windowsills, play stalk-and-pounce games before meals, and watch carefully to be sure she doesn't dive for the door any time it's opened. Outdoor cats usually adapt to being indoor-only cats within several weeks.

Choosing Your New Pet

You've evaluated your home situation and your commitment. You've talked it over with everyone in your household. You've decided that you want to get a cat or kitten and have a pretty good idea as to what kind you'd like. Congratulations! You are about to begin what will most likely be a wonderfully fulfilling adventure in feline love and responsibility. Now you need to find just the right cat. Don't be in a rush. Remember, you may be living under the same roof with this animal for the next fifteen to twenty years. To be fair to everyone involved, do some research following the guidelines presented here and visit with at least a few different cats. If you are considering a purebred, carefully study the Reference Guide to Cat Breeds and decide which type of cat will best fit in with your household and lifestyle. Then confer with your family and make your choice.

A carefully selected pet will make a loving family companion.

How to Hold a Cat

Some cats like to drape themselves over your shoulder, surveying what's behind you; some prefer to be tucked up against your chest in an upright position; and a few even enjoy being cradled like a human infant. In time your cat will let you know exactly how he prefers to be held. There are cats that simply can't tolerate being held at all and will wiggle and squirm every second they are in your arms.

If you must handle a fractious cat, grab him by the scruff of the neck with one hand and place the other hand between the rear legs to restrain the hindquarters (illustration on page 318). Keep the legs facing away from your body. Use this safety hold only to move the cat a short distance—for example, from a veterinarian's exam table into a carrier. Never pick up a cat by the front legs or tail.

Pick up a kitten or cat by placing one hand on the chest right behind the front legs while using your other hand to gently scoop up the rear end and hindlegs.

Cradle the cat against your body.

Finding a Domestic Shorthair

Domestic shorthairs, or common house cats, far outnumber purebred cats. There are millions of these cats in the world, in all shapes and colors and with all kinds of personalities. The safest place to get a domestic shorthair is an animal shelter, where the staff knows the cats on hand and will work to find the right match for you. Adopting from a shelter is also a great way to provide a loving home to a homeless cat.

Adopting a Shelter Cat

Animal shelters are a convenient, reliable, and inexpensive means of acquiring a pet. Many shelters provide initial vaccinations, parasite treatment, and tests for fatal infections caused by feline leukemia virus and feline immunodeficiency virus, and offer free or low-cost neutering. Good shelters are clean and well ventilated and are staffed by caring, knowledgeable employees and volunteers.

If you find a cat that you like, see if the shelter has a private room where you and other members of your household, including children, can spend some time with the cat. Some cats are fearful when caged in a noisy, open area but will warm up if treated kindly in a separate, quiet room. Follow the guidelines given beginning on page 48 for evaluating a cat's health and temperament. Find out everything the staff knows about the cat's background, such as why he was given up and what his early environment was like. Before leaving with the cat, find out what shots and parasite treatments he has had and whether he has been neutered.

Shelters are a wonderful source of nonpurebred cats, like this handsomely patterned one.

Special-Needs Shelter Cats

The majority of cats available at animal shelters are even-tempered felines that have lost their homes through no fault of their own. Often a member of the household has developed an allergy, or the owners have moved, or an unplanned litter of kittens arrived. A small fraction of shelter cats may have been abused or neglected by a previous owner and need special care. These cats, which

Young kittens from unplanned litters swamp shelters in the summertime.

often wind up in shelters again and again, may be fearful or aggressive. They are not appropriate pets for a family, as the natural boisterousness of children may unnerve them and lead them to strike out. Only adults with cat-owning experience, who know how to read feline body language and know when to approach and when to retreat, should consider adopting such cats. A fearful young cat may blossom into a well-adjusted adult in a household with a stable, outgoing resident cat or a low-key older dog that either pays no attention to felines or has a healthy respect for them.

If you want to do a mistreated cat a real kindness by taking her into your home, you will have to go to extra lengths to make the relationship work. When you bring her home, confine her to one room along with a litter box, food, and water. Leave a cat carrier or a box in the room that she can use as a safe haven. Give her some time to hide out and assess her new home. Do not attempt to pull her out of hiding unless absolutely necessary. Spend time in the room to let the cat get used to you; read aloud, sing softly, and talk quietly to her. Don't approach her; let her come to you first. This may take just a few days or as long as several months.

A sociable cat that greets you at the front of his cage is a good choice for a family pet.

Finding a Purebred Cat

If you are looking for a pedigreed, or purebred, cat, the most important part of the process is finding a reputable breeder, one that breeds for physical and mental soundness and refuses to breed any animal that exhibits a poor temperament or hereditary problems.

A reputable breeder is unquestionably the best source for high-quality purebred kittens and cats. An excellent way to meet breeders is to visit a cat show, where you can see a wide array of breeds and also ask questions. Many veterinarians work with breeders and can offer advice. You can find breeders and show schedules in cat magazines, on the Internet, and by contacting cat registries (see the Breed Registries appendix). The Cat Fanciers' Association and the International Cat Association award certificates to catteries (cat breeding operations) that adhere to certain standards. Both programs are fairly new, so many high-quality catteries have not yet been certified.

Evaluating a Breeder

The first step in purchasing a healthy, well-socialized cat is to visit catteries to observe the environment. Overcrowding, bad odors, and a general lack of cleanliness (dirty food and water dishes and unclean litter boxes) are bad

Reputable breeders conscientiously breed cats not only to meet high aesthetic standards, which this lovely Burmese certainly achieves, but also physical soundness and good temperament.

signs. Observe and handle the cats to gauge their physical conditions and temperaments and take the opportunity to ask questions and evaluate the breeder.

Reputable breeders will, in all likelihood, check you out as you check them out. They will ask you about your lifestyle, your experience with cats, and why you want one of their cats. They may also ask you for references. If you have children, they may want to see them interact with the chosen animal before finalizing the adoption. A reputable breeder will expect you to request a tour of the area where the cats are kept (to make sure it is clean) and to ask questions.

The following questions will help you evaluate each breeder you visit. If a breeder doesn't answer questions willingly, you should assume she has something to hide. If you suspect that you have run across a breeder who is in it for the money rather than the health of the breed, do not support her business by buying one of her animals.

Before purchasing a purebred, find out if there are any breed-related health problems. Devon Rexes (above) are susceptible to hereditary baldness.

Can you tell me about the breed? What are its best and worst qualities? Good breeders are knowledgeable about their breed and will be enthusiastic about sharing their knowledge with you. No breed is without its quirks, and a reputable breeder will not hesitate to admit this. A responsible breeder will want you to understand both the pros and cons of the breed so that you will be prepared for what lies ahead. Be sure to ask about the breed's temperament, grooming needs, and any health problems to which it may be prone.

How long have you been breeding this particular type of cat? The most experienced breeders will often have the best litters and will have a number of references at the ready. However, sometimes newer breeders are more careful and enthusiastic, although they do not yet have a track record.

How often do you breed your cats? For health reasons, most female cats should not be bred more than once every nine months to a year between the ages of one and seven years. Those who breed their cats more often may be more interested in financial profit than in feline health.

Do you show your cats? Breeders who show their cats will be proud to show you awards their cats have won. Remember that awards and certificates alone are not evidence of a breeder's reputability. Make sure that the breeder is concerned not only with characteristics that will win awards but also with the overall health and temperament of the cat.

Are the cat's parents or other relatives on the premises? Usually just the mother will be present with the litter; the father has often been involved only for the mating. Ask about the father's temperament and ask to see pictures. Observe the other cats on the premises.

If socialized properly, the kittens will develop temperamental characteristics similar to those of their relatives.

Do you screen for hereditary diseases? Which ones? Ask whether the breeder screens for hereditary diseases, such as polycystic kidney disease in Persians and Himalayans. Breed-related health problems are noted in the Reference Guide to Cat Breeds; look for a ① symbol in the entries for the breeds that interest you. Make sure the cattery is free of the deadly feline leukemia virus and feline immunodeficiency virus by asking to see veterinary test results. Find out how often the breeder tests his cats.

Are your kittens examined and vaccinated by a veterinarian? Although many breeders vaccinate their litters themselves, the kittens should be seen by a veterinarian who can also examine them for congenital problems, such as heart defects, deafness, and eye problems. The kittens should receive their first vaccinations at six to eight weeks of age.

How long will I have to wait for a kitten? Responsible breeders often do not have extra kittens on hand. They breed only at specific times of year or after they have commitments from prescreened buyers. They sell their kittens at eight to sixteen weeks of age. Kittens younger than eight weeks will not have been properly socialized.

May I have the names of people who have purchased cats from you? Confident breeders should be willing to give you the names and telephone numbers of a few individuals with whom they've place

When choosing among a litter of purebred kittens, such as these Turkish Vans, you will usually have the opportunity to meet the mother cat as well.

cats in the past. Call at least two or three people and inquire about the health and temperament of their cats. Ask how responsive the breeder has been to any problems.

What kinds of instructions will you provide when I take the kitten home? A concerned breeder will give you information about feeding and grooming, and tips specific to the health and happiness of your particular breed. Be sure to find out what brand of food and litter the cat is accustomed to.

Expect a responsible breeder to want to see how your children treat a cat or kitten.

Do you provide a contract? You should insist on a contract. It should have a health guarantee and provisions for returning the cat to the breeder if necessary. You may be required in the contract to have a veterinary examination performed within a certain period after the purchase and to have the cat neutered. A reputable breeder will offer you another kitten or a refund if your veterinarian diagnoses a serious problem within the specified period. If you are buying the offspring of a show cat, you may be asked to sign a co-ownership agreement with the breeder; it is wise to have a lawyer review such a contract.

Do you have "papers" for the cats you sell? You should receive pedigree documentation and health and vaccination records. The pedigree documentation (a diagram of the family tree) will list your cat's ancestors for three or more generations, including awards they have won. Breed association registrations indicate only that the cat is the product of a registered purebred male and female of the same breed; it says nothing about the quality of the cat you are buying. The breeder should provide you with an application to register the kitten or a certificate to transfer ownership of a named and registered cat to you.

Other Sources for Cats

Animal shelters and reputable breeders are the best sources for obtaining healthy, well-socialized cats that will fit in with your particular household. People do get wonderful family pets from other sources, but most of these are hit or miss. Some promote poor breeding practices, while others encourage the overpopulation that results in the killing of millions of animals yearly.

Stray Cats

Although some of the best feline friends are homeless cats that wander into loving homes, it is always risky to adopt a street cat. Strays often have serious medical or behavioral problems that can take time and money to correct. Before handling a stray animal, find out from the local health department what the risk of rabies is in your area. Never handle a vicious animal.

If you find a stray cat and want to keep him, isolate him from your other pets and take him to a veterinarian. If he is intact, have him neutered as soon as possible. If you find a stray cat that you do not want to keep, take the cat to a shelter or animal control agency. If you want to take a more active role, file a found report with animal .control, run advertisements in local publications, post "Found Cat" signs, and take the cat to a veterinarian for a checkup. If no one claims the cat, start trying to find him a new home; it may take as long as a year to

A stray cat can make a fine companion, but be sure to have any stray animal checked out by a vet as soon as possible.

find a home for an adult cat. Some neighborhood cat rescuers may be fine sources for stray cats, as long as they take the cats to the veterinarian and have them neutered and de-wormed before adoption.

Feral Cats

Stray cats that were once pets can make suitable family pets. Feral cats, which have never been tamed or lived with humans, usually do not. Such cats are never entirely predictable, and often, after months of socialization, may still strike out whenever they feel anxious. Often unneutered, feral cats can invade a yard and home, urine mark, and pick fights with resident cats. If you are bothered by feral cats, contact animal control or a local rescue

Feral cats usually do not make suitable pets for households with children.

center. Keep your pet's vaccinations up to date and keep him away from feral cats. If you are interested in helping feral cats, see the Resources appendix for organizations to contact.

Pet Shops

Many cats sold in pet shops are the products of kitten mills, wholesale operations that breed animals in large numbers purely for economic gain, often with little concern for the behavioral or physical health or happiness of either the parents or the offspring. It is not impossible to get a healthy cat from a pet shop, but in general it is a bad idea to support shops that sell animals (as opposed to stores that sell pet supplies and sometimes help shelters or rescue groups promote adoption of animals needing homes).

Commercial Breeders

Large-scale commercial catteries that breed so frequently they always have animals for sale may not provide all animals with the daily one-on-one attention they need and deserve. As a result, kittens that come from these sources often suffer from medical and behavioral disorders. Some of these breeders supply pet stores; others sell directly to the public.

Backyard Breeders

Although there are many reputable breeders who run their businesses out of their homes, it is not a good idea to obtain cats from "backyard breeders," people who are not conscientious about their breeding programs and are more concerned with financial gain than with the health and well-being of their animals. A few red flags: breeders who are not knowledgeable about their breed; who do not check you out as well as you check them out; who are not active in cat associations or local animal welfare organizations; who do not register their cats; or who keep their cats isolated in basements, garages, or other unpleasant spaces.

Free to a Good Home

Finding a kitten through newspaper ads or posted signs may be slightly less of a gamble than rescuing a stray off the street, but it is still an unreliable means of obtaining a family pet. Often, kittens advertised in this way are the result of an unplanned pregnancy (this is one reason why it is so important for all cat owners to have their pets neutered), and sometimes the father is not even known, which makes it difficult to assess what the kittens' adult temperaments might be.

There are, of course, situations in which someone cannot keep a healthy cat (perhaps someone in the home has developed an allergy to the cat) and will advertise its availability. If you are interested in adopting a family cat, speak with the owner, find out the cat's routine and habits, observe her in her home, and call the veterinarian that has been caring for her. If you like the cat and feel that she will fit into your household, consider going forward with the adoption.

Choosing a Healthy Cat

Regardless of what kind of cat you wish to acquire, choosing a healthy individual with an agreeable temperament is important. While unhealthy and unsocialized cats need homes, too, they are likely to place greater demands on an owner (in terms of both time and money) and may never be able to develop the kind of comfortable relationship sought by many cat owners.

Judging Temperament

Look for a cat that moves toward people rather than away and that enjoys being held in all sorts of positions. Avoid cats that bite or

Healthy, well-socialized kittens are active and people-oriented.

extend their claws too readily. If you are trying to choose from a litter of kittens, refrain from choosing one that is inactive or avoids people. Normal kittens are inquisitive and active (those that are not may have a physical disorder), and well-socialized cats tend to make the best pets.

Judging Physical Condition

The cat's body should be neither too skinny nor too potbellied; a slight potbelly is usually normal in a kitten but may be a sign of an intestinal parasite infection or a more serious disease. The coat should be shiny and healthy looking, with no bald spots, and the eyes and nostrils should be free of discharge. Even if your new cat seems to be quite healthy, be sure to have her examined by a veterinarian as soon as possible, ideally before bringing her into your home. It is especially important to ascertain whether the newcomer is carrying any infections if you have other cats.

A healthy cat has bright eyes and an alert expression.

A shiny, full coat is a sign of good health.

Preparing Your Home
for Your New Cat

Picking up and bringing home a new cat or kitten is an exciting and happy event for people, but it is a stressful time for the newcomer being whisked away by a stranger from a familiar environment. Prepare for his arrival ahead of time by cat-proofing your home, shopping for essential items, and setting up a space for him. Make plans to pick him up at the be-

Thoughtful preparation for the arrival of your new pet is a vital step toward years of happy, healthy companionship.

ginning of the weekend or some other time when you'll be able to spend a few days helping him acclimate to his new surroundings. Make an appointment to bring the cat to the veterinarian within twenty-four hours of his arrival.

Setting Up a Space

Prepare a spare bedroom or bathroom to serve as the new cat's temporary home; confining him to a small area will be less overwhelming than giving him free rein over the entire house right away. Place all the necessary supplies—litter box, food and water, scratch post, and a warm, soft place to sleep—in the room, and set up some safe places to hide, such as a cat carrier or a cardboard box laid on its side. Place the litter box in a location that is quiet yet easy to reach, and don't put it too close to the feeding and drinking area.

Cat-Proofing Your Home

Even indoor-only cats do not live free of risk. Kittens and younger cats are more apt to be injured indoors because of their inquisitive and rambunctious natures, but even older, more experienced cats are vulnerable to injury or poisoning. Critically examine the areas where your cats will live—and the nature and habits of your individual cat, once you have him—and take measures to cat-proof your home.

Prevent access to range-top burners, wood stoves, electrical cords, poisonous houseplants, and household medicines and chemicals (see Household Poisons, page 330, and Poisonous Plants, page 328).

High-Rise Syndrome

Cats can tumble from apartment windows either by slipping out accidentally during a catnap or falling while trying to nab an insect or a bird. Injuries sustained in such falls have become so common that a term has been created to classify them: "high-rise syndrome."

Cats have been known to survive falls from great heights, partially because of their ability to right themselves in midair but also because of their tendency to "spread eagle" their limbs, so that when they hit, the force is more evenly distributed over the whole body rather than just in the limbs. But all too often their injuries—broken jaws and front legs, and internal bleeding, for example—are severe, disabling, and painful, if not fatal.

Feline poise and agility notwithstanding, many cats are seriously injured in falls from windows and fire escapes.

Keep the clothes dryer door shut when it's not in use, and carefully check inside before starting it.

Remove such enticing but potentially deadly articles as rubber bands, plastic bags, string, yarn, tinsel and other holiday decorations, staples, needles, pins, and buttons. Even lengths of dental floss left in an open wastebasket pose a hazard for curious cats. Use a waste receptacle with a tight-fitting cover for disposing of cat-dangerous items.

Keep all windows closed or install screens made of sturdy material (metal screen wire is much better than plastic). Make sure screens are in good repair and that they are securely fastened. Window guards provide additional security by keeping screens from popping out when leaned on.

Keep the toilet lid down; very young kittens have been known to climb up shower curtains and then fall off into the toilet bowl.

Keep doors to the garage closed at all times. If your cat has access to your car, make sure you know his whereabouts before you start the engine. Cats sometimes climb up under the hood of a car to sleep and are then injured by the engine when the car starts.

Place bird cages, fish tanks, and other small pet homes in secure, well-anchored places, and be sure they are tightly closed or covered. Do not give your cat the opportunity to express his natural predatory instincts at the expense of your other pets.

The best way to keep cats from sharpening their claws on the furniture is to provide an alternative scratching surface.

Shopping List

A cat's needs are fairly humble, but there are some essential supplies you'll want to have prior to your cat's arrival.

Food and Water Dishes

You will need separate food and water bowls. They should be easy to clean, with a wide top, low sides, and a base broad enough to prevent tipping. Stainless steel, glass, or ceramic dishes are best; plastic bowls may cause skin irritation. Some cats don't like to place their face into a bowl so narrow that it bends their whiskers.

Food

Buy a supply of the same brand of food the cat has been eating. After a week or two, you can begin to switch to a different food by combining the two kinds, then gradually decreasing the amount of the old food and increasing the new. See page 234 for information on choosing a cat food.

Scratch Posts

Scratch posts come in a number of different styles and materials, including sisal, nubby fabric, and even natural wood. The basic vertical post works well for most cats. It must be tall enough to allow the cat to stretch his entire length, with a base wide and sturdy enough to prevent tipping. For cats that prefer to scratch on a horizontal surface, place corrugated cardboard scratch boxes or pieces of carpeting turned underside out (so that the sisal is facing up) flat on the floor.

Cat Carriers

A cat carrier is an essential piece of equipment, whether you use it for extensive travel or only for trips to the veterinarian. Choose a sturdy carrier that is easy to clean and open and that has no sharp, protruding edges on the inside. It's easier to get a cat in and out of a carrier that opens on the top or side—not the end—but these carriers are hard to find and are not approved by airlines. A hard plastic, rectangular carrier placed under a table can be left open with some bedding inside to make a comfortable den. Soft luggage-type carriers are light and comfortable to carry and allow a little extra room for the cat who is traveling on-board an airplane with her owner.

Help your cat get used to the carrier when she is a kitten. Leave the carrier out at home, and keep the door open so your cat can climb inside to explore. Put a favorite toy and a soft item inside for her to rest on. Feed her in the carrier from time to time. Eventually, she will regard the carrier as a safe haven rather than a scary cage.

Litter Boxes and Filler

Many cats dislike covered boxes because they tend to trap odor inside, and the hood may prevent them from assuming a comfortable position; other cats appreciate the privacy afforded by covered boxes. Such boxes also help keep dogs and children out. Boxes that automatically sift litter may frighten some cats. Plastic litter liners make cleaning the box easier for the owner, but urine may seep through scratched-up liners and allow odors to build up. Some cats dislike boxes with liners and will take their business elsewhere.

When choosing a litter box, simpler is usually better.

There are many types of litter available, but most cats seem to prefer the unscented, clumping style. However, if your new cat is already accustomed to a different type, it's best to stick with that for a while (see page 240 for advice on switching litter types). Any type of sturdy litter scoop is fine.

Toys

Cats get the most fun out of toys that can move in a fashion that mimics the motions of prey. Some of the most popular toys resemble a fishing pole with line and lure attached; few cats can resist at least a few pops as the lure swings by or scurries along the ground. These kinds of interactive toys are especially appreciated by more mature cats. Objects that just lie around the house become much less interesting to cats as they get older.

Kittens can find amusement in just about anything.

Never permit your cat to play with yarn, string, rubber bands, ribbon, or Christmas tree tinsel. Objects such as these can become lodged under the tongue or in the stomach or intestines, creating serious problems and possibly leading to death.

Grooming Equipment

All cat owners need a flea comb (a fine-toothed metal comb available from most pet supply stores), a nail trimmer, a styptic pencil or powder (to stop bleeding in case of nail trimming mishaps), a special toothpaste for cats—don't use human toothpaste!—and a cat toothbrush or finger brush (your veterinarian can supply one). For a long-haired cat you need a wide-toothed comb, a stiff natural bristle brush or pin brush (a brush with metal bristles), and a pair of blunt-tipped scissors for removing hair mats. For a shorthaired cat, a slicker brush (a fine-toothed brush for removing loose hair) or a rubber brush should suffice. See Grooming Your Cat (page 241) for grooming, bathing, nail trimming, and tooth brushing instructions, as well as photographs of equipment.

Identification

Even indoor cats can slip out a door unnoticed and become lost, so it is important for all cats to have some sort of identification. The simplest form is a metal identification tag hanging from a collar. Your name, address, and telephone number, as well as those of the veterinarian, should be on the tag. Another option is a metal stud engraved with identifying information that your veterinarian attaches to your cat's ear, like an earring. Yet another option is a microchip implant containing an identification number. Check with your veterinarian or local animal shelter to find out if microchip scanners are in place in your community. If your cat gets lost, check shelters regularly, call outside at mealtimes, place posters with the cat's photograph (make one ahead of time and keep it in your feline first aid kit) around the neighborhood, and check with your neighbors.

Cats will nap wherever they find a comfortable spot.

Bedding

There is little need to purchase a special cat bed because your cat will pick her own favorite sleeping spots anyway. If you choose to buy a cat bed, make sure it is easy to clean. The cat is most likely to use it if you place it in an area where she has already chosen to sleep. If you don't want your cat to sleep on your bed or a child's bed, keep the bedroom door closed from the outset.

An Urgent Reminder:
Have Your Cat Neutered

It is very important to have your cat neutered at the first safe opportunity, which may be as early as eight to fourteen weeks of age, to help curb feline overpopulation. Far too frequently, cats reproduce before their owners get around to having them neutered. Millions of homeless cats are euthanized every year, largely because there are too many cats and not enough homes.

The sexual behaviors of intact adult cats can be extremely unpleasant; yowling and urine marking are to be expected in both sexes, while males will also roam and fight with other cats. When in heat, female cats ovulate in response to mating, which means that there are always eggs available for fertilization, and mating almost always results in pregnancy. Neutering of a female cat (also called spaying) involves removing the ovaries and uterus. A neutered female is less likely to develop breast cancer and is protected from uterine and ovarian cancers. Neutering (removing the testicles) of a male

Have your cats neutered so that you do not contribute to the feline overpopulation problem.

prevents testicular cancer. Regardless of their age when neutered, male cats do not become more prone to urethral obstructions after their operation.

Neutered cats require fewer calories to maintain their body weight than intact ones; if they continue to eat the same amount they ate before their operation, they will put on weight. They do not, however, get lazy or lose their original personalities.

To locate a low-cost neutering facility in your area, contact the local shelter or humane society or call 1-800-248-SPAY.

Welcoming Your New Family Member

The big day has arrived—it's time to bring your new family member home. Prepare for the arrival ahead of time (see page 50), so that you can devote the day to the cat's peace of mind. Remember to make plans to take him to the veterinarian for a checkup within the first twenty-four hours; meanwhile, keep him isolated from other cats.

Advance preparation allows you to concentrate on giving the newcomer the comfort he needs.

Picking up Your New Cat

It's easy to get swept up in the excitement when picking up a new pet, so it's a good idea to prepare a checklist reminding you to get the following information from the breeder or shelter: a list of the vaccinations, parasite treatments, and any special tests the cat has had; the name and telephone number of the veterinarian who has examined the cat; the name of the food the cat has been eating; the type of litter he's been using; pedigree and breed association papers, if applicable; and the shelter or breeder contract.

Bring along a cat carrier lined with a soft, absorbent, washable material. Either place the carrier on the car seat and secure it with a safety belt or put it on the floor of the car.

Easing the Transition

Most cats will settle in comfortably if given some time to acclimate to the new environment. This may take from several days to a couple of weeks for an adult cat, considerably less time for kittens. Place your new cat in the room you have prepared in advance (see page 50) and keep the door closed for a few hours, or until she calms down a bit. If she meows for attention, go in and give her some, but if she doesn't, just leave her alone. If she's the only cat in the household, after she's relaxed let her explore her new home on her own. You don't need to keep her in the confined area any more, but do keep it accessible. If your home is large and the cat is less than four months old, keep her in one or two rooms when you can't watch her. You'll need to continue to do this until she's about four months old to be sure she doesn't stray too far from the litter box and start eliminating elsewhere. If there are other resident cats

Set up a litter box in a quiet area and give your new kitten some time to acclimate herself.

or dogs, keep them apart at first. See specific instructions (on page 60) for introducing the newcomer to the resident pets.

Embarking on a new routine in an unknown environment can be particularly daunting to an adult cat. It is not unusual for a mature feline to deal with new surroundings by going into hiding and coming out only to eat or use the litter box when you are asleep or away. Don't force a relationship. Continue to provide food and water on a schedule, but otherwise ignore the cat until she begins to seek some attention from you.

Introducing a New Cat to a Resident Cat

Even if your cat is friendly to you and quickly accepts other people, you cannot assume that she will be as accepting of other cats. Most animal behaviorists agree that if the resident cat is a male, the new cat should be a female, and that introducing a kitten rather than another adult is preferable. Bringing in a second cat is not wise if you already own an older cat (ten years of age or older) who has never had feline companionship.

A new cat will almost invariably meet with antagonistic behavior from the others. Expect hissing, swatting, chasing, and actual attempts to drive the newcomer away. The social balance of even long-term residents can be upset; cats that previously got along well may begin to fight with each other, and other behavior problems, such as urine marking, may develop. Be sure to pay extra attention to the resident cat or cats during this time of social upheaval, just to reassure them and ease their anxiety. Expect them to be somewhat withdrawn. It may take as long as a few months for two adult cats to learn to get along. If aggression, house soiling, fasting, or withdrawal persist, it may be kindest for you to find another home for the new cat.

In most cases, following the steps described on the next page will help ease a new cat into the existing hierarchy.

A kitten is the wisest choice for an additional pet in a home with a cat already in residence.

Keep the Cats Apart   Isolate the newcomer from the other cat or cats in a spare bedroom or bathroom. (If the resident cat's litter box is in your only bathroom, move it just outside the bathroom several weeks before the new cat comes; this way the path to the box is the same, but the cat gets there faster.) Provide food, water, and a litter box for the new cat, and keep the door shut. Pay lots of attention to the new arrival, as well as to the residents. The strangers will be aware of each other's presence, but keeping them physically apart will prevent altercations.

Introduce the Cats Gradually   After at least two weeks of isolation, place the newcomer in a cage or carrier in the doorway of his room, or behind a screened barrier, or crack the door slightly, making sure the cats can't push it open the rest of the way. For the next several days, either move the carrier from room to room or allow the newcomer to explore the house periodically while the resident is confined to a separate room. This allows the new cat to establish his presence but does not give the cats the opportunity to fight. You may want to feed the cats simultaneously near each other, with the newcomer in his carrier or behind the screened barrier. This gives them a pleasurable experience to associate with their early encounters.

Hold a Meeting   Feed both cats; when they're satiated and feeling a little lazy, take the newcomer out of the carrier or remove the barrier and let the cats find one another. Make sure exits to other rooms are open so the cats can escape if necessary. Expect some sniffing, and even some hissing, growling, and swatting. Don't try to intervene unless it looks as if bloodshed is imminent, in which case you should separate the cats with a thick blanket and carefully place the newcomer back in his own area. Go back to the first step, and try another meeting in a week or so. Repeat the process until fighting no longer occurs.

Until you're certain that your dog and your new cat are safe together, keep them separated when left alone.

Introducing a New Cat to a Resident Dog

If you are bringing a cat into a household with a dog, isolate the new-comer for at least a week so that the cat can become comfortable with her new surroundings before meeting the dog. During the first meet-ing, keep the dog leashed and make sure the cat has a clear avenue of escape, preferably over a gate into a safe haven that the dog does not have access to. While dogs and cats do not actually have a natural antagonism to one another, a dog's instinct may be to chase anything that runs, while the cat's nature tells her to run from something bigger that is chasing her. Do not allow fighting, as the consequences of a dog-and-cat fight can be serious.

Don't force the relationship. Over time, a peaceful coexistence usually develops. For the first month or so, keep cat and dog separated when you can't be home to supervise, even if they seem to be getting along well together. If you want to have both a dog and a cat under the same roof, it is often easiest to raise them together from puppyhood and kittenhood.

Now What?

You've chosen a cat, prepared your household, and brought the cat home. You've introduced the cat to her new surroundings. Now what? Turn to Section III, What Makes a Cat a Cat? (beginning on page 171), to read about how a cat works from the inside out. Turn to Section IV, Taking Care of Your Cat (beginning on page 231), to learn about the daily care that will keep your new companion happy and healthy for a long time to come.

This American Shorthair kitten has something to say. See page 214 for information on how cats communicate.

II

Reference Guide to Cat Breeds

Once you have read Section I of this book and have decided to bring a cat into your life, you will be faced with several more decisions. Do you want a domestic shorthair as a family pet or a purebred cat for showing? Do you want to adopt a kitten or an adult cat from a shelter or obtain a specific breed from a breeder?

Most people's cats are not purebred; in fact, 90 percent of pet cats in North America—be they tabby or solid, tortoiseshell or bicolor, orange or black—are called domestic shorthairs, a blanket term applying to nonpurebred house cats, some of which could also be called domestic medium-hairs or domestic longhairs.

It is quite likely that in your search for the perfect cat you will choose a domestic shorthair. However, domestic shorthairs have much in common with purebred cats. The Reference Guide to Cat Breeds therefore begins with an overview of feline features shared by all domestic cats. This overview gives you a basic vocabulary for describing what your cat looks like and explains why it looks that way. It also describes where various coat colors and patterns originated and how they have evolved. Photographs of these common feline coat patterns and colors, and the classic shapes of heads, eyes, and bodies, will give you clues to the ancestry of your cat, whether purebred or not.

Following the Overview of Feline Features are entries that introduce fifty cat breeds. If you are looking for a cat with a very specific appearance and personality, or a cat to show, you may want to acquire one of the breeds. Each entry provides information about the breed's origins, its appearance and temperament, any special grooming needs, its energy level, whether it is a lap cat or prefers to keep some distance, its vocal qualities, and other traits.

With all this information in hand, you can return to Section I for help in finding a breeder, assessing a cat's health and temperament, preparing for the cat's arrival in your home, and the other delightful details of bringing a cat into your life.

Overview of Feline Features

Cats attended to their own breeding until about a hundred years ago, when people got involved. By then, nature had created numerous varieties of coat colors, patterns, textures, and lengths that have served cats well for millennia. From this rich genetic soup cat breeders have developed the fifty or so contemporary cat breeds, commonly known as purebred cats, by purposefully selecting, "capturing," and refining traits already contained within the feline gene pool.

Though nonpurebreds are often called "mixed breeds," these cats are not "mutts" or mixes of different breeds, but rather are the basic, or "pure," cats from which come all the characteristics seen in the purebreds. ("Mixed breed" is a more apt term for dogs because almost every random-bred pooch shows the stamp of one or more purebreds, and there is not a single basic type of nonpurebred dog.) The virtually limitless array of colors and patterns seen in domestic shorthairs—among them the familiar tabby, tortoiseshell, calico, black, white, and piebald—does not signify differences of breed but simply of appearance. The purebreds are for the most part carefully contrived variations on the common domestic shorthair theme.

Even the so-called natural breeds—generally cats of ancient origin that evolved in a particular geographical location, such as the Persian and the Manx—have been refined and altered through years of selective breeding. The Persian's body is much more compact and its face much flatter than it was a hundred years ago, and the body of the Manx has also become shorter.

It is fitting, then, to introduce the breeds with a review of the most common features, coat colors, and patterns seen in all cats, from the humblest house cat to the most exalted champion show cat.

Original Cats

Every domestic cat alive today most likely traces its heritage back to the tabby-patterned African Wildcat, a light brown shorthaired cat with black stripes. When cats were first domesticated in ancient Egypt, they all probably had tabby-patterned coats. Over the thousands of years since, naturally occurring mutations—spontaneous, accidental alterations in genetic material—created variations in color and pattern. Such mutations are the engine that drives evolution itself, producing variety within a species and occasionally giving rise to an entirely new species. Without mutations, all cats would still look like tabbies.

Despite the incredible variety in colors and patterns seen in cats today, all domestic cats carry their ancestors' tabby genes. Cats that don't look like tabbies have other (mutated) genes that merely prevent the tabby coat pattern from showing. In other words, all domestic cats are genetically tabbies.

Facing page: The African Wildcat *(Felis lybica)* is probably the ancestor of all domestic cats. It is the most common wildcat in Africa.

Coat Palettes

There are two basic palettes of feline coat colors: deep colors and dilute colors. The basic deep colors are black, orange (called red by cat fanciers), dark brown (chocolate), and light brown (cinnamon), and are seen when color is evenly distributed along the shafts of the cat's hairs.

When the same color is unevenly distributed in microscopic clumps along the hair shafts, the cat has a dilute-colored coat of gray (commonly called blue) instead of black, cream instead of red, lilac or lavender instead of dark brown, or fawn instead of light brown. It typically takes selective breeding to produce cats that are solid-colored in most of these shades except black and gray. Non-purebred cats tend to have a combination of colors and markings.

Red/Orange
(deep)

Cream
(dilute)

Black
(deep)

Gray/Blue
(dilute)

Dark Brown
(deep)

Lilac
(dilute)

Light Brown
(deep)

Fawn
(dilute)

How the Tiger Cat Got Its Stripes

Wildcats display the same array of tabby markings seen in domestic cats, so it seems evident that the process of natural selection had a hand in designing these coat patterns by favoring mutations that enhance an animal's chances for survival. In the wild, cats catch their meals by lying in wait, assessing their prospects, then charging and pouncing on their prey. While waiting for dinner to appear, cats need to be nearly invisible to their prospective entrée. The habitats of different wildcats provide excellent clues about where each domesticated tabby pattern might have proved most successful.

For example, the tiger hunts at the edge of the forest, where tall grasses and reeds create vertical shadows alternating with lighter vertical bands where sunlight reaches the ground; the original mackerel tabby cat, the African Wildcat, was domesticated along the banks of the Nile, where similar shadow patterns prevail. The lion and the cheetah are savannah cats that, in their different ways, blend in with dry grass; the ticked-tabby-patterned cat and the spotted tabby were discovered on open plains in Africa and India. Leopards are forest cats whose blotchy markings blend in with the dappled shade cast by leafy trees; classic tabbies were first documented in deeply forested northern Europe.

It may have taken a spontaneous mutation to produce each new kind of tabby, but the continuation of each new coat pattern probably depended on whether it served its owner well as a "hunting outfit." Cats that survived longer had a better chance of reproducing and passing their advantageous markings on to subsequent generations.

The cheetah's bold spots serve as camouflage in savannah grasses.

Coat Patterns

Solid-Colored Cats

All cats have genes for the tabby pattern, whether they look like tabbies or not. For a cat to show its true tabby stripes (or spots), it must receive at least one gene from one of its parents for the agouti, or banded, hair type. Cats that appear uniform in color have coats composed almost entirely of solid-colored nonagouti hairs because they have inherited from both parents the recessive gene for unbanded hairs. But the tabby genes that all cats carry can still exert some influence, even in solid-colored cats. When viewed in bright light, a solid-colored cat may show a faint tabby pattern called ghost markings. A ghost tabby marking is sometimes visible in solid-colored newborn kittens.

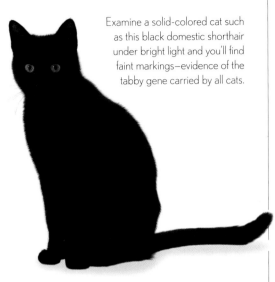

Examine a solid-colored cat such as this black domestic shorthair under bright light and you'll find faint markings—evidence of the tabby gene carried by all cats.

All-White Cats

Genetically speaking, an all-white cat is like a whitewashed wall. Although all-white cats may have genes for colored fur, they also have a gene that masks all color. Some-times a young white cat has a colored patch on her head that shows her masked color, but this usually fades with time. Because an all-white cat can still pass her masked color genes to offspring, her kittens may be living clues to her other hidden colors. However, a cat that inherits an all-white gene from both parents will have only all-white kittens. The color-masking gene also influences eye color, giving many all-white cats blue irises.

White cats can pass along masked color genes to their offspring, resulting in kittens of different colors.

The color-masking gene is also associated with deafness. Seventeen to 22 percent of white cats with nonblue eyes are deaf; 40 percent of white cats with one blue eye are deaf; and 65 to 85 percent of white cats with both eyes blue are deaf.

Tabby Patterns

There are four basic types of tabby pattern (as shown in the photographs on these pages), but generally speaking, tabby is a pattern of dark markings on a lighter-colored background. The tabby pattern is formed by the combination of two different types of hairs: agouti hairs, which have alternating bands of dark and light color; and solid-colored dark hairs, also known as nonagouti hairs. Concentrated areas of the solid-colored dark hairs appear as dark stripes or spots, giving the cat its pattern.

Spotted Tabby

The spotted tabby pattern may be just a mackerel or classic pattern with breaks in the stripes or blotches. These cats have varying degrees of striping on the face, legs, and tail. The Ocicat (page 130) and the Egyptian Mau (page 116) are breeds that have been bred for this pattern, which shows up only rarely in nonpurebreds.

Mackerel Tabby

The original tabby pattern from which variations have evolved is striped. This coat pattern is known as mackerel tabby because narrow dark streaks radiate downward from the middle of the cat's back like a fish skeleton. Mackerel tabbies are commonly known as "tiger" cats.

Classic Tabby

Classic tabbies, also called blotched tabbies, have swirls or circles on the sides of the body; in these cats, the darker areas are broader and blotchier than in mackerel tabbies.

Ticked Tabby

Cats with the ticked tabby pattern, exemplified by the Abyssinian breed (page 86), have coats composed nearly entirely of agouti (banded) hairs. They lack the solid-colored nonagouti hairs that make stripes and whorls in other tabbies, and so have a minimal coat pattern. In nonpurebreds, the ticked pattern is usually combined with other markings.

All tabby cats have a distinctive "M" marking on the forehead.

Piebald Cats

Cats with areas of white on their bodies are known as piebald or particolor. The colored areas of piebald cats can be many different hues and patterns, and the amount of white can vary tremendously. Different genes or combinations of genes give cats different forms of white-spotting, including bicolor, mitted, and van patterns.

Bicolor

Bicolor cats are usually one- to two-thirds white and typically have patches of color on their heads and torsos.

Tortoiseshell Cats

The tortoiseshell (or "tortie") pattern is typically a coat with both black and red hair, but it may also come in other versions, including dilute blue and cream. Tortoiseshell cats are almost always female because the gene that determines whether a hair will be red or black is carried only by the X chromosome. Females have two X chromosomes and so can have both black hair and red hair (one color not being dominant over the other), whereas normal males have only one X chromosome and so can be either black or red—but not both. There are rare cases of tortoiseshell males (with two X chromosomes and one Y), but these cats are usually sterile.

Blue and Cream Tortoiseshell

The blue and cream tortoiseshell is a dilute version of the red and black tortoiseshell.

Tortoiseshell

The tortoiseshell pattern is nearly always found in female cats, which can carry genes for both black and red hair.

Van

Van cats are mostly white with patches of color mainly on their heads and tails.

Mitted

Mitted cats have white on their paws, chin, chest, belly, and back legs.

Lockets

"Lockets" or "buttons" are small spots of white on an otherwise colored cat.

Calico

A calico cat is essentially a tortoiseshell with patches of white. The white part of the coat is usually most prominent on the underside of the body, and the red and black patches are larger and more distinct than in the tortoise-shell pattern. Those with blue and cream patches instead of orange and black are called dilute calicos.

Torbie

A tortoiseshell cat that also has any of the four tabby patterns is called a torbie or a patched tabby.

Patterns of Inheritance

Like all animals, a cat gets its genetic material—including genes for coat color, coat pattern, eye color, and hair length—from its parents. One of the factors that determines which of the contributed genes will be expressed in the offspring is whether the gene is dominant or recessive. A dominant gene will overrule recessive genes.

Suppose a female cat that is genetically 100 percent mackerel tabby, having gotten the mackerel tabby gene from both her parents, were to mate with a male that was genetically 100 percent classic tabby. Which type of tabby pattern would the kittens have? All the kittens would be mackerel tabbies because the mackerel tabby gene is dominant to the recessive classic tabby gene. Similarly, the shorthair gene in cats is dominant over the longhair gene.

A recessive trait will be evident only if the cat has inherited two copies of that gene—one from each parent. There is no way of knowing just by looking at a cat (or any animal) if it carries one hidden recessive gene that, combined with a similar recessive gene from another cat, will produce offspring showing the recessive trait. This is why a litter of kittens sometimes contains surprises.

Tortie Lynx Point
Cats with both striped and tortoiseshell patterns on the points are called tortie lynx points.

Colorpoint
Cats with unpatterned or solid points are called colorpoints.

Tortie Point

Cats with a tortoiseshell pattern on the points are called tortie points.

Lynx Point

Cats with a striped pattern on the points are called lynx points.

Pointed Cats

Most people associate the pointed coat pattern—a light-colored torso with dark-colored areas on the paws, ears, muzzle, and tail—with Siamese cats (described on pages 148 through 157). The pointed coat pattern is the result of several mutated genes that cause hairs on the coolest parts of the body—the extremities—to have extra color. Points are not evident at birth but become prominent as kittens mature. The lighter body color typically darkens as the cat ages but never becomes as dark as the points.

Points can be solid (solid points are often called colorpoints) or patterned, and can come in any of the basic feline colors and their dilutions. Pointed cats are described in terms of their points. Cats with seal-colored points are called "seal points," those with chocolate-colored points are called "chocolate points," and so on.

There are pointed nonpurebred domestic short- and longhairs, but they are fairly rare.

Smoke

In solid-colored cats, the silver gene lightens or even whitens the base of all the hairs, as in this beautiful black smoke.

Silver Cats

Another mutation can affect the appearance of any color or pattern by removing the yellowish-tan pigment from the cat's hair. The silver gene transforms an ordinary tabby into a showy silver tabby, a commonplace solid-colored cat into a rare smoke, and, perhaps most impressively, a plain ticked tabby into a glistening shaded or chinchilla cat.

Chinchilla

Chinchillas are basically shaded cats in which the lighter bands of the hairs are even further widened, leaving only the tips of the hairs colored. Red chinchillas such as this one and red shaded cats are sometimes called cameos.

Silver Tabby

In tabbies, the silver gene further lightens the lighter bands of the agouti (banded) hairs, while the dark bands are unaffected, as in this silver classic tabby American Shorthair.

Many-Toed Cats

Polydactyly (literally, "many fingers") is an inherited trait resulting from a mutation that causes cats to have extra toes. Polydactylous cats usually have additional "thumbs" or first digits on the front feet, but there is considerable variation. Some cats may have what appear to be only enlarged first digits; others may have up to three or four extra toes. The hindfeet can have extra first digits, too, but they rarely occur unless at least one of the front limbs has extra toes. Most polydactylous cats experience no ill effects, but because of the location of the claws on the extra digits, it may be difficult for cats to keep their claws healthy. Ingrown nails can be the painful consequence.

In most of the United States, polydactyly is fairly uncommon, but there are pockets of many-toed cats in various parts of the country, most notably in Boston, Massachusetts, and elsewhere in the Northeast. The high percentage of many-toed cats around Southampton, England, the port from which many early settlers embarked, suggests that polydactylous cats were brought from England in the 1630s. Many cats in Halifax, Nova Scotia, also have many toes. Founded in the mid-1700s, Halifax received a majority of its initial supplies off ships originating from—not surprisingly—Boston.

Shaded

Shaded cats are cats with ticked tabby coats in which the lighter bands of all the hairs have been both lightened (or whitened) and widened, while the dark bands have been narrowed, as in this shaded silver Persian.

The Feline Physique

Nature loves averages, and so most randomly bred domestic shorthairs are rather average in appearance. Their bodies tend to be neither overly short nor extremely elongated, their heads are usually neither perfectly round nor triangular, and their eyes tend to be somewhere between round and almond-shaped. Purebred cats are bred for particular features, including the extremes of body, head, and eye shape illustrated on these pages.

Feline Body Types

Feline body types range between the two extremes of cobby and oriental. Cobby cats are short-bodied and heavy-boned, while cats described as oriental are fine-boned and svelte, with long, fine legs. Cats with oriental bodies tend to have long, slender, pointed tails, while the tails of cobby cats are generally shorter and stouter.

Cobby
This Manx cat epitomizes the short, compact, cobby body type.

Feline Head Shapes

Feline head shapes range from round to wedge-shaped (also called triangular), with a wide variety in between, including rounded wedge shapes, ovals, and rectangles.

Wedge
This Oriental Shorthair's head is wedge-shaped, as are the heads of all cats in the Siamese family.

Round
The head of this Scottish Fold is nearly perfectly round.

Rectangle
This domestic shorthair's head is rectangular in shape.

Intermediate

Most domestic shorthairs are neither extremely short-bodied nor long, but are intermediate in conformation.

Oriental

Siamese are the prototypical oriental cats—long, lean, and tubular.

Feline Eye Shapes

Feline eyes range between the two extremes of round and almond-shaped (a narrow oval), with an assortment of variations on these shapes in between.

Almond

Round

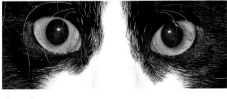

Oval

How to Use the Breed Entries

The following pages offer an indispensable reference guide to the fifty breeds. The breeds are presented in alphabetical order, beginning with the Abyssinian and ending with the York Chocolate. Breed "families" are covered together, even if the family members go by another name. For example, the Colorpoint is basically a Siamese cat with a different coat, and so it is discussed alongside the Siamese. The Nebelung, a Russian Blue with short hair, is covered along with the Russian Blue.

Each breed entry gives a brief overview of the breed, with a personality assessment, a physical description, grooming advice, a concise account of the breed's ancestry, and notes on problems with the breed or other important considerations. The photographs, drawings, and text combined give a complete review of each breed's physical attributes, including overall body conformation, coat colors, and coat texture.

Although every cat must be evaluated individually, when choosing a cat it is helpful to learn about the characteristics that are often shared among cats of a breed—for example, specific behavioral and personality tendencies. The entries that follow are about the breed's tendencies as a whole. Individual cats will depart from the standard in various ways. A cat's personality depends less on breed type than on how it was socialized as a youngster and what its parents' personalities were.

Each breed account includes the components described below.

Photographs

There are one or more photographs of each breed. Many breeds come in a vast array of coat colors, as indicated by the text; in those cases, a sampling is shown.

Opening Paragraph

The first few lines of each entry provide an assessment of the breed's personality; information on how the breed gets along with children; how vocal, active, and sociable it is; whether or not it is a lap cat; and any other characteristics of temperament that tend to define the breed. A cat's voice is described only when distinctive. Note that less can be said with confidence about the temperaments of many of the relatively new and/or rare breeds as compared to the more popular (and therefore more populous) cats.

Appearance

A number of physical features distinguish each of the breeds, among them coat color and pattern, shading, length, and texture. Other distinguishing features are body type, which ranges from cobby (short and compact) to oriental (long and lean); head shape, which ranges from round to rectangular to triangular (wedge-shaped); and eye shape, which may be round or almond or somewhere in between these extremes. These shapes are further described and illustrated on pages 80–81.

Special Grooming Needs

Nearly all cats should be groomed once a week. Regular grooming sessions provide a good opportunity for checking on your cat's overall physical health and well-being. (See page 241 for specific suggestions on grooming your cat and page 268 for a step-by-step mini–physical exam that you can perform at home.) Some cats have special grooming requirements: they may need more frequent brushing, monthly bathing, or perhaps they should be groomed less frequently than most cats (as with the American Wirehair, whose hair is easily damaged). Any such grooming considerations are discussed here.

Origins
Each account includes a brief recounting of the breed's ancestry.

Special Alerts
(!) Certain medical conditions are seen with greater frequency in some breeds of cats than in others. The most common or best-recognized conditions, or those of most concern to prospective owners, are mentioned. Be aware that some of the most popular breeds have the longest lists of medical conditions—partly for the simple reason that problems become much more apparent when there are more cats to observe. Far less is known about the

potential problems in some of the rarer or newer breeds. Health concerns that are discussed at length in the Common Feline Health Problems chapter have a page reference; others have a brief definition.

Also listed here are other considerations that prospective owners of the breed should be aware of—for example, its suitability for indoor/outdoor life or extreme personality traits that might make the cat inappropriate for certain households.

Margin Notes
The following information appears in the outer margin of each new breed page.

Body shape At the top of the margin is a drawing of each breed in full profile to show the cat's overall body shape.

Icons Icons are displayed in the margin only when a breed ranks exceptionally high in the category represented. It cannot be overemphasized that cats vary tremendously, even within a breed, depending on such critical factors as kittenhood experiences and genetics. The icons indicate only that there is a strong tendency for a particular characteristic within a breed and are not meant to be taken as absolute truths about the qualities of that breed.

Balinese can be noisy cats.

TALKATIVE These are chatty cats. This icon does not refer to the quality of a cat's voice, however. If a cat's voice is distinctive, it is described in the opening paragraph of the breed account.

LAP CAT

The Lap Cat icon is given to those cats that enjoy or even crave physical contact with their owners. Many cats that are sociable, affectionate, and people-oriented (and are described as such in the opening paragraph of the breed account) nonetheless prefer not to be *on* their owners, but simply to be *near* them. These cats are not true lap cats and so are not assigned the Lap Cat icon.

HIGH ENERGY

These are cats that seem to be in constant motion, always sticking their noses someplace, checking things out—the prototypical curious cat. Such cats, especially if they are youngsters, require more attention and playtime than calm, sedate felines.

GOOD WITH KIDS

A healthy cat of any breed will be fine with children if he was properly socialized with children as a kitten and if both of his parents were even-tempered. The Good with Kids icon is meant to call attention to the breeds that are particularly easygoing and tolerant. Only breeds that tend to be exceptionally accepting of children who are not rough will bear this icon. Of course, some of those without the icon will also be good family cats and get along well with your children. Cats that do well with children are also generally accepting of the family dog and of other cats in the home.

SPECIAL GROOMING NEEDS

Cats that need to be brushed more than once a week get the Special Grooming Needs icon. Note that not all longhaired breeds need more than once-weekly grooming; those with thin undercoats are not prone to forming mats. On the other hand, short-haired cats with particularly dense coats should be brushed two or three times

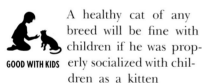

Cats of the Oriental breed are typically inquisitive and energetic.

a week to remove loose hair, thereby limiting the amount of hair that winds up on your furniture (or on you) or that is ingested by the cat during grooming and subsequently coughed up as a hairball. Cats with other sorts of extra grooming needs—

Birmans make great companions for children.

the Sphynx, for example, which needs to be bathed regularly to avoid greasy buildup—will bear the grooming icon as well. All special grooming requirements are detailed in the Special Grooming Needs text (as described on page 82).

Weight A weight range indicating the average size of a typical adult male of the breed appears at the bottom of the margin. In contrast to dogs, cat breeds differ little in body size. While breeds of dogs may differ in weight by as much as 200 pounds, the largest of the purebred cats (the Siberian) and the smallest (the Singapura) differ by a mere fifteen pounds. Most of the other breeds weigh between eight and twelve pounds, with males tending to outweigh females by about 10 to 20 percent.

In the larger breeds, such as Maine Coons, Norwegian Forest Cats, Ragdolls, and Siberians, the difference in size between the sexes is quite dramatic. The larger breeds also mature more slowly than the smaller ones and often do not reach full size until four or five years of age.

Breed Club Standards

The descriptions here are meant to help people choose a pet rather than a show cat. The text does not specify the exact breed standards required by different breed associations, such as the Cat Fanciers' Association (CFA) and the International Cat Association. Each association has its own list of cats that it "accepts" and its own standards for each breed. Furthermore, different associations may classify a particular cat in a different way; the CFA, for example, classifies the Himalayan as a color division within the Persian breed, while most other registries recognize it as a separate breed. Contact the association of your choice if you are interested in showing a cat and need to know the official standards. (See also the Breed Registries appendix if you want to show your cat.)

Abyssinian and Somali

Abyssinians and Somalis are gentle, bold, playful, and extremely busy, always seeking to be part of household activities. They are freedom-loving and dislike close confinement or restraint. Although not lap cats, they are companionable, people-oriented, and sociable with other animals. Their voices, though rarely used, are bell-like and pleasant.

Appearance The Abyssinian is a lithe, muscular cat of medium length. It has a rounded wedge-shaped head, expressive gold or green almond-shaped eyes, and large, moderately pointed ears. A rounder head and longer hair—especially on the fluffy, foxlike tail, the britches, and the neck ruff—are the only features that distinguish the Somali from the Aby.

The Aby's most striking feature is its beautiful ticked tabby coat, which is medium in length and fine in texture. The characteristic tabby "M" typically appears on the forehead.

Ruddy Abyssinian

Left to right: ruddy, blue, and red Abyssinian kittens, about six weeks old. The color on their heads will lighten as the kittens mature.

Four colors are recognized by the major U.S. breed associations: ruddy (the darkest and most common of the colors), red (sorrel or cinnamon), blue, and fawn. European breed registries recognize additional colors.

Origins No one knows where the first Abyssinian came from, but there are several theories. Some literature supports the theory that progenitors of today's Abys accompanied British troops returning from Abyssinia (modern Ethiopia) in the late 1800s. Other evidence suggests that the ancestors of the breed may actually have been natives of India imported to England by British merchants passing through Calcutta.

Blue Somali

Red Abyssinian

An equally plausible theory holds that the Aby's ancestors were native British cats and that cat fanciers developed the breed by carefully mating indigenous ticked-coated cats. Somalis appeared in the 1950s as offspring of Abyssinian matings with other breeds. Initially these longhaired Abys were considered undesirable and were not taken seriously. But in the 1970s, an American breeder recognized their beauty, named the breed (calling it Somali because of Somalia's geographic proximity to Ethiopia), and began an extensive breeding program. Since then its popularity has spread from the United States to other parts of the world.

! Breed-related health problems: patellar luxation (page 294); renal amyloidosis (page 307); retinal atrophy (a rare eye condition that ultimately leads to impaired vision).

Fawn Somali

American Bobtail

American Bobtails are intelligent, good-natured, friendly cats, although they are somewhat shy with strangers. Many Bobtails play fetch and come when called.

Appearance The American Bobtail is a stocky, muscular, medium to large cat, with hindlegs that are longer than the forelegs. The head is broad, with large, almond-shaped eyes and moderately large ears set low on the head. The unique tail, which reaches about halfway down to the hock (the "ankle" of the hindleg), is probably the result of a genetic mutation similar to that responsible for the lack of a tail in the Manx cat.

Bobtails come in both long- and shorthaired varieties; the coat of the shorthair is actually medium in length. The coat is best described as shaggy, with a dense undercoat. All colors and patterns are recognized.

Special Grooming Needs Bobtails should be groomed at least twice a week to remove loose fur.

Origins In the 1960s, an Iowa family mated their Siamese with an orphaned male tabby that had a short, upraised tail. Some of the kittens had their mother's long tail, while others had their father's short

Brown mackerel tabby longhaired American Bobtail

tail. One of the short-tailed cats mated with a long-tailed one, and their whole litter had short tails. These remarkable kittens were designated a new breed: the American Bobtail.

WEIGHT 10–12 LBS.

American Curl

BODY SHAPE

LAP CAT

GOOD WITH KIDS

The American Curl is another of nature's gifts to cat fanciers; the distinctive curled ears are the result of a natural, or spontaneous, mutation. Curls are friendly, affectionate, people-oriented cats, and make playful companions. They are even-tempered cats that adapt well to other pets in the household and actually seem to enjoy being around children.

Appearance The American Curl is a medium-size, moderately muscular cat. It has a rounded wedge-shaped head and large, walnut-shaped eyes. This cat's most compelling feature is, of course, the backward-curling ears. Kittens are born with "normal" ears (that is, folded down, not standing up until the end of the first week or so), but by three weeks it's evident which kittens are destined to have curled ears. By four months the curl is permanent.

Curls may be longhaired or shorthaired; in both varieties, the undercoat is sparse, which means that even longhaired Curls are not likely to develop matted coats. Longhairs have a silky, semi-long, close-lying topcoat. Coats are acceptable to breed registries in any color or pattern.

WEIGHT 7–10 LBS.

Brown spotted tabby shorthaired American Curl

Blue torbie and white longhaired
American Curl kittens

Origins The American Curl is a relatively new breed. In 1981, an unusual stray found her way into the California garden of Grace and Joe Ruga. She was a black kitten with longish fur and striking ears that curled back in a graceful arc. The Rugas adopted her, naming her Shulamith. Shulamith had four kittens, two of which inherited her remarkable curled ears. Today, all American Curls trace their pedigree back to Shulamith.

American Shorthair

BODY SHAPE

GOOD WITH KIDS

SPECIAL GROOMING NEEDS

The American Shorthair is a robust, well-proportioned cat of fine intelligence and disposition—the quintessential American breed. Affectionate and sociable, the American Shorthair adapts well to children and other animals. It can be playful, romping with the kids, or it may be satisfied just to watch the action from a distance. American Shorthairs are the ideal hearth cats, happy to share a cozy spot (next to you, or at your feet perhaps, rather than on your lap) and communicate their contentment with loud purring.

Appearance Shorthairs are medium to large in stature, powerfully built, and athletic. Their faces are wide and full-cheeked, with large, nearly round eyes. The ears are widely spaced and slightly rounded at the tips. The American Shorthair's coat is short and very dense. Breed associations recognize more than eighty colors and patterns; most common is the classic tabby pattern in silver, brown, or red.

Brown classic torbie American Shorthair with a magnificent tabby pattern and the sweet expression the breed is known for

WEIGHT 9–12 LBS.

Red silver classic
tabby American
Shorthair

Special Grooming Needs Because of their dense coats, American Shorthairs need to be combed about two or three times a week to remove loose fur.

Origins Domestic cats first arrived in America aboard the Pilgrims' boats early in the 17th century and quickly asserted their position as rodent destroyer in both rural areas and settlements. Over time, the American domestic cat developed characteristics of temperament, appearance, and constitution that were admired by fanciers.

By the beginning of the 20th century, however, the unique qualities of these shorthaired American beauties were in danger of being lost due to breeding with popular longhaired and exotic cats from around the world. Hoping to rescue the breed, fanciers selected the

Silver classic tabby kittens

best specimens for controlled breeding programs. The first American-bred Domestic Shorthair to be registered as a pedigreed cat was a blue smoke named Buster Brown, registered in 1904 by Jane Cathcart. Breed standards for the Domestic Shorthair were eventually developed and improved, and the finest qualities of the hardy, now pedigreed, cats were preserved. In order to better differentiate these cats from their nonpedigreed domestic cousins, the breed was renamed the American Shorthair in 1966.

(!) A vigorous cat with a hearty appetite, the American Shorthair should be encouraged to exercise daily, and its diet should be monitored to avoid obesity.

Black and white bicolor
American Shorthair

American Wirehair

BODY SHAPE

The Wirehair is similar to the American Shorthair in disposition. This is a quiet, sweet-natured, easygoing cat that gets along well with children and other pets.

GOOD WITH KIDS

Appearance The American Wirehair is a muscular cat with a distinctive wiry coat; even its whiskers curl. The ideal cat is medium to large and well-muscled, with a dense, coarse coat that has a curly appearance. Wirehairs have round heads with large, widely spaced eyes and medium-size ears that are rounded at the tips.

SPECIAL GROOMING NEEDS

Each hair is thin and wiry or bent, resulting in the crimped coat that is the hallmark of this breed. Breeders strive for coats that are dense, resilient, and coarse. They routinely cross Wirehairs with American Shorthairs, resulting in similar colors and patterns among the two breeds.

Special Grooming Needs The wiry hair is easily damaged, so brushing or combing is not advised except during the spring shedding season.

Origins The American Wirehair breed was developed from a farm cat named Adam discovered in 1966 in upstate New York. This male of nonpedigreed parents (some authorities claim the parents were American Shorthairs) was the only one of six kittens with dense, wiry fur. When Adam was mated with one of his littermates, Tip-Toe, he passed along the mutated gene for coat texture, and subsequent litters produced more of these wonderful wirehaired kittens.

WEIGHT 8-11 LBS.

Brown classic tabby and white
American Wirehair

Bengal

BODY SHAPE

HIGH ENERGY

Described by the breed founder as the "domestic reproduction of a leopard," the Bengal descends from crosses between a wildcat and a domestic cat. Bengals are intelligent, friendly, assertive, and active cats. Some like to retrieve objects, and many have a fondness for climbing and playing in water. They also enjoy cat-and-mouse games and will find their own toys if none are provided. Their voices are sometimes rather wild-sounding.

Appearance The Bengal is a medium to large cat with a head that is longer than it is wide. It is bred to retain its wild appearance: sleek, long, and muscular, with the hindquarters slightly higher than the shoulders. The black-tipped tail is carried low. The Bengal has short, rounded ears; oval, wide-set eyes; prominent whisker pads; and rounder nostrils than other domestic cats.

The Bengal's most defining characteristic is its spotted or marbled coat with thick, peltlike fur.

WEIGHT 9–12 LBS.

Brown spotted Bengal

Brown marble Bengal

In spotted Bengals, the spots appear randomly or in horizontal patterns and stand out in extreme contrast to the background color, which may be a bright shade of tan, gold, or mahogany. Marbled cats have horizontal stripes arranged randomly, like waves of color running through a piece of lighter-colored marble.

Spotted snow Bengal

Origins Hoping to produce an animal with the appearance of a spotted wildcat and the sweet disposition of a house cat, in the 1980s an Arizona woman began a breeding program with eight female descendants of crosses between Asian Leopard Cats and domestic cats. She named the new breed Bengal after the scientific name *(Felis bengalensis)* of the wildcat forebear.

(!) Breed-related health problems include entropion (page 288).

Birman

The Birman, also called the Sacred Cat of Burma, is sometimes described as puppylike—it is playful and will follow its owner everywhere. These loving, placid cats make great companions for children: they can be carried around in all sorts of positions and don't mind being held on their backs. They are not particularly vocal.

Appearance Birmans are large, powerfully built cats, stocky in body and legs. The head is broad and rounded, with round, vividly blue eyes and medium-size ears that are as wide at the base as they are tall.

The Birman's coat is medium to long and silky in texture, with a relatively sparse undercoat that is not prone to matting. Some breed associations recognize only the traditional Siamese point colors: seal, blue, chocolate, and lilac. Others allow a number of other solid point colors, lynx points, and tortie points. The feet are white and, ideally, the fur is tinged with gold.

Blue point (two at left) and seal point (right) Birman kittens

WEIGHT 8–11 LBS.

Origins According to an ancient Burmese legend, one hundred pure white cats with yellow eyes served as sacred companions to the priests of a temple that held a golden statue of a blue-eyed goddess. Following an attack on the temple, one of the cats assumed the characteristics of the idol at the moment of his master's death: his fur became tinged with gold and his eyes turned sapphire blue. His extremities darkened to the color of the earth, but his feet, which touched the body of his master, stayed white. The remaining cats also acquired the coloration that is seen in the Sacred Cats of Burma (modern Myanmar) to this day.

The modern history of this breed is not quite as fanciful as the legend. Many sources agree that French breeders crossed one of the temple cats with either a Persian or a Siamese, thereby initiating the breed we know as Birman. Some skeptics argue, however, that the breed did not originate in Burma at all but was created by French breeders. This theory is not very popular.

Lilac point Birman

Bombay

BODY SHAPE

LAP CAT

GOOD WITH KIDS

Although the Bombay retains the look of a wildcat, it is really a calm, gentle, and affectionate breed. Some owners describe these cats as doglike: they are very companionable, they can be leash trained, and they enjoy playing fetch. Bombays are fine companions for children and they readily accept the family dog. In a multicat household, though, Bombays expect to dominate.

Appearance Like Burmese cats, Bombays have round heads and widely set ears, but they are slightly larger, with longer bodies and longer legs. Bright, copper-colored eyes are considered more desirable than gold eyes.

The Bombay is the quintessential black cat, from the tip of the nose to the bottoms of the feet. The fur, jet black to the roots, is shiny and close-lying, accentuating the muscular build.

Origins In 1953 a breeder from Louisville, Kentucky, bred black American Shorthairs with sable Burmese, intending to produce cats with the sleek, shiny coat of the Burmese and the rich black tones of the American Shorthair. After years of selective breeding, the Bombay, named for the black leopard of India, achieved championship status.

(!) Bombays have hearty appetites, and some tend to overeat. Owners can cope with this problem by rationing food or providing a lower-calorie diet.

WEIGHT 8-11 LBS.

Black Bombay
with gold eyes

British Shorthair

BODY SHAPE

LAP CAT

GOOD WITH KIDS

SPECIAL GROOMING NEEDS

The British Shorthair, oldest of the English breeds, is easygoing, untemperamental, and reserved, yet also extremely affectionate. These adaptable cats take children and other animals in stride. Although British Shorthairs enjoy the occasional romp, they are not rowdy cats and do not require a lot of attention. Their voices are soft and sweet.

Appearance The British Shorthair is most remarkable for its roundness: it has a large, round head; round, wide-set eyes and ears; and round paws. It is a solidly built, medium to large cat with a broad chest.

Blue British Shorthair. This breed's coat is so dense that it looks padded.

The coat of the British Shorthair is dense and plush, yet crisp rather than soft. Although the traditionally favored color is blue—hence the original name of the breed, British Blue—the British Shorthair is now recognized in a virtual rainbow of different colors and patterns.

Special Grooming Needs As with other dense-coated cats, twice- or thrice-weekly grooming will limit the amount of hair that winds up on the furniture.

WEIGHT 9–12 LBS.

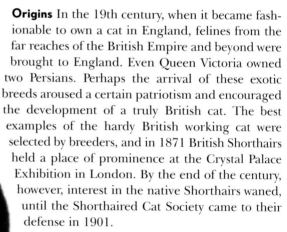

Black British Shorthair

Origins In the 19th century, when it became fashionable to own a cat in England, felines from the far reaches of the British Empire and beyond were brought to England. Even Queen Victoria owned two Persians. Perhaps the arrival of these exotic breeds aroused a certain patriotism and encouraged the development of a truly British cat. The best examples of the hardy British working cat were selected by breeders, and in 1871 British Shorthairs held a place of prominence at the Crystal Palace Exhibition in London. By the end of the century, however, interest in the native Shorthairs waned, until the Shorthaired Cat Society came to their defense in 1901.

During World War II, the population of British Shorthairs diminished significantly. After the war, some breeders crossed Shorthairs with Persians in an attempt to replenish the Shorthair stock. American associations were at first reluctant to recognize the British Shorthair because, with its

Left to right: blue, black, and cream mackerel tabby British Shorthair kittens

Persian blood, it was genetically similar to the Exotic Shorthair, a cross between the Persian and the American Shorthair. But in 1980 the British Shorthair achieved championship status in America.

(!) Breed-related health problems include hemophilia B (a hereditary bleeding disorder).

Dilute calico British Shorthair

Burmese

BODY SHAPE

TALKATIVE

LAP CAT

GOOD WITH KIDS

Left to right: platinum, blue, champagne, and sable Burmese kittens

Ideal lap cats, Burmese enjoy people and love to cuddle. They are also playful (they're born acrobats), intelligent, and good with children and other animals. Burms require more attention than many Western breeds; females are generally more bossy and demanding than males. Burmese have deep, rumbling voices and do not hesitate to use them.

WEIGHT 7-9 LBS.

Appearance A Burmese is a stocky cat of medium size with good muscular development, short legs, and round feet. The head is exceptionally round, with a short muzzle and wide-set, golden eyes.

The Burmese coat is short, fine, and silky and lies close to the body. The solid, dark sable brown Burmese is in a league of its own, but a dilute division includes cats with lighter coats: champagne

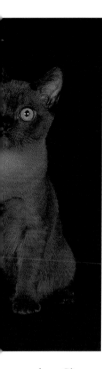

(light brown), blue (gray), and platinum (lilac). While some breed registries recognize Burmese in a host of colors and patterns, others classify these cats as Foreign Burmese (as described on page 107).

Origins Burmese are thought to descend from sacred brown cats kept by student-priests in the palaces and temples of ancient Burma (modern Myanmar). Harrison Weir, organizer of the first modern cat show, described two variants of the Siamese cat in 1889. One type he described as light-colored with darker points, and the other—an accidental deviation, in his opinion—as a chocolate variety. The lighter, pointed cats invariably beat the chocolate ones at shows, and over time the "chocolate Siamese" disappeared from competitions. Looking back, many people believe these "chocolate Siamese" were not Siamese at all, but descendants of jealously guarded cats from ancient Burma.

Sable Burmese

In 1930 a retired Navy doctor procured a brown female cat named Wong Mau from Burma that turned out to be a Siamese-Burmese hybrid. Wong Mau was bred to a seal point Siamese. When one of her offspring was mated with her, three types of kittens resulted: some that were light in color with typical dark Siamese points, some that were brown with darker points, and a third kind that was brown with no markings. These unmarked brown kittens became the foundation stock of the modern Burmese breed in North America.

ⓘ Breed-related health problems: corneal dermoids (a small patch of skin and hair attached to the cornea, usually near the corner of the eye, that can be fixed surgically); cherry eye (page 288).

Champagne Burmese

Foreign Burmese

BURMESE FAMILY

The Foreign Burmese, also known as the European Burmese, is essentially a Burmese with coats of many colors. These colorful Burms are as intelligent, lively, chatty, and affectionate as their traditionally colored kin. Loyal and friendly, they enjoy the company of both animals and humans.

TALKATIVE

LAP CAT

Appearance Though slimmer and longer nosed than the Burmese, the Foreign Burmese has the same medium-size, muscular build as its American counterpart. The head is a short, rounded wedge with wide-set ears that are rounded at the tips. The large, rounded eyes slant slightly inward and are colored shades of yellow to amber.

GOOD WITH KIDS

The Foreign Burmese's coat is, like that of the Burmese, short, fine, glossy, and close-lying. In addition to the traditionally accepted coat colors of sable, light brown (called champagne in the Burmese), blue, and lilac (called platinum in the Burmese), the Foreign Burmese is recognized in red, cream, seal tortie, blue tortie, chocolate tortie, and lilac tortie.

Origins In the 1960s, British breeders who imported Burmese to England expanded the gene pool by crossing them with red point Siamese and British Shorthairs. The introduction of the red gene expanded the palette to include six additional colors.

WEIGHT 7-9 LBS.

Lilac Foreign Burmese

Burmilla

BODY SHAPE

LAP CAT

GOOD WITH KIDS

Lilac-tipped
Burmilla

Similar in temperament to Burmese, Burmillas are sociable, playful, and affectionate. Like their Burmese cousins, they appreciate cuddling and companionship and do well with other animals and children.

Appearance Breeders have worked to maintain the Burmese body type and the tipped coat of the chinchilla progenitor. Like the Burmese, Burmillas are medium-size cats with compact, muscular bodies and round faces with short muzzles.

The Burmilla has a soft, short, close-lying, light-colored coat with hairs tipped with a contrasting color. Many colors are recognized.

Origins Burmillas are the happy result of an accidental breeding between a chinchilla Persian named Sanquist and a lilac Burmese named Faberge. Their four kittens, born in 1981, became the foundation stock of a new breed.

WEIGHT 8-10 LBS.

Black-tipped Burmilla

California Spangled Cat

BODY SHAPE

A recently developed breed similar in concept to the Ocicat, the Spangled Cat is a spotted, wild-looking creature. But this is a purely domestic breed, not a hybrid between a wildcat species and a domestic variety. Sweet-natured, intelligent, and energetic, Spangles enjoy companionship but are not demanding of their owners' attention.

Appearance Spangles are large, well-muscled cats with long bodies and a "wild," low-slung gait. They have prominent cheekbones and pale, well-developed whisker pads. The forehead is slightly rounded, the eyes are almond-shaped, and the ears are rounded at the tips and set high on the head. The tail is dark-tipped and blunt.

The Spangle's spotted tabby coat is shorthaired, with slightly longer fur on the tail and underbelly.

Origins California Spangled Cats were developed in the 1980s by a California breeder who was determined to create a domestic breed to mimic endangered spotted wildcats. A complex breeding program including an Abyssinian–domestic shorthair cross, a British Shorthair, an American Shorthair, a feral cat from Cairo, a spotted Manx, and a Siamese produced the anticipated results after eleven generations.

Blue silver California Spangled Cat mother with brown kitten

WEIGHT 12–16 LBS.

109

Chartreux

BODY SHAPE

LAP CAT

GOOD WITH KIDS

SPECIAL GROOMING NEEDS

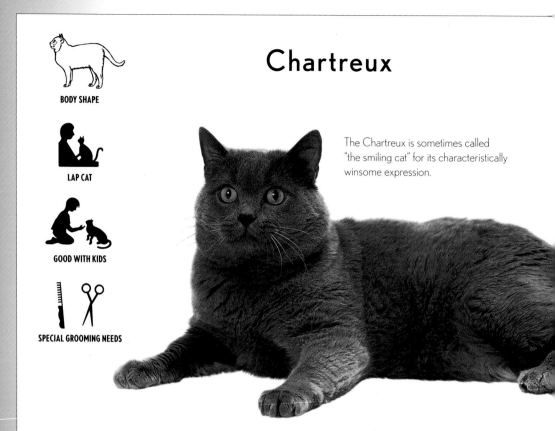

The Chartreux is sometimes called "the smiling cat" for its characteristically winsome expression.

Chartreux make gentle, devoted pets that get along quite well with other household animals, children, and even strangers. They are affectionate and loyal, and like to be near (or on) their human companions, whom they will follow everywhere. Some Chartreux like to climb, and, if given the opportunity, they are excellent hunters. Chartreux are rather quiet cats. Some never meow, while others have thin, high-pitched voices.

Appearance This is a husky, muscular cat with broad shoulders, an oval head, and a short muzzle. Proportionately small feet give the Chartreux the appearance of walking on tiptoe. The large, round, wide-set eyes range in color from copper to gold; the ears are small to medium and stand erect and close together.

WEIGHT 9–12 LBS.

The Chartreux boasts a luxuriant, dense, and woolly blue-gray coat of short to medium length.

Special Grooming Needs The Chartreux's heavy coat should be brushed twice a week to remove loose hair and more frequently during the spring shedding season.

Origins Thought to be the predominant domestic cat variety in France at one time, the Chartreux (possibly named for the fine-quality Spanish wool called *pile de Chartreux* that was imported by France) had nearly disappeared by the 1800s. In the 1920s, however, a large colony of these cats was discovered on Belle-Ile-sur-Mer, off the coast of Brittany. The breed nearly disappeared again after World War II, so nonpurebred cats, Blue Persians, and, later, British Blues were used to reestablish it. Chartreux were imported to the United States in 1970.

⚠ Breed-related health problems include patellar luxation (page 294).

The adult Chartreux's eyes are a bewitching pumpkin orange; the kitten's eyes have not yet completely changed from their original blue.

Cornish Rex

BODY SHAPE

TALKATIVE

LAP CAT

HIGH ENERGY

SPECIAL GROOMING NEEDS

WEIGHT 6–8 LBS.

Cornish Rexes make very playful, affectionate, fun-loving companions that enjoy being part of a busy household. Their acrobatic abilities are extraordinary; with their extremely powerful thighs, they can easily leap from the floor to the top of the refrigerator in a single bound. Because they lack one of the two kinds of hair that make up the topcoat, Cornish Rexes seek warmth and love to cuddle. Some have sweet voices, others have more strident ones, but all are talkative.

Appearance The Cornish Rex has a slender body, a deep chest, and long, fine legs. Especially long hindlegs and a naturally arched back contribute to the breed's athletic appearance. The head is egg-shaped, with medium to large oval eyes and large, erect ears set high on the head.

The short, soft coat has a wavy washboard appearance caused by bent, abnormally short awn and down hairs and the absence of guard hairs. Even the whiskers curl. There is a plethora of coat colors and patterns.

Black and white bicolor Cornish Rex

Tortoiseshell Cornish Rex

Special Grooming Needs The breed's wavy hairs are easily damaged. Overly vigorous brushing can break the delicate hairs and create bald spots. Cornish Rexes shed minimally.

Origins The Cornish Rex's remarkable wavy coat first occurred as a natural mutation in a barn cat born in Cornwall, England, in 1950. Cat fanciers used inbreeding to select for the wavy coat gene and then crossed Rexes with other breeds to strengthen the stock, refine the build and features, and increase the color varieties.

(!) The Cornish Rex's delicate coat does not protect these cats from cold or sun, so don't allow them outdoors. Breed-related health problems include hypotrichosis (hereditary baldness).

Devon Rex

BODY SHAPE

LAP CAT

HIGH ENERGY

SPECIAL GROOMING NEEDS

WEIGHT 7-9 LBS.

Devon Rexes are busy, inquisitive, playful, affectionate, and extremely people-oriented. They are exceptional leapers and have been known to jump into their owners' arms and ride happily on their shoulders. Some wag their tails and follow their owners around. They communicate in quiet chirps and trills.

Appearance The Devon Rex is a slender, muscular cat with long forelegs and a broad chest. It is stockier than the Cornish Rex and has a broader head. The Devon Rex's muzzle is short, the eyes are large and wide-set, and the ears are large. The whisker pads are prominent, the whiskers curly, sparse, and short.

The coat is soft, short, and wavy, with a looser curl than the Cornish Rex. There is great variability in coat texture, color, and pattern.

Special Grooming Needs Groom these cats gently, as their hair breaks easily. In some Devons, an oily or waxy secretion tends to build up around the nails and in the folds of skin; affected cats require bathing every few weeks.

Tortoiseshell Devon Rex

Origins The Devon's wavy coat was a natural mutation in a field cat found in Devon, England, in 1960. As with the Cornish Rex, fanciers inbred to select for the wavy coat, then outcrossed for vigorous health and color variety.

① The Devon's delicate fur will not provide protection from cold or sun, so don't allow them outdoors. Breed-related health problems: hypotrichosis (hereditary baldness); patellar luxation (page 294).

Red point (left) and blue-eyed white (right) Devon Rex kittens. Their bald bellies will grow furry as the kittens mature.

White Devon Rex

Egyptian Mau

BODY SHAPE

HIGH ENERGY

Egyptian Maus are similar to Abyssinians in temperament: playful, busy, and sociable. Early Maus were reportedly wild and unpredictable, but thanks to generations of selective breeding, they are now loyal, even-tempered cats.

Appearance The Egyptian Mau is a medium-size cat with well-developed muscles, a rounded wedge-shaped head, and erect, medium to large ears. The almond-shaped eyes are light green.

The Mau's spotted coat, which is of medium length, is its most distinctive feature. In fact, the Egyptian Mau is the only naturally occurring spotted breed of domestic cat. The spotted pattern is randomly distributed, and the spots, which vary greatly in size and shape, are deeply colored and contrast distinctly with the background color. Maus come in three colors: silver with charcoal markings, bronze with dark brown to black markings, and smoke with black markings.

Origins Egyptian Maus (*mau* is Egyptian for "cat") are descended from cats brought from Cairo to Rome in the early 1950s by the Egyptian ambassador to Italy. A Russian expatriate princess who admired the cats obtained a silver female, bred her to another of the ambassador's cats, and increased her population to three. The princess came to New York with her Egyptian cats in 1956 and sparked the interest of American breeders. All Maus in the United States were descended from her original three cats until the early 1980s, when additional Maus were finally imported from Egypt and India, thus enlarging the gene pool.

WEIGHT 7-9 LBS.

Bronze Egyptian Mau
with black markings

Havana Brown

BODY SHAPE

LAP CAT

These elegant cats make intelligent, affectionate, playful companions. True to their Siamese ancestry, Havanas can be demanding, but they are not as vocal as Siamese and have softer voices. Sometimes described as coy, Havana Browns are also much subtler than Siamese, often sneaking up onto their owners' laps unnoticed.

Appearance The Havana Brown is a muscular, medium-size cat with a distinctive rectangular muzzle, said by imaginative breeders to resemble the base of a lightbulb or a corncob. The rich brown coat is accented by large, striking green eyes. The hair, both on and in the large, round-tipped ears, is sparse.

Havanas have a short to medium-length glossy coat that is deep mahogany or chestnut brown. Even the whiskers are brown. Some registries recognize the color dilution lilac.

Origins These cats were named either for the popular brown Cuban cigar or for a breed of brown rabbit previously named for the cigar. They are not Cuban at all, however, but an English creation. In the early 1950s, a British woman crossed a black shorthaired Persian-Siamese hybrid with a seal point Siamese and came up with a solid brown male, the first Havana to be registered in England and the progenitor of the modern Havana breed. A California breeder imported the first Havana Browns to the United States in 1956; her cats became the foundation stock for the breed in North America.

Havana Brown kitten—even the whiskers are brown.

WEIGHT 8-10 LBS.

Japanese Bobtail

BODY SHAPE

LAP CAT

HIGH ENERGY

GOOD WITH KIDS

Bobtails are friendly, intelligent, very affectionate, and among the happiest breeds of cat. They're wonderful with children—and just about anyone else. They are also playful cats and enjoy carrying objects in their mouths and romping in water. Their voices are chirpy and soft.

Appearance The Japanese Bobtail is a medium-size cat, slender and well muscled. The legs are long and fine, with the hindlegs slightly longer than the forelegs. The stumpy tail, the result of a naturally occurring mutation, is covered by a fan of thick fur and resembles a rabbit's tail. The kinks and curves of the tail are unique to each individual cat, and the length ranges between one and three inches. Bobtails have triangular heads, high cheekbones, long noses, and oval eyes. Odd-eyed and blue-eyed cats are not uncommon.

Black and white bicolor shorthaired Japanese Bobtail displaying its distinctive pom-pom tail

WEIGHT 7–9 LBS.

Red and white bicolor longhaired Japanese Bobtail

Japanese Bobtails come in short- and longhaired versions. The most popular coat pattern is the tricolor calico (also called *mi-ke*, Japanese for "three-fur"): red and black in bold contrast to a vivid white background. Black on white and red on white are also popular, and tortoiseshell and solid coats in black, red, or white are also acceptable.

Origins For centuries, the Bobtail was the closely guarded pet of Japanese nobility. In 1602, however, the Japanese authorities ordered all privately owned cats to be released into the countryside to combat the rodents that were threatening the lucrative silk industry. Since that time, Japanese Bobtails have been celebrated in folklore and art and are considered to bring good fortune. An American breeder brought Bobtails to the United States in 1968, and the breed was fully recognized ten years later.

Calico shorthaired Japanese Bobtail

Korat

Korats are sweet, gentle, and quiet. They like to be around people—or, if possible, on them—especially a chosen favorite, though they can be shy around strangers. They are stubborn cats and will give up toys reluctantly; they may also try to dominate other cats in the household. Korats do not like to be left alone and require lots of attention.

Appearance The Korat is a muscular, medium-size cat with a relatively compact body. The face is heart-shaped; the luminous green to amber eyes are large and round; and the ears, which are large and round-tipped, sit high on the head.

Korats are shorthaired cats with a sparse undercoat. They come in only one color: blue-gray with a silver tipping that lends a shine to the close-lying fur.

Origins The Korat has been highly valued in its native Thailand for centuries. To Thai farmers, the Korat's blue-gray coat resembled a rain cloud; to Thai merchants, the silver tipping prophesied good luck in business; to a young bride, a wedding gift of a pair of Korats ensured a prosperous future.

The breed was first exhibited in 1896 at a London cat show, where it was entered in the Siamese class. Although truly from Siam, the blue-gray cat did not look like a Siamese and was disqualified. In 1959, a pair of Korats was given to the American ambassador to Thailand and ultimately ended up in Oregon. A breeding program began, and more cats were imported from Thailand in the early 1960s.

WEIGHT 8-10 LBS.

Blue-gray Korat with silver tipping

La Perm

BODY SHAPE

LAP CAT

La Perms, which owe their curly coats—or perms—to a naturally occurring mutation, are outgoing, affectionate, and inquisitive. Unless they're trying to get your attention, they tend to have quiet voices.

Appearance Medium-size, curly-coated cats, La Perms have rounded heads with prominent, round muzzles and full whisker pads. The wide-set ears are also rounded and the eyes are large and almond-shaped.

La Perms display a great diversity in hair length and fullness. Both short- and longhaired varieties have soft, curly coats; the hair is curliest at the base of the ears, and the whiskers may also curl. Longer-haired cats have ringlets of curls over the entire body, accented by a long, curly, plumed tail; they develop a neck ruff at maturity. Shorthaired varieties have more of a permanent wave; the hair is not long enough to form ringlets. All colors and patterns are represented.

Origins One kitten in a litter of Oregon barn cats was born hairless. The odd-looking kitten survived and grew a coat of curly hair. Curly, the aptly named tabby female, became the foundation female of this new breed. Baldness still occurs in some kittens, and is reported by breeders to occur most commonly during infancy or in females prior to their first heat. Some kittens born with straight hair shed their coat, which is later replaced by the unique curly coat.

WEIGHT 7-9 LBS.

Brown mackerel tabby shorthaired La Perm

121

Maine Coon

BODY SHAPE

GOOD WITH KIDS

SPECIAL GROOMING NEEDS

The Maine Coon's easygoing nature makes it a fine companion for children and other pets. Maine Coons are gentle, affectionate, and playful. They are also good mousers and like to retrieve objects. They communicate with quiet, chirplike trills.

Appearance The Maine Coon is a large cat, broad-chested and muscular, with a long, rectangular body and a long, plumed tail. The feet are round and tufted—well suited to snowy climates. Large, tufted ears; large, wide-set eyes; and a regal neck ruff contribute to the impressive aspect of this American beauty.

The Maine Coon is traditionally a long-haired brown tabby with a silky coat. The coat is heavy and water-resistant, with hair longest on the tail, ruff, stomach, and hindquarters. Maine Coons come in all patterns and colors except chocolate, lilac, and Siamese point patterns.

Special Grooming Needs The Maine Coon's coat will mat unless it is groomed two or three times a week. Special attention should be devoted to keeping the tail, ruff, stomach, and hindquarters free of snarls and debris.

WEIGHT 14–18 LBS.

Brown classic tabby Maine Coon on the prowl. The hunting instinct remains strong in this breed.

Origins The Maine Coon's exact origins are not known. Contrary to popular myth and the implications of the breed name, the distinctively bushy, often ringed tail does not come from crossing a cat with a raccoon (which is genetically impossible). It is likely that the breed resulted from intermixing between indigenous American shorthaired tabbies and imported longhaired cats. Several historical accounts link the origin of the Maine Coon with Angora cats that were dispatched to North America by Marie Antoinette. Another theory proposes that the Maine Coon's progenitors were Norwegian Forest Cats brought to the Americas by the Vikings. The breed's shaggy, water-resistant coat is well suited to the long, harsh winters of Maine, where farmers have long valued this cat's mousing ability.

Red mackerel tabby Maine Coon

! Breed-related health problems include hypertrophic cardiomyopathy (page 302).

BODY SHAPE (MANX)

BODY SHAPE (CYMRIC)

LAP CAT

GOOD WITH KIDS

SPECIAL GROOMING NEEDS

WEIGHT 9–12 LBS.

Manx and Cymric

Black Manx

The tailless Manx is a friendly, affectionate, relaxed companion—an easy feline to share a home with. According to some sources the Manx is somewhat doglike in its habits; it will play "fetch," growl at an unidentified disturbance, and may follow its owner around. These cats are also known for their love of shiny objects—keep an eye on your jewelry! Manxes like to snooze in laps and high places. Children, dogs, and other cats are taken in stride. The Cymric, whose name is derived from the Gaelic word for Wales, is a longhaired version of the Manx.

Appearance The Manx is a solidly built, medium-size, cobby cat with a round head, widely spaced ears, and large, round eyes. The powerful hindlegs are longer than the front legs, so the short back arches upward to the rounded rump. A completely tailless Manx is called a "rumpy"; the "rumpy riser" appears to be tailless but has one to three vertebrae fused to the end of the spine; the "stumpy" has one to five normal vertebrae, which give the cat a short, moveable tail stump; the "longy" is a cat with a shorter-than-normal tail, but a tail nonetheless.

Brown classic tabby Manx

The Manx's coat is very thick and glossy, with a dense undercoat. The Cymric has a soft, semi-long outercoat that gradually lengthens from head to rump. Many colors and patterns are accepted for both short- and longhairs, including tabby, solid, bicolor, shaded, tortoiseshell, and calico.

Special Grooming Needs Both the Manx's and the Cymric's dense coats need to be combed two or three times a week to remove loose fur.

Origins One of the oldest natural breeds of cats, the Manx is native to the Isle of Man, an island in the Irish Sea between England and Ireland. According to a biblically inspired Celtic folktale, the Manx was the last of God's creatures to climb aboard the ark, barely making it before Noah slammed the door shut. A variation portrays Noah's dog as the

Brown mackerel tabby Manx kitten

Brown mackerel tabby and white Cymric. The high rump, rounded back, short body, and widely spaced ears distinguish the breed.

culprit responsible for the loss of the cat's tail. In exasperation, the tailless cat fled the ark and swam from Ararat to the Isle of Man, where it found a home. Another tale claims that the Irish, or alternatively the Vikings, stole kittens to use their tails as good luck charms. In order to save their kittens, wise mother cats bit off the tails of their young, thus producing the tailless cat.

But how did the Manx really lose its tail? Geneticists have determined that taillessness occurred as the result of a spontaneous mutation. The breed was easily established due to the genetic nature of the tailless trait and centuries of inbreeding in an isolated island environment. Both long- and shorthaired cats existed on the Isle of Man before the appearance of the mutant gene for taillessness. When the tailless Manx appeared, the recessive longhair gene may have been part of the package.

① Some Manx cats experience neurologic disorders and defecation problems due to spinal defects associated with the gene for taillessness. The rabbitlike hop that is sometimes seen in Manx cats is probably due to some degree of spinal deformity. Spinal abnormalities can be discerned in kittens before they reach four months of age.

Munchkin

BODY SHAPE

The feline version of the Dachshund, this controversial new short-legged breed (named after the little people of Oz) is friendly, confident, talkative, and intelligent, with a wonderful sense of humor. Munchkins are extremely easygoing and so make great companions for children.

Short legs apparently do not handicap Munchkins, which can run with considerable speed and climb trees—although their jumping ability is somewhat limited. Countertops may be beyond their reach, but some owners may consider this an asset. They are able to groom themselves, and can stretch with hindlegs to scratch behind their ears.

TALKATIVE

Appearance Apart from its shortened limbs, the Munchkin resembles a domestic long- or shorthaired cat. All patterns and coat colors are acceptable.

LAP CAT

Origins The Munchkin breed descends from a stray cat with unusually short legs. Since cat fanciers got their first glimpse of this dwarfish feline at a show at New York's Madison Square Garden in 1991, the breed has created quite a stir, and its acceptance is not unanimous.

The Munchkin's shortened legs are caused by a spontaneous dominant mutation that has appeared before—in England in the 1930s and in Russia in the 1950s. Munchkins are still a breed in progress; most major breed associations do not recognize them for competition.

GOOD WITH KIDS

WEIGHT 8–10 LBS.

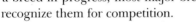

Brown mackerel tabby shorthaired Munchkin

Norwegian Forest Cat

BODY SHAPE

GOOD WITH KIDS

SPECIAL GROOMING NEEDS

Norwegian Forest Cats are gentle, friendly cats that enjoy climbing and, according to one source, fishing. They thrive in a busy household with lots of children, other animals, and plenty of action. While these cats love to be *with* people, they don't necessarily want to be *on* them.

Appearance The Norwegian Forest Cat is large, sturdy, and boxy, with back legs that are slightly longer than the front legs and paws tufted with fur between the toes. The head is triangular, with widely spaced ears and large, almond-shaped eyes that range in color from green to hazel to gold. White cats may have blue eyes or odd eyes.

The Wegie's coat is well designed to withstand the harshest of winters, but by spring it sheds its dense, woolly undercoat, leaving only the magnificently plumed tail and the tufts of its ears and feet to remind you that this is indeed a long-haired cat. Wegies come in all coat colors and patterns except the Siamese point patterns.

WEIGHT 8–10 LBS.

Dilute calico Norwegian Forest Cat showing off its voluminous tail

Brown mackerel torbie and white
Norwegian Forest Cat

Special Grooming Needs
Apart from periods of heavy shedding (less pronounced with indoor cats), the Norwegian Forest Cat does not generally require daily grooming; combing once or twice a week is recommended.

Origins The domestic cat appeared in Norway sometime after A.D. 1000. The Siberian and the Turkish Angora, natural longhaired breeds from Russia and Turkey, respectively, have been named as possible precursors of the large, densely furred Norwegian Forest Cat, as have descendants of crosses between Angoras and Scottish Wildcats. Whatever the breed's true origins were, the development of the Norwegian Forest Cat probably paralleled that of longhaired breeds elsewhere. In cold, wet environments, cats with woolly undercoats and long, water-repellent outercoats survived by adapting well to harsh climates.

⚠ Breed-related health problems include glycogen storage disease (a rare and fatal nervous system disorder).

Cream Norwegian Forest Cat

Ocicat

BODY SHAPE

TALKATIVE

HIGH ENERGY

GOOD WITH KIDS

Although bred to look like wildcats, Ocicats have the dependable temperament of a domestic cat—they are playful and sociable and make devoted companions. Their Siamese and American Shorthair ancestry contributes to their wonderful way with children. From their Abyssinian forebears, they inherited a high energy level. Ocicats are also eminently trainable; they will play fetch, walk on a leash, or ride on your shoulder. These cats tend to be vocal, though they are not quite so chatty as their Siamese progenitors.

If you are a frequent traveler, obtain a feline companion for your Ocicat, as these cats do not like being left alone.

WEIGHT 12–15 LBS.

Cinnamon Ocicat

Appearance The Ocicat is a long, muscular, medium to large cat with almond-shaped eyes and erect, wide-set ears. The head is a rounded wedge.

The Ocicat's lustrous, close-lying coat is randomly spotted. Each hair is banded: those within the spots are darker at the tip than those of the background. The spots can be tawny, chocolate, cinnamon, blue, lavender, and fawn on a silver or nonsilver background.

Origins The first Ocicat came about accidentally as the result of a breeding program designed to produce a pointed Siamese with a ticked tabby pattern. A chocolate point Siamese male was bred with a female that was part Siamese and part Abyssinian. The litter produced the intended Abyssinian–pointed Siamese, but also Tonga, an ivory kitten with golden spots resembling an Ocelot. A mating of Tonga's father and mother again yielded spotted offspring, which were used to form the foundation for the new spotted Ocicat breed. American Shorthairs were subsequently introduced into the Ocicat breeding program, adding mass and size.

Chocolate silver Ocicat

Persian

BODY SHAPE

LAP CAT

GOOD WITH KIDS

SPECIAL GROOMING NEEDS

WEIGHT 9-12 LBS.

The Persian is one of the most placid breeds. Gentle, quiet, and sweet-natured, Persians will not necessarily play with the kids, but neither will a houseful of children bother them—not much does! Just keep in mind that sticky-fingered kids can wreak havoc with the Persian's voluminous coat. These cats seem to be one of the least vocal breeds, although some owners describe their voices as melodious.

The Persian—or Longhair, as the breed is known in the United Kingdom—is an extremely popular breed; three-quarters of all registered pedigreed cats are Persians.

Copper-eyed cameo Persian

Appearance Beneath all that beautiful fur is a cobby, well-muscled, medium to large cat with short, thick legs. The roundness of the body is emphasized by a massive, round head, a short nose, and large, round eyes. The ears are small, widely spaced, and set low on the head. Eye color depends on the color of the coat.

The Persian's dense coat is exceptionally soft and silky; the hairs of both the undercoat and the .outercoat are quite long. The Persian's luxurious long hair extends from its ear tufts down to its bushy tail.

To accommodate the more than fifty Persian colors and patterns, some North American breed associations organize the Persian into seven divisions: solid, silver and golden, shaded and smoke, particolor, bicolor, tabby, and Himalayan. English registries still categorize each color as a separate breed.

Special Grooming Needs The Persian's voluminous coat must be combed daily to prevent mats from forming. Monthly baths are recommended.

Calico Persian kitten

Origins Many sources credit the 17th-century Italian traveler Pietro della Valle with introducing the first longhaired cats to Europe. In 1614, Pietro encountered a unique breed of cat with long, silky gray hair in the Persian province of Chorazan and imported a number of these cats to Italy. Soon after, white longhaired cats from Angora (modern-day Ankara, Turkey) were exported to Britain and France, where naturalist Georges Louis Leclerc de Buffon compared them to the Persian, noting that, except for their color, the Persians resembled the cats from Angora.

Descendants of these two longhaired breeds exhibited different physical characteristics. Angoras had finer features and were smaller boned than the stockier Persians. By the beginning of this century, cat fanciers in England had chosen the Persian over the Angora. In the United States, Persians replaced the indigenous Maine Coon as the longhaired darling of the cat fancy.

Over the years, the Persian has become more stylized in appearance, especially in the United States. Persians today have broader, flatter faces than they did one hundred years ago. Breed standards differ significantly from country to country.

Bicolor cream and white Persian kitten with copper eyes

Copper-eyed red Persian

① Breed-related health problems: tear overflow (page 287); constricted nostrils (which may lead to noisy breathing and may also make the cat less able to cope with high temperatures); dental malocclusions (teeth that fail to meet each other properly, possibly causing more rapid buildup of plaque and tartar); cherry eye (page 288); entropion (page 288); polycystic kidney disease (page 306); seborrhea oleosa (a skin condition that causes itchiness, redness, and hair loss); susceptibility to ringworm (page 291). Persians are also notorious for litter box lapses, at least in part because they dislike having litter granules stuck to their feet and in their fur.

Exotic Shorthair

PERSIAN FAMILY

The Exotic resembles the Persian in temperament—quiet, unobtrusive, and gentle—as well as in appearance. Exotics are lap cats, but, like other pets with dense coats, they may prefer sleeping on a cool floor. These cats are good with children, as they are not easily ruffled.

Appearance The Exotic is basically a shorthaired Persian. Exotics look like Persians with the notable exception of the thick, medium-length coat. They are medium to large, heavy-boned cats with a short, compact body; soft, round lines; short legs; and a short tail. Exotics have massive round heads, round eyes set well apart, the characteristic Persian snub nose, and small, rounded, widely set ears.

A dense, plush coat lends the Exotic a teddy bear look, while nearly one hundred patterns and colors give the breed an extensive wardrobe.

Blue mackerel tabby Exotic Shorthair kitten

WEIGHT 9-12 LBS.

Copper-eyed white Exotic Shorthair

Special Grooming Needs The Exotic Shorthair has been called the lazy man's Persian, as its coat does not mat or tangle readily. However, because the coat is so dense, it should be brushed a couple of times a week to remove loose fur.

Origins Breeding programs designed to improve the lines of American Shorthairs in the 1950s resulted in the creation of the cat now known as the Exotic Shorthair. In these programs, Persians crossed with American Shorthairs sometimes produced shorthaired offspring that were decidedly exotic in appearance. These first shorthaired Persians caused quite a controversy when they successfully competed with American Shorthairs in the show ring. Other shorthaired Persians also emerged when Persian breeders tried to create new coat colors.

Before 1967, Persians were also crossed with Burmese, Abyssinians, British and American Shorthairs, and Russian Blues to introduce the short coat length to the breeding line. Those shorthairs that most resembled shorthaired Persians were designated Exotic Shorthairs, and the new breed was established.

① The same health problems seen in Persians afflict this breed (page 135).

Red classic tabby Exotic Shorthair with copper eyes. Note the Persian-like tiny ears and short body.

Himalayan

PERSIAN FAMILY

BODY SHAPE

LAP CAT

GOOD WITH KIDS

SPECIAL GROOMING NEEDS

The Himalayan, a Persian cat with Siamese coat colors, borrows heavily from the Persian side. This is a gentle, docile breed that copes quite well with children and other animals. Himalayans are, for the most part, quiet creatures that rarely vocalize. However, their strong voices, when used, may remind you that there is indeed Siamese in the gene pool.

Appearance The Himalayan is a medium to large cat with a short, compact body; short, thick legs; and a short, thick tail. These cats have the typically Persian broad face, snub nose, rounded ears set low on the head, and large, vividly blue eyes.

As with other Persians, Himalayans have a voluminous coat of long, dense fur that covers

Seal point Himalayan

WEIGHT 9–12 LBS.

the entire animal, from ear tuft to toe tuft. A gorgeously showy neck ruff lends a regal quality to their demeanor. Especially distinctive are the contrasting points, which may be solid, tortoiseshell, or lynx. Body color ranges from white to beige.

Special Grooming Needs The Himalayan's dense undercoat will mat unless the cat is combed daily. White-coated cats can get dirty even indoors and require monthly bathing.

Origins In the 1920s, breeders from several countries attempted to create a cat with all the attributes of the Persian coupled with the distinctive color-point markings of the Siamese. They were somewhat successful, but it wasn't until the 1950s that persevering breeders in California and Great Britain achieved the success that resulted in a new breed, the Himalayan.

ⓘ The same problems seen in Persians afflict this breed (page 135).

Seal lynx point Himalayan kitten

Ragdoll

BODY SHAPE

GOOD WITH KIDS

SPECIAL GROOMING NEEDS

WEIGHT 14–18 LBS.

Ragdolls, named for their willingness to go limp in your arms, have an easy-going, docile temperament that makes them particularly good with children and other pets (though young children must be instructed not to take advantage of the Ragdoll's accepting nature by being too rough). Some breeders claim that they are so nonaggressive they won't even defend themselves when attacked. These gentle giants are sociable, playful, soft-voiced, and affectionate.

Appearance Ragdolls, long and muscular cats, are slow to mature—they do not reach their (large) adult size and weight until they are three to four years old. The head is broad and softly triangular; the ears are broad-based and sit atop the head with a slight forward tilt; the large, oval, wide-set eyes are blue.

The silky, semi-long coat comes in four colors—seal, chocolate, blue, and lilac—and three patterns—mitted, bicolor, and color-point. Mitted Ragdolls have dark points that end where white mittens and boots

Chocolate bicolor Ragdoll displaying its gentle, playful disposition

begin. Bicolors have dark tails and ears, and masked faces interrupted by an inverted "V" of white between the eyes; they have a white ruff, stomach, legs, and feet. Colorpoints have dark extremities contrasting with lighter bodies and no white markings. Coats do not achieve full color until the cat is about two years old.

Special Grooming Needs If you would like to own a fluffy cat but do not want to commit to daily grooming, here's your opportunity. Combing or brushing just once or twice a week is recommended, as the Ragdoll's coat is not prone to matting.

Blue mitted Ragdoll

Origins Since a California breeder developed the Ragdoll in the 1960s, there has been much disagreement regarding the breed's history. Some sources claim that it is descended from a Persian-Birman cross, with a touch of Burmese. Others claim that all Ragdolls descend from the matings of two feral toms with the same Persian-type female.

Seal point Ragdoll

Russian Blue and Nebelung

BODY SHAPE (RUSSIAN BLUE)

BODY SHAPE (NEBELUNG)

HIGH ENERGY

SPECIAL GROOMING NEEDS

Russian Blues are an intelligent breed, well mannered and fastidious, with quiet voices to match their gentle demeanor. Owners describe them as shy yet affectionate. They've also been described as somewhat flighty, perhaps not the best quality in a cat if you have children. Russians are sprightly cats; many will retrieve objects and some reportedly can open doors. They love to drink water from faucets. The Nebelung, essentially a longhaired Russian Blue, is named for the luminous quality of its silver-tipped coat: *Nebelung* is German for "creature of the mist."

Appearance The Russian Blue is a long, fine-boned, graceful cat. Round green eyes are prominently featured on a triangular head with a blunt muzzle and erect, widely spaced ears.

The Russian's lustrous, silver-tipped gray coat is one of its most distinctive features. The short, dense coat is so plush that it stands out from the body. It is said that the Russian's exquisite coat, prized by trappers, put it at considerable risk during the long subarctic winter. The Nebelung's fluffy tail distinguishes the breed from the Russian Blue.

WEIGHT 6–8 LBS.

Russian Blue

Russian Blue

Special Grooming Needs These dense-coated cats should be brushed twice a week to remove loose fur.

Origins British sailors probably brought these cats from the White Sea port of Arkhangelsk in the subarctic region of northern Russia to northern Europe and Britain in the 1860s. American breeders imported them from both England and Scandinavia, and by combining the best traits from each line, achieved the standard admired in the United States today. In the 1980s in the United States, a Russian Blue male was crossed with a female that carried the longhair gene. The foundation stock for the new longhaired breed, the Nebelung, was taken from two litters of that cross.

Nebelung

Scottish Fold and Highland Fold

BODY SHAPE (SCOTTISH FOLD)

BODY SHAPE (HIGHLAND FOLD)

GOOD WITH KIDS

SPECIAL GROOMING NEEDS

WEIGHT 10–12 LBS.

These quiet, sweet-natured, easygoing cats are most content when they are around people and dislike being alone. Although Folds prefer the company of humans, another cat will satisfy their need for companionship if nobody is at home for much of the day. Their laid-back temperament makes them very good with children. The Highland Fold is a longhaired version of the Scottish Fold.

Appearance Folds are medium-size cats with a robust, rounded appearance. They have rounded heads, short necks, and large, round, widely spaced eyes. Kittens are born with "normal" ears, but at about two to four weeks of age, some begin to develop a noticeable bending forward of the ears; by three months of age, the fold, which varies in degree from cat to cat, is permanent, giving the cat an owlish look.

Scottish Folds have dense coats that stand out from their bodies. Highland Folds have coats of variable length, from medium to long; hair is longest on the ruff, leg britches (the long hair along the rear part of the back legs), and plumed tail. Both Folds come in many colors and patterns.

Left to right: black and white bicolor, silver mackerel torbie and white, cream mackerel tabby, and silver mackerel tabby Scottish Fold kittens. For health reasons, two fold-eared cats are not usually mated, and so litters often include straight-eared kittens such as the one in this litter at the far right.

Special Grooming Needs Folds should be brushed two to three times a week—long-hairs to prevent matting and shorthairs to remove loose fur.

Origins Today's Scottish Folds trace their ancestry to Susie, a white barn cat born in Scotland in 1961 with uniquely folded ears. Susie had a litter of kittens that included a female with folded ears, which in turn produced a fold-eared male. A London breeder determined that a dominant mutant gene was responsible for the folded ears.

Red mackerel tabby Scottish Fold

Silver classic tabby and white Highland Fold

Longhaired kittens have appeared in Scottish Fold litters from the beginning. Susie probably produced longhaired kittens, as did her daughter Snooks. Early breeding programs in the United States paired the fold-eared imports with British and American Shorthairs. Many British Shorthairs carry a longhair gene, which may have found expression in the new long-haired Folds. Some sources also suggest that Persians were used in the early development of this longhaired breed.

(!) Some kittens born to two fold-eared parents experience a crippling skeletal abnormality called congenital osteodys-trophy, a progressive stiffening and fusing of the joints that ultimately makes walking painful.

Calico Highland Fold. Tightly folded ears and round eyes give this cat an owlish expression.

Selkirk Rex

BODY SHAPE (LONGHAIR)

GOOD WITH KIDS

SPECIAL GROOMING NEEDS

Selkirks are similar in temperament to the affable British Shorthair and the gentle Persian. While they are not lap cats per se, they are tolerant, easygoing creatures that happily cohabitate with people and other animals.

Appearance The Selkirk Rex, which may be bred with Persians, Exotics, or British and American Shorthairs, are rectangular, heavy-boned, muscular cats with a round, broad head and a short muzzle. The wide-set eyes are large and round; the ears are also set well apart and are rounded with pointed tips.

Selkirk kittens are born with curly hair and whiskers; when the kittens reach about six months of age, the curly coat is replaced by a sparser, straighter coat until they reach maturity. Adults tend to lose the curly whiskers they had as kittens. The adult Selkirk's coat is dense, full, and soft as lamb's wool. The loosely coiled curls are most prominent on the neck, tail, and stomach. The coat may be either long or short. Cats with the Selkirk gene on both sides have sparser, tighter coats than cats with only one Selkirk parent. Selkirks come in any number of colors and patterns.

Special Grooming Needs These dense-coated cats should be brushed a couple of times a week to remove loose fur.

Origins The foundation for this new breed of rex (curly-coated) cats was a unique, curly-coated calico kitten found in a Wyoming animal shelter in 1987. Bred with a champion black Persian in 1988, she produced three curly-coated kittens in a litter of six, proving that the rex gene was dominant. The breed was named after Wyoming's Selkirk Mountains.

WEIGHT 9–11 LBS.

Black smoke shorthair Selkirk Rex

Siamese

BODY SHAPE

TALKATIVE

LAP CAT

HIGH ENERGY

GOOD WITH KIDS

Siamese cats are loyal, energetic, and intelligent. They are also sociable and affectionate, and tend to follow their chosen human(s) around the home. They like to be held and to ride on their owners' shoulders. They expect their affection to be returned, and dislike being left alone for long periods of time. Siamese are also very vocal, with a distinctive, deep, nasal voice. The persistent chattiness of this breed may be irksome to some, but Siamese-lovers find these cats' voices endearing. Siamese are excellent with kids; they will tolerate being dressed up and carried around, though rough play is not appreciated. They generally dominate other cats in the household.

Lilac point Siamese

WEIGHT 7-9 LBS.

Seal point Siamese

Appearance The Siamese has the prototypical oriental physique: long and svelte from its wedge-shaped head to its tapering tail, with long, delicately boned legs supporting a tubular body. The nose, too, is long, while the ears are large and the eyes are deep blue and almond-shaped.

The Siamese's short, silky, close-lying coat is most remarkable for the pointed pattern of colored extremities—face, ears, legs, and tail—which contrast with the paler body. Until the 1930s, breed registries recognized only the seal point color form (deep, seal brown points and a pale, fawn-colored body). Blue points (a bluish-white body with slate blue points), as well as chocolate points and lilac points, are now recognized.

Origins Siamese cats have been around for centuries in their native land of Siam (now Thailand) but were unknown in the West until the 19th century, when it became fashionable

Seal point Siamese showing its tubular body and athletic nature.

to own a Siamese cat. The first Americans to own Siamese cats had to be fairly affluent, as it cost about a thousand dollars to import one from England at the turn of the century. Siamese remained immensely popular until the 1960s, when supply exceeded demand. By then, the Siamese gene pool had been on loan to enterprising breeders for some time. Colorpoints, Oriental Shorthairs and Longhairs, Balinese, Javanese, Tonkinese, Havana Browns, and Himalayans all owe some component of their genetic make-up to the Siamese. With all the competition, the Siamese's unparalleled reign in popularity came to an end.

ⓘ These are active, demanding cats that require lots of attention and space to play. Provide them with an interesting environment where they can climb, scratch, and run, and anticipate spending some playtime with them every day. Breed-related health problems: crossed eyes due to an inherited neurological defect; nystagmus (a slight but very rapid jerking back-and-forth of the eyes); congenital heart defects (page 302).

Chocolate point Siamese kitten that has not yet grown into its ears.

Balinese

SIAMESE FAMILY

BODY SHAPE

Named for graceful dancers from the island of Bali, Balinese are very similar in temperament to Siamese: busy, extroverted, curious, affectionate, demanding, loyal, intelligent, and very good with children. They like to talk and can be noisy cats.

TALKATIVE

Appearance The Balinese, a longhaired Siamese, is a slim, medium-size cat. The head is long and triangular, with large, pointed ears and blue, almond-shaped eyes. The tail is long and plumed. The medium-long, silky coat is not particularly prone to matting. The Balinese comes in the four Siamese point colors—seal, chocolate, blue, and lilac.

LAP CAT

Origins Some believe the longhaired Balinese derives from Siamese-Angora or Siamese-Persian crossing begun in the 1920s; others credit a spontaneous mutation as the source of the longhaired gene. In the 1950s, a California breeder began a program to develop the Balinese into a new breed.

HIGH ENERGY

(!) These cats crave companionship and affection and need plenty of exercise and opportunities for scratching. They have the same breed-related health problems as the Siamese (page 150).

GOOD WITH KIDS

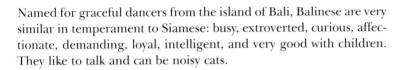

Lilac point Balinese

WEIGHT 7–9 LBS.

Colorpoint

SIAMESE FAMILY

BODY SHAPE

TALKATIVE

LAP CAT

HIGH ENERGY

GOOD WITH KIDS

WEIGHT 7-9 LBS.

The Colorpoint is Siamese in temperament and intelligence—active, demanding, vocal, loving, and smart. These cats love to play; give them a paper bag and you'll provide both cat and human with an evening's entertainment. They're also likely to end up under the covers with you on a cold night.

Appearance The Colorpoint, a Siamese in nontraditional colors, is a svelte cat with a wedge-shaped head; large, flaring ears; and blue, almond-shaped eyes. The short, glossy fur comes in a wide variety of colors, and the mask, ears, legs, and tail can be solid or patterned.

Blue-cream point Colorpoint

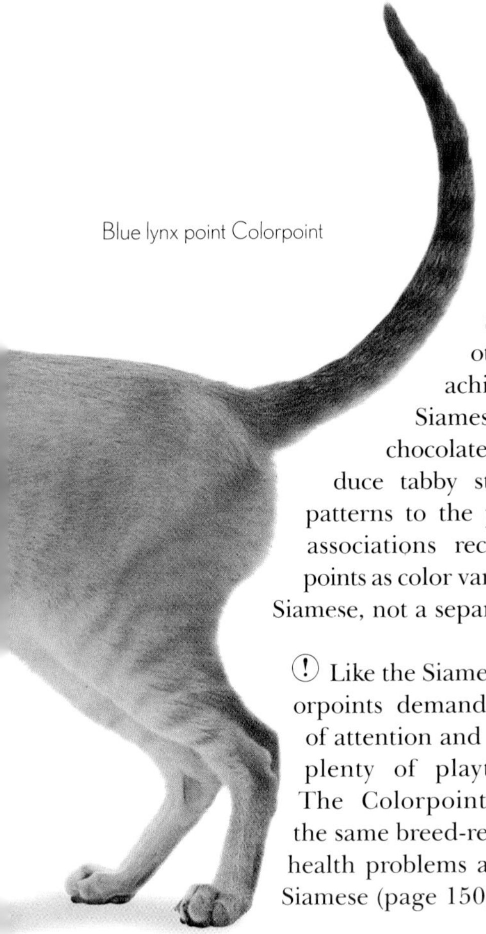

Blue lynx point Colorpoint

Origins In the late 1940s, British breeders crossed Siamese cats with American Shorthairs, Abyssinians, and other shorthairs in order to achieve colors beyond the Siamese's traditional seal, blue, chocolate, and lilac, and to introduce tabby striping and tortoiseshell patterns to the points. Some breed associations recognize Colorpoints as color varieties of the Siamese, not a separate breed.

(!) Like the Siamese, Colorpoints demand a lot of attention and need plenty of playtime. The Colorpoint has the same breed-related health problems as the Siamese (page 150).

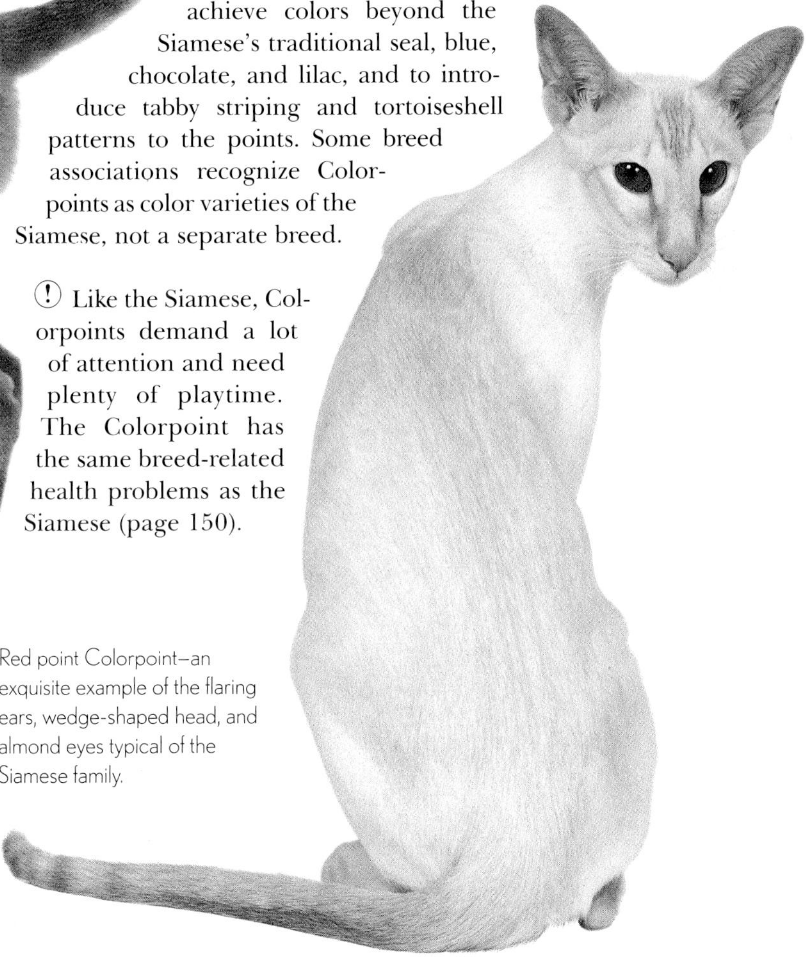

Red point Colorpoint—an exquisite example of the flaring ears, wedge-shaped head, and almond eyes typical of the Siamese family.

153

Javanese

SIAMESE FAMILY

BODY SHAPE

TALKATIVE

LAP CAT

HIGH ENERGY

GOOD WITH KIDS

WEIGHT 7-9 LBS.

Like Siamese, Javanese are busy, talkative, curious cats that demand lots of attention. They enjoy playing and are partial to high spaces. Once they have settled down, these affectionate cats are happy to curl up on your lap.

Appearance The Javanese has a sleek, tubular body; long, thin legs; a wedge-shaped head; blue, almond-shaped eyes; large, pointed ears; and a tapering, plumed tail.

The medium-length coat is close-lying and silky and does not mat easily. Essentially a long-haired form of the Colorpoint, the Javanese may have points that are solid red or cream, lynx-patterned in red or cream (as well as in the traditional Siamese colors), or tortie-patterned.

Chocolate lynx point Javanese

Seal lynx point Javanese

Origins Breeders long recognized that when Siamese were crossed with domestic shorthairs to produce Color-points, the recessive gene for long hair sometimes found its way into the gene pool. These longhaired Colorpoints were effectively recycled as Javanese—longhaired Siamese in nontraditional colors. Other breeders began with Balinese—the longhaired Siamese in traditional Siamese point colors—and crossed them with Colorpoints to produce kittens that were longhaired, pointed, and splashed with color.

 Javanese need lots of play-time and companionship, either human or animal. The Javanese has the same breed-related health problems as the Siamese (page 150).

Red lynx point Javanese

Oriental

SIAMESE FAMILY

TALKATIVE

LAP CAT

HIGH ENERGY

GOOD WITH KIDS

Orientals are cuddly, loquacious, and inquisitive cats. They like to climb and to retrieve objects, and are ingenious at finding new toys to play with. They are extremely people-oriented, which means that they are always underfoot. Orientals do well with children as long as play sessions are not too rough.

Appearance The Oriental is a nonpointed Siamese that comes in hundreds of combinations of color and pattern. Orientals are long, lean cats with long, triangular heads; large, flared ears; and green, almond-shaped eyes (white Orientals may have blue, green, or odd eyes).

WEIGHT 7-9 LBS.

Ebony ticked torbie Oriental Shorthair

Orientals may have short or long hair. Shorthairs have short, finely textured, close-lying fur. Longhairs have medium-length, silky, close-lying fur and a plumed tail.

Origins In the late 1960s, fanciers created the Oriental Shorthair by breeding Siamese to American Shorthairs and Abyssinians. Oriental Longhairs were developed in the late 1970s by crossing Oriental Shorthairs with Balinese and Javanese.

⊙ Orientals need lots of human interaction and love to play. They have the same breed-related health problems as the Siamese (page 150).

Blue mackerel tabby Oriental Longhair

Siberian

BODY SHAPE

GOOD WITH KIDS

SPECIAL GROOMING NEEDS

These gentle, friendly, loyal cats from northern Russia are good with kids and adjust well to other pets. They love to climb, so provide ample opportunity for them to explore high places. Some purr magnificently, endearing themselves to their owners.

Appearance Siberians are large cats that give the appearance of strength and power. A rounded body shape differentiates the breed from the boxier Norwegian Forest Cat and the Maine Coon. The yellow-green eyes are large, round, and wide-set, the ears large and wide with rounded tips.

Siberians have a short, dense undercoat and a moderately long outercoat enhanced by a neck ruff. They exhibit many coat colors and patterns; brown tabbies are the most popular.

Special Grooming Needs Twice-weekly combing should keep the Siberian's coat free from tangles.

Brown mackerel tabby Siberian

WEIGHT 15-20 LBS.

Brown tabby and white
Siberian

Origins Siberians lived unobtrusively in their northern homeland for centuries; Russian cat fanciers have only recently dedicated themselves to this gentle breed. These cats have not been unknown to Westerners, however; Siberians competed in early-19th-century cat shows in England, but they could not vie with the ever-popular Persians, and promotion of the breed subsided.

Following the renewed interest of European cat associations in the 1980s, breeders in Russia began to focus attention on their neglected native cat, and a registry for Siberian cats was formed in St. Petersburg. In 1990, the first Siberians were imported to the United States, where they have since become a small but growing presence.

Blue and white (left) and red classic tabby (right) Siberian kittens

Singapura

BODY SHAPE

LAP CAT

HIGH ENERGY

The Singapura's tail is tipped in black.

The smallest of the domestic cat breeds, Singapuras are quiet, affectionate, curious, and intelligent. They love to play fetch, and generally like to join in their owners' activities. They crave human companionship; plan to spend some time with this perky feline.

Appearance Singapuras are small, muscular, moderately stocky cats. The head is rounded, with prominent hazel, green, or yellow eyes and large, moderately pointed ears.

The most remarkable aspect of this wee cat is the subtle coloration of the short, silky, close-lying coat: It is a pale ivory color with sepia ticking covering the entire body except the stomach, chest, and muzzle.

Origins These cats were allegedly discovered on the streets of Singapore and imported to the United States in the early 1970s. Because they were not accompanied by official papers recording their origin or place of entry, some people question this history. Most breed associations accept the Singapura for registry.

WEIGHT 5-7 LBS.

Singapura with hazel eyes

Snowshoe

BODY SHAPE

This breed possesses the unflappable, easygoing temperament of its American Shorthair forebears, making it a fine companion for children or other pets. Affectionate and people-oriented, the Snowshoe is an amiable and loving friend and companion. Although not as vocal as a Siamese, the Snowshoe can be quite a talker, albeit with a softer, more melodic voice.

TALKATIVE

Appearance A medium-size cat, the Snowshoe combines the stocky, robust appearance of the American Shorthair with the length of the Siamese. The pleasing result is a powerful, agile cat of intermediate body type. The head is a rounded wedge shape, the eyes are oval and bright blue, and the ears are medium-size, with slightly rounded tips.

LAP CAT

The Snowshoe is a shorthaired cat with a pointed coat pattern, white markings on the feet (for which the breed is named), and an inverted white "V" on the face, which begins in the middle of the forehead and descends to the muzzle. These cats come in two color combinations: seal point and white, and blue point and white.

GOOD WITH KIDS

Origins Philadelphia breeder Dorothy Hinds-Daugherty developed this breed in the 1960s by crossing a Siamese with a bicolor American Shorthair. Breeder Vikki Olander saw the breed's potential, wrote the first breed standard, and persevered until the new Snowshoe was accepted for registration in 1974.

Seal point and white
Snowshoe

WEIGHT 8–10 LBS.

Sphynx

BODY SHAPE

LAP CAT

GOOD WITH KIDS

SPECIAL GROOMING NEEDS

This all-but-hairless breed may look bizarre, but all sources indicate that the Sphynx's easygoing disposition quickly wins over many detractors. Very loving and affectionate, the Sphynx makes an amiable and patient companion to dogs, other pets, and children.

Brown mackerel tabby and white Sphynx

Appearance Barrel-chested and muscular, the Sphynx has a medium-long body. Oversize ears give the breed a batlike appearance, while large, round eyes give the face a startled expression. The whiplike, tapered tail may end in a surprising puff of hair.

The Sphynx's wrinkled, chamois-soft skin is covered with nearly imperceptible down; short, soft, densely packed hair is sometimes found on the ears, muzzle, feet, tail, and scrotum. Whiskers and eyebrows may be broken or absent. All colors and patterns are possible.

Special Grooming Needs Because the Sphynx's skin quickly becomes greasy, weekly sponge-bathing with an anti-seborrheic shampoo (which you can obtain from a veterinarian) is recommended.

WEIGHT 8–10 LBS.

Brown tabby and white Sphynx

Left to right: brown tabby and white, brown and white, calico, red and white, and seal point and white Sphynx kittens

Origins In 1975 in Wadena, Minnesota, a farm cat named Jezabelle bore two hairless kittens in two succeeding litters. The ancestry of many of today's Sphynx cats can be traced to one of these cats.

A few years later, three hairless strays were rescued from the streets of Toronto. The two females were sent to a breeder in the Netherlands, who crossed them with a Devon Rex. The descendants of these cats became the foundation for the Sphynx in Europe.

⚠ Sun and extreme temperatures can be hazardous for the Sphynx, so indoor living is vital for its survival. Some cats enjoy the extra warmth of a sweater in the winter.

Brown tabby and white Sphynx. Note the short, dense hair on the edges of the batlike ears.

Tonkinese

BODY SHAPE

TALKATIVE

LAP CAT

HIGH ENERGY

GOOD WITH KIDS

WEIGHT 7-9 LBS.

The Tonkinese was developed to combine the best characteristics of the Siamese and the Burmese. Tonks are sociable, intelligent, and curious like their Siamese side, and calm and adaptable like their Burmese ancestors. They like to talk, but their voices are less strident than the Siamese. These are engaging, entertaining creatures.

Appearance Tonks are medium-size cats with good musculature; they are surprisingly heavy for their size. The head is a rounded wedge, and the ears are medium in size. Tonkinese that exhibit the mink pattern (described below) have distinctive aquamarine eyes.

The short, silky, close-lying coat may be one of three patterns— solid, mink, or pointed— and one of as many as eight colors—natural, champagne, platinum, blue, cinnamon, fawn, red, and cream. Solid Tonkinese have the dark body color of the Burmese; pointed

Blue pointed Tonkinese

Champagne mink
Tonkinese

cats have the pale body and dark points of the Siamese; and mink Tonkinese have an intermediate body color with darker points. Solid and pointed Tonks do not compete in most show rings but are indispensable in Tonkinese breeding programs. When a pointed Tonkinese is crossed with a solid Tonkinese, all the offspring display the mink pattern.

Origins In the early 1960s, a Canadian breeder crossed a sable Burmese with a seal point Siamese, which produced a cat of intermediate type and coloring. She renamed this hybrid Siamese a Tonkanese. The spelling was changed in 1971 to Tonkinese after the Bay of Tonkin in Southeast Asia.

(!) True to their Siamese lineage, Tonks are active cats that need room to play, climb, and jump; they also need plenty of attention and companionship.

Natural (right) and champagne (left) mink Tonkinese

Turkish Angora

BODY SHAPE

HIGH ENERGY

The Turkish Angora is an ancient natural breed that has enjoyed a resurgence in popularity since its reintroduction to the West in the 1960s. Graceful, playful, loving, loyal, and gentle are words enthusiasts use to describe this cat. Angoras are also extremely busy, always on the move. They'll check in with you for about five seconds—until something else catches their attention. These resourceful cats will invent their own toys if none are provided and have been known to play with dust motes.

Appearance The Angora is a small to medium cat, lithe and fine-boned, with a long, graceful body and a long, plumed tail. The large, erect ears sit high on the head and close together. The eyes are large and almond-shaped. The head is wedge-shaped.

The glossy coat is medium-long and silky, with a thin undercoat that is not prone to matting. Hair is longest on the tail, ruff, and

Blue-eyed white Turkish Angora

WEIGHT 8-10 LBS.

back legs. All-white Angoras may have been the most popular representative of the breed in the past, but Angoras of many colors and patterns are gaining in popularity.

Origins The Angora was found residing in Turkey by the 1400s in the region surrounding the city of Angora, later named Ankara. This aristocratic-looking cat was exported to the estates of European nobility during the Renaissance. Angoras and Persians competed against one another at the early cat shows in England, but by the end of the 19th century, the Persian had edged out all other longhaired competitors, including the Angora.

In the 1940s the Turkish government (in conjunction with the Ankara Zoo) began a program to collect, preserve, and protect the traditional all-white Angoras. In 1962 an American couple bought a pair of the zoo's Angoras and imported them to the United States. Other breeders followed suit, and by 1970 the Turkish Angora was reintroduced to the show ring.

(!) All-white Angoras with one or two blue eyes may be partially or totally deaf, a tendency common to blue- and odd-eyed white cats of other breeds as well.

Black and white bicolor
Turkish Angora

Turkish Van

Tortoiseshell and white Turkish Van

The Turkish Van is an energetic, intelligent, soft-voiced, and affectionate breed. Also known as "the swimming cat," the Turkish Van is famous for its love of water. It will swim or just lie in the water—most unusual for a cat. Its fluffy, foxlike tail is in perpetual motion.

Appearance The Turkish Van is a large, muscular cat, wide-bodied and large-boned. Like the Turkish Angora, the Van has long legs, but its feet are larger than its cousin's. A broad, wedge-shaped head supports large, wide-set ears. Vans may have amber or blue eyes, or one of each.

The Van's semi-long, silky coat is somewhat heavier than the Angora's but is also not prone to matting. British and North American cat fanciers favor white Vans with colored markings on the head and a fully colored tail. The colored areas may be red, cream, black, blue, tortoiseshell, calico, brown tabby, torbie, or silver/smoke versions of all the above colors and patterns.

Origins In 1955, two British women vacationing in the Lake Van region in eastern Turkey were given a pair of white kittens with auburn markings on their heads and tails. The women imported more of the cats and began a breeding program. The Turks consider a true Van cat to be all white with odd eyes. This cat is rare in its native Turkey today.

WEIGHT 10-13 LBS.

York Chocolate

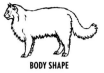

BODY SHAPE

The York is a true lap cat, one that is happy to be held and cuddled. This is not to imply that Yorks are sedate and docile; in fact they are active, intelligent, and curious, constantly monitoring the activities of their owners.

LAP CAT

Appearance The York Chocolate is a medium to large cat, big-boned and muscular. Some Siamese ancestry is assumed, as the head is a rounded wedge, longer than it is wide. The large, pointed ears tilt forward; the almond-shaped eyes may be green, gold, or hazel.

HIGH ENERGY

Yorks are solid or bicolored in chocolate or lilac. The medium-long, glossy coat is silky and close-lying, with a thin undercoat that is not prone to matting. Yorks have a plumed tail, toe tufts, and a modest neck ruff.

Origins The owner of a New York State goat dairy had a farm cat named Blackie that in 1983 presented her with a litter of kittens. One of these kittens, named Brownie, had her own litter of kittens, and so appeared a longhaired black male named Minky. Minky and Brownie produced Teddy Bear and Cocoa. Their owner, who was running out of names for brown cats, noticed a consistency in body and coat type among the kittens and initiated a breeding program.

WEIGHT 14-16 LBS.

Chocolate and white bicolor York Chocolate

III

What Makes
a Cat a Cat?

The more you understand about what makes a cat a cat, the more interesting and rewarding an experience it will be to live with and care for your feline friend, and the more responsible an owner you can be. This section of the *ASPCA Complete Guide to Cats* opens with a bit of evolutionary history (how domestic cats probably came to have their present form) and an account of the relatively recent development of the special bond between cats and humans. A guide to how cats are built and how they work follows. Next is an exploration of feline behavior: How smart are cats? What do they do all day? How do they communicate?

The three chapters in this section are:

This introduction to the inner life of your cat is followed by the section Taking Care of Your Cat, a comprehensive guide to keeping your cat healthy and happy throughout her life.

History of the Domestic Cat

Cats are by far the most popular pet in North America. In fact, in the United States there are 10 million more pet cats than dogs. But cats are not and never have been universally admired. It has been estimated that one out of four Americans harbors a distinct distaste for cats. This ambivalence toward cats probably dates all the way back to the dawn of civilization. Some early cultures venerated cats as benevolent deities, while others believed them to be agents of evil—and a few associated them with both fertility and death. In spite of humans' contradictory feelings for cats, a wild ancestor nonetheless developed—through close contact with people over thousands of years—into the house cat we know today. A brief account of that history follows.

By about 1500 B.C., the cat was considered sacred in Egyptian society. This bronze of a mother and kitten dates from the Saite period (730-332 B.C.).

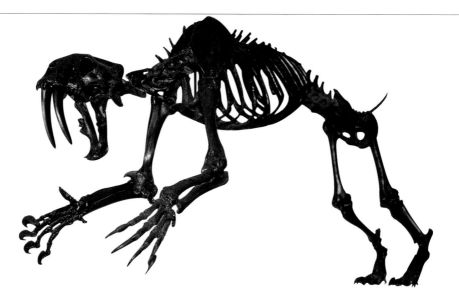

The saber-toothed tiger was the last in one line of prehistoric cats.

The Cat's Early Ancestry

The domestic cat (*Felis catus*, scientifically speaking) bears a strong resemblance to its prehistoric prototype, *Proailurus* ("early cat"), a bobcat-size creature of about twenty pounds that roamed Eurasia and Africa some 34 million years ago. The cat's evolution over the millennia was largely a process of fine-tuning. From early on, much of the key equipment was in place: keen vision, a flexible spine and front limbs, retractable claws, and powerful jaws with flesh-cutting teeth.

One branch of the ancient cat clan reached a dead end with the fearsome saber-toothed cats about 10,000 years ago. From the other branch evolved the present-day cat family, which includes the big cats—panthers, lions, tigers, leopards, and cheetahs—as well as numerous smaller wild species, such as ocelots, bobcats, and lynxes. In all, thirty-eight cat species (thirty-seven wild, one domestic) are known today.

Wildcats such as this Barbary leopard and the domestic house cat all follow the same basic blueprint.

Cats by Category

Ever since the ancient Greeks divided all living organisms into two major groups—the plant kingdom and the animal kingdom—scientists have endeavored to further classify plants and animals according to characteristics that define their similarities and differences. Modern classification systems follow the scheme formulated by Swedish botanist Carolus Linnaeus (1701–1778), which subdivides the plant and animal kingdoms into major groups called phyla. Phyla are divided into classes, classes into orders, orders into families, families into genera (singular: genus), and genera into species. The species is the basic unit of classification and is generally what we have in mind when we talk about a kind of animal. The domestic cat belongs to the phylum Chordata, which includes all vertebrates; the class Mammalia, warm-blooded animals with hair; the order Carnivora, a diverse group consisting mainly of meat-eaters; the family Felidae, the cats, both wild and domestic; the genus *Felis*; and the species *catus*—hence the scientific name of the domestic cat, *Felis catus*.

From Wildcat to Lap Cat

Felis catus appeared about 7,000 years ago; it is probably a relative of the African Wildcat (still found in the Middle East and Africa), which is less timid than other wildcat species and to this day often lives close to human settlements. Most likely, domestication first occurred in Egypt around the time when agriculture developed and humans began to live in permanent settlements. Our ancestors' stores of grain attracted rodents—providing a steady food supply for the local wildcats. Shelter from weather and predators was a further advantage of life among humans, who may at first have appreciated cats solely for the purpose of pest control. Over thousands of years, the relationship between humans and cats grew closer, and cats became better suited to life with people.

The African Wildcat *(Felis lybica)* is the likely progenitor of the modern domestic cat.

By about 1600 B.C. domesticated cats were well integrated into Egyptian society. Sometime after 1500 B.C., the cat became a sacred religious symbol associated with the goddess of fertility and sexuality. At first, the Egyptians forbade export of the sacred animal, even going so far as to retrieve felines that had been taken abroad. The Phoenicians, eastern Mediterranean seafarers and merchants of legendary status, are known to have traded with the Egyptians. Historians believe that cats were brought aboard Phoenician ships and carried to various Mediterranean and Indian ports of call before 500 B.C. Dates of the cat's arrival in most of Asia are uncertain.

The Egyptians were inordinately fond of household pets. In contrast, the Greeks were unsentimental about animals. While some dogs in ancient Greece were valued for their hunting or herding skills, cats had no such status, and we know nothing about their daily lot. Greek cats probably earned their keep as rodent police, dining on their own kills and on the odd kitchen scrap.

In ancient Rome, cats had a little more to purr about. The Romans doted on their dogs, and they also found cats endearing. Nonetheless, cats still had to earn their keep by protecting food supplies. With the rise of the Roman Empire, barter and exchange distributed cats throughout Europe and Asia. Wherever people traveled, cats were carried along. As rats and mice were inadvertently spread by the international shipping trade, its rodent-killing prowess made the cat a valuable commodity. The cat eventually replaced the European polecat, or ferret, as the vermin destroyer of choice. Aboard ships, cats came to be regarded as ambassadors of good fortune. Sailors believed that cats could foresee bad weather, so they brought cats with them to all points of the compass.

Bast, ancient Egyptian goddess of love and fertility, was often represented as a cat. This bronze figure dates from the Saite period (730-332 B.C.).

Faith and Felines

Dedicated cat fanciers are often accused of "cat worship," but their devotion to felines pales compared to that of the ancient Egyptians, to whom the cat was literally a sacred animal. The cat was immortalized in Egyptian temple art and linked to Bast, the goddess of love and fertility. Anyone who killed a cat might be sentenced to death. When an Egyptian family lost its beloved cat, family members entered a period of ritual mourning, shaving their eyebrows to make their grief obvious to all. Family pets were mummified and buried in special cat cemeteries; but not all mummified cats had spent their lives as pampered pets. There was a thriving industry for the breeding and sacrifice of kittens, which would then be mummified and sold by priests of the Bast cult to pilgrims at the goddess's shrine. Hundreds of thousands of mummified cats have been found at one burial site, and scholars believe that many, perhaps all of them, were bred to be sacrificed.

Cats are welcome in Buddhist temples such as this one in Bangkok, Thailand.

Cats didn't always fare well in Christendom, either. In 1484, Pope Innocent VIII proclaimed that witches used animals as "familiars," or helpers in their service to the devil. The familiars of choice were believed to be cats. Suddenly, owning a cat—or even feeding a stray—became a capital offense, punishable by burning at the stake. The cats, too, of course, were put to death.

Cats have not suffered in the name of faith universally. Among Muslims, for example, cats have always held a place of honor because of the prophet Muhammad's great fondness for them. Several legends tell of the Prophet's tenderness toward his own cats. One tale relates how a cat saved Muhammad from a deadly serpent.

In India, Hinduism emphasizes reverence for all living things, cats included, as do the Parsi faith and Jainism. In fact, devout Hindus keep at least one cat in their homes as a religious obligation. Buddhism, too, is famous for its teachings about compassion toward all creatures—but in early Buddhism, compassion toward cats was optional at best. Standoffish and self-centered, according to one legend, the cat had failed to grieve at the Buddha's funeral (snakes were the only other animals to behave so badly). However, Buddhists have long since forgiven cats their lapse in manners.

Cats in ancient Egypt were revered in life and in death. This mummified cat dates from the Saite period (730-332 B.C.).

Renaissance painter Francesco Ubertini rendered his subject and her beloved pet with equal care.

The Renaissance ushered in far better times for cats (and humans) in Europe. People who had kept cats secretly could now do so openly. In the households of nobles and the rising merchant class, cats were pampered and adored. While not all cats were so privileged, at least officially sanctioned cruelty to cats had become a thing of the past.

Cats reached North America in large numbers during the eighteenth century, earning their keep on farms overrun by rodents. As in Europe, a favored few enjoyed a sedentary, sheltered lifestyle, but the vast majority worked for a living. It was not until the nineteenth century that a new type of domestic feline emerged: the cat as companion animal and object of aesthetic admiration.

Almost everywhere it went, the cat was well received because of its practical value and, no doubt, because of its often endearing nature. But at times—especially in medieval Europe—its welcome wore thin. Leaders of the Church—guided by superstition rather than the Bible—demonized black cats as consorts of the devil, and the faithful responded by killing them. While black cats bore the brunt, there weren't enough of them to go around, so tabbies and torties suffered as well.

In one of history's great ironies, cats were slaughtered en masse during the bubonic plague of 1347–1348, when one out of every three Europeans perished. But the Black Death, as the pandemic was called, was spread by flea-infested rats and not by cats, as was widely presumed. Those felines that survived the dubious public-health strategy of cat extermination helped save Europe by eradicating vermin. Had more cats lived, fewer people might have died.

Eliot Gregory painted this portrait of Robert and Catherine Jacobs with the family kitten in 1848.

A young Marlon Brando with his pet cat

that first best-in-show award. Today the cat fancy is alive and well, and hundreds of cat clubs worldwide sponsor cat shows.

While barn cats still guard their territory against rodent intruders, nowadays working cats are far outnumbered by beloved household pets whose main responsibility is to keep humans company. There are even "glamour" cats whose job is to delight cat lovers on the show circuit. Many homeless and abandoned cats still populate our streets, alleys, and animal shelters—and millions of them are destroyed each year. But tens of millions of cats are fortunate enough to live in good homes. Cats have, when one looks at the history of the feline–human relationship, never had it so good. Perhaps this is what cats had in mind all along when they adopted us thousands of years ago.

With the rise of an urban middle class in the nineteenth century, many cats no longer had to serve as full-time mousers. Increasingly, they were kept by owners who simply liked having them around for their beauty, grace, and the affection they could offer (when they felt like it). A phenomenon called the "cat fancy" followed. The pets of "fanciers" competed for ribbons at cat shows, and breeders began to refine existing breeds and develop new ones. The first recorded cat show—with 170 cats on exhibit—was held in 1871 at London's Crystal Palace. Just eighteen years later, more than three times as many cats were shown, and 20,000 cat fanciers attended. American cat lovers soon followed suit with a show of their own, at New York's Madison Square Garden in 1895. Perhaps not surprisingly, a Maine Coon, a breed of Yankee ancestry, won

The human–feline relationship is mutually beneficial.

How the Cat Works

In the words of Leonardo da Vinci, "the smallest feline is a masterpiece." The cat is one of nature's most elegant examples of form following function. The design of the feline physique is perfectly suited to a predatory carnivore's needs: detecting, pursuing, catching, killing, eating, and digesting prey. In fact, the cat's basic form has changed relatively little since wildcats first appeared some 30 million years ago. The many species that now inhabit the world's jungles, forests, deserts, couches, and armchairs all follow the same basic blueprint. Although most domestic shorthairs aren't likely to catch anything more exotic than a few extra hours of sleep, today's pet cat is built very much like its wild relatives.

Thick paw pads and intricately constructed wrist and foot joints help ensure a safe landing.

Framework: Bones and Muscles

As any cat owner knows simply by watching, the cat is built for grace, flexibility, and power. From a sitting start, it can jump up to nine times its own height. It can make its chest and shoulders narrower, to squeeze through almost impossibly tight spaces. It can sleep curled into the shape of a letter O and, immediately upon awakening, stretch and form an inverted C, pressing its chest almost to the floor.

As in all mammals, a cat's skeleton supports the body, providing a framework for the muscles and allowing movement only at special points (the joints). It also protects fragile internal organs. Special bone structures—the vertebral column and the skull—enclose the delicate spinal cord and brain, vital components of the nervous system. In the illustration below, the major bones are labeled.

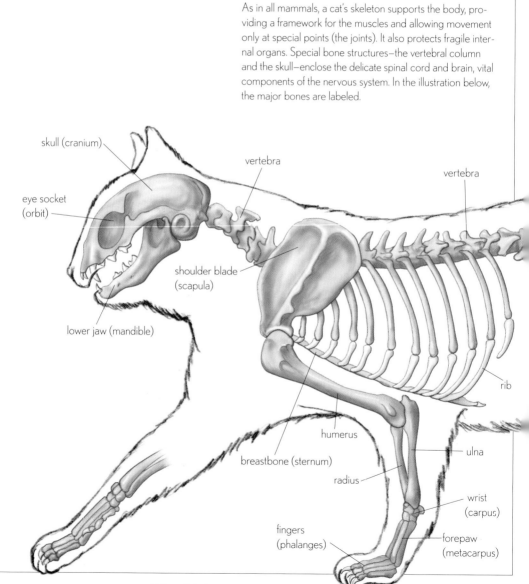

skull (cranium)

eye socket (orbit)

vertebra

vertebra

shoulder blade (scapula)

lower jaw (mandible)

rib

humerus

ulna

breastbone (sternum)

radius

wrist (carpus)

fingers (phalanges)

forepaw (metacarpus)

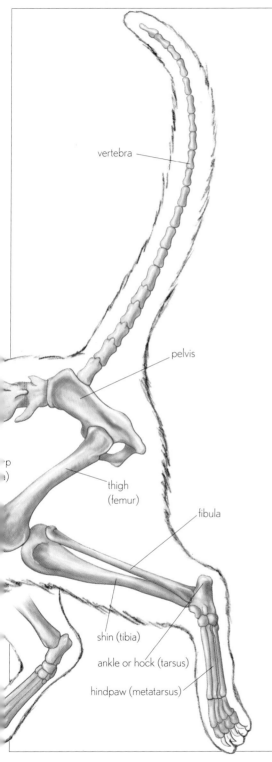

vertebra

pelvis

thigh
(femur)

fibula

shin (tibia)

ankle or hock (tarsus)

hindpaw (metatarsus)

Sinuous Spine

Where does a cat get its remarkable elasticity, both in motion and at rest? The first place to look is the animal's spine. Because cats' vertebrae are flexibly connected and have particularly elastic cushioning disks between them, the feline spine is extremely supple. A cat's ability to right itself in midair so that it can land on its feet and to make rapid changes in direction while pursuing or capturing prey are both made possible by the flexibility of its spine.

The flexibility of the cat's spine also contributes to its fluidity and speed as a runner. To reach top speed—about thirty miles an hour—a domestic cat depends on its spine as much as on its feet and leg muscles. When running, cats can lengthen their stride, and thus increase their speed, by alternately extending and flexing their vertebral column. When the cat's feet push off to start a new stride— the claws serving as spikes for traction— the cat's body stretches to its maximum length. The cat's running style thus resembles a series of elongated jumps or bounds. The cat increases its speed by lengthening its stride with each bound, until every stride carries it about three times the length of its own body. Many other mammals, especially humans, rely on a more pistonlike sprinting style, in which the key factor is how often the feet make contact with the ground.

Stretching and Squeezing

Another special feature that contributes to feline flexibility is the tiny, rudimentary collarbone, which helps cats to lengthen their stride when sprinting by allowing them to extend their forelegs fully. The lack of a long, anchored collarbone (as humans have) gives cats the ability to squeeze through tight openings by literally compressing themselves to fit the available space. Moreover, the feline shoulder blade is attached to the rest of the body only by muscles, not by bone. This gives the shoulder blade tremendous freedom to move as the cat moves, enhancing the cat's flexibility and grace and extending its long running stride.

Tail

The tail is an extension of the backbone. While tailless cats seem to live their lives quite unimpaired, the tail may help cats keep their balance during athletic maneuvers. The tail serves as a stabilizer and a counterweight, and is quite useful when a running cat quickly changes direction. The position of the tail also helps communicate a cat's emotional state to others. (See Feline Body Language on page 217.)

The tail serves to balance this cat, which is sitting up on his haunches.

Legs and Toes

Whether running or walking, cats land on their toes. Such digitigrade locomotion is the hallmark of a sprinter. Animals that land on the full soles of their feet, using plantigrade locomotion, are better suited to sustained exertion. Bears and humans, for example, have a plantigrade footfall. Cats hunt using great bursts of speed (after which they often end up panting).

The spring in a cat's legs is phenomenal, thanks in part to the construction of its hip, knee, and ankle joints. These joints have very little give from side to side. They are very stable and strong and can withstand great force applied in one direction: forward. When the cat's hind-leg muscles contract, the three joints extend in an instant, giving the animal enormous thrust to carry it either high or far. The cat's landing is cushioned by the thick pads on its feet, and by the bones of its feet and wrists, whose intricate construction makes a stable two-point landing on its forepaws possible.

Cats are able to rotate their spines more than many other animals and can twist their bodies to a much greater extent.

Powerful rear legs and an extremely flexible spine give the cat its explosive power and speed.

Explosive Power

One look at a cat in profile provides an obvious clue as to why cats are such marvelous, explosive athletes. In proportion to its overall body size, a cat's hindleg muscles are enormous, as is its "launching pad," an exceptionally long rear foot. These anatomical features translate into tremendous power and mechanical advantage when a cat springs or leaps.

The cat's particular type of athleticism may also come partly from the many "fast-twitch-fatiguing" cells contained in its skeletal muscles. As their name suggests, these cells produce explosive movement, but they use up their energy stores in a flash and tire easily—as does the cat, which has relatively few "slow-twitch" fibers to give it much endurance.

Energy Conservation

Because cats lack the staying power of plantigrade long-distance runners, conserving energy is a must for them. Even the way a cat walks can save energy, as the contralateral gait cats sometimes use—left hindfoot moving more or less in tandem with the right forefoot, and right hindfoot moving with left forefoot—is mechanically very efficient.

The best energy-saving strategy, of course, is to stay put, and cats are masters at it. Their brain chemistry makes it possible for them to spend more of their time asleep than awake.

Lightning Fast Nerves

When cats are awake, an intricate network of nerves radiating from the brain and the spinal cord operates in high gear, receiving and transmitting information and governing sensations, reflexes, and motor functions throughout the cat's body. The lightning speed at which the cat's nervous system operates is illustrated by the well-known feline "righting reflex" (illustrated on page 207). Thanks to this and its remarkably flexible spine, a cat held feet upward and dropped will have its feet pointed downward, ready to land, before it has fallen twenty-four inches.

Facing page: Domestic cats have remarkable jumping abilities on a par with those of their wild relatives.

Dexterity

A cat's wrist bones and their associated tendons and ligaments give the cat a measure of manual dexterity—not close to matching our own, or even a raccoon's, but enough to enable the cat to get mice out of hiding places (or food out of its dish) with a handlike scooping motion and to hold onto trees. This ability to pronate the wrist (carpus)—turn the bottom of the paw toward the midline of the body—is not common in the animal kingdom. But then, neither are most creatures as graceful and nimble, yet powerful, as cats.

Heart and Lungs

Cats have typical mammalian respiratory and circulatory systems. The air they take in through the mouth and nostrils travels down the windpipe (trachea) to the lungs. Encased in the protective rib cage and separated from the abdomen by the diaphragm, the heart and lungs then work together to circulate oxygen, via the blood, throughout the body.

Conducted along an intricate system of arteries and veins, blood distributes oxygen, nutrients, and disease-fighting agents and takes up carbon dioxide and other waste products. When the blood makes its way back to the lungs, the blood vessels of the circulatory system and the branches of the respiratory system (called bronchi and bronchioles) make a vital exchange of newly inhaled oxygen for carbon dioxide to be exhaled.

The feline heart is well adapted to a predatory lifestyle, capable of accelerating from a resting heart rate of about 150 beats per minute to more than 240 beats per minute (four beats per second) to provide the circulation needed for sudden bursts of speed.

The ability to rotate the forearms is a necessity for animals that capture small prey and climb trees.

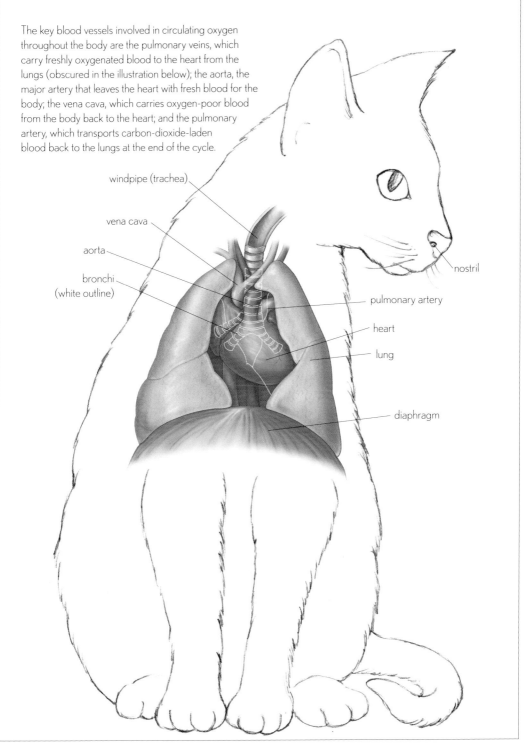

The key blood vessels involved in circulating oxygen throughout the body are the pulmonary veins, which carry freshly oxygenated blood to the heart from the lungs (obscured in the illustration below); the aorta, the major artery that leaves the heart with fresh blood for the body; the vena cava, which carries oxygen-poor blood from the body back to the heart; and the pulmonary artery, which transports carbon-dioxide-laden blood back to the lungs at the end of the cycle.

windpipe (trachea)

vena cava

aorta

bronchi
(white outline)

nostril

pulmonary artery

heart

lung

diaphragm

How the Cat Works **189**

As in most carnivores, the feline intestinal tract is short but efficient, allowing cats to digest food rapidly and avoid carrying excess weight.

Digestive and Urinary Systems

The cat's digestive system works in much the same way as a human's: food is broken down into small pieces in the mouth by the teeth and saliva and then swallowed. It travels down the esophagus to the stomach, where acids and enzymes break it down further. It then passes through the small intestine, where food is further digested and water and nutrients are absorbed and enter the bloodstream. The remaining undigested solid waste material is carried out of the body via the large intestine and anus in the form of feces. Other contributors to the digestive process are the liver, which assists in the digestion of fat, and the pancreas, which produces digestive juices and some hormones.

The urinary system is responsible for such vital functions as helping to maintain the proper amount of water in the body and helping to keep the body's overall chemistry in balance. The kidneys filter various waste products into urine, which is carried along the ureters to the bladder and out of the body via the urethra.

esophagus

The liver is an amazing organ that performs many vital roles in various systems. It stores nutrients and vitamins, breaks down sugars, and eliminates toxins. It also produces bile, which assists in the absorption of fats, and manufactures important hormones.

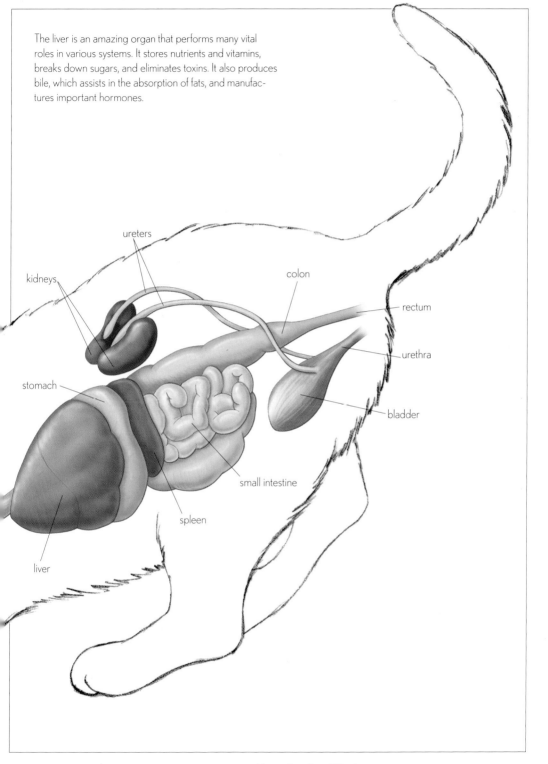

ureters

kidneys

colon

rectum

urethra

stomach

bladder

small intestine

spleen

liver

Cats' teeth are perfectly suited for their job—killing prey and shearing and slicing meat. The upper jaw (maxilla) is immobile, while the lower jaw (mandible) moves freely up and down. Together the jaws function as scissors to prepare food for swallowing.

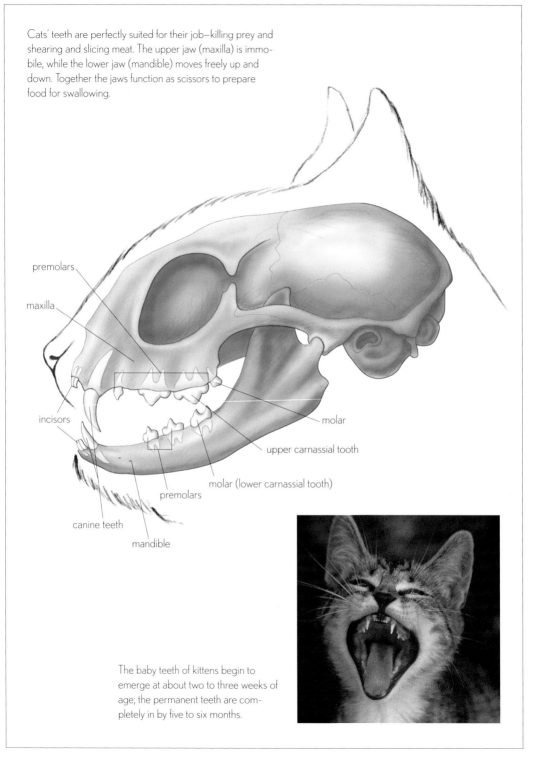

premolars

maxilla

incisors

molar

upper carnassial tooth

molar (lower carnassial tooth)

premolars

canine teeth

mandible

The baby teeth of kittens begin to emerge at about two to three weeks of age; the permanent teeth are completely in by five to six months.

Teeth

A cat's teeth serve as a solitary carnivore's survival kit, with each tool closely tailored to specific tasks. The four long, strong canine teeth, or fangs, are used for seizing and killing prey with an efficient bite to the neck. The twelve small incisors are useful for nibbling to clean either one's own coat or to remove feathers and fur from prey and pull meat from bones. The ten premolars and four molars, including the four large, sharp carnassial teeth, which move together like the blades of scissors, are for shearing and chewing meat. When your cat eats with his head tilted to one side, he is shearing food with one set of molars and premolars; after a short time, he may tilt his head the other way, moving the food to the other side of his mouth for shearing by the other set.

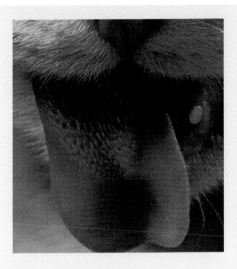

Tongue

The upper surface of the cat's tongue is carpeted with sharp, backward-pointing, bristlelike projections called filiform papillae. Used with force, this rasplike surface can remove flesh from bone; used more gently, it can serve as a "hairbrush" for grooming.

Like dogs, cats lap up liquids by curling the tip of the tongue back to form a "ladle"; by quickly withdrawing the tongue, they are able to flip water into the mouth.

Reproductive System

Cats reproduce sexually, as all mammals do, and have the standard mammalian reproductive 'system. Like many other domestic animals (including dogs), the female cat has reproductive (or estrous) cycles during certain times of the year—her "breeding season." Most female mammals release eggs at certain times in their estrous cycles, but female cats conserve their eggs until mating stimulates their release. This makes cats extremely efficient reproducers, as whenever eggs are released from the ovaries, the sperm is there to fertilize them, virtually guaranteeing pregnancy. Kittens are born about sixty-three days after the eggs are fertilized. (See The Beginning and End of Life: Times for Special Care on page 333 for more on mating, pregnancy, and birth.)

Female cats usually have their first breeding season of the year in late winter or early spring, when the hours of daylight begin to lengthen. During periods of "heat" (or estrus)—the part of the estrous cycle when the female is fertile and will allow mating (and which usually lasts about seven days)—female cats advertise their availability by calling loudly, rolling about provocatively, and scent-marking with urine.

Female cats reach puberty—and begin egg production in their ovaries—at five to twelve months. (Burmese and other Oriental breeds tend to reach puberty at an earlier age than other breeds; Persians tend to be older.) Females born late in the breeding season tend to come into "heat" at an earlier age than others, as they are younger when the springtime heat season begins than kittens born earlier.

As for the tomcat, he is always ready to mate once he reaches puberty, which is generally between nine and twelve months of age. The desire to mate, to roam in search of receptive females, to fight with other males, and to scent-mark with urine accompany puberty.

Neutering

When male cats are neutered (or castrated), the testes are removed and the vas deferens and blood vessels are tied. In females, the ovaries and much of the uterus are removed (this procedure, ovariohysterectomy, is commonly called spaying). Both neutering procedures are performed under general anesthesia, usually at around five to six months of age, but can safely be done as early as two months of age. (See also An Urgent Reminder: Have Your Cat Neutered on page 57.)

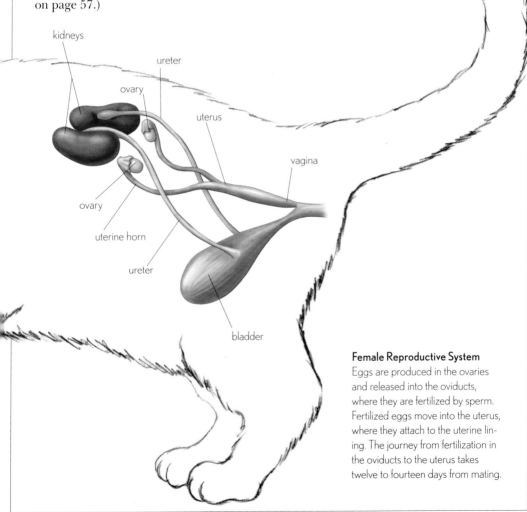

kidneys

ureter

ovary

uterus

vagina

ovary

uterine horn

ureter

bladder

Female Reproductive System
Eggs are produced in the ovaries and released into the oviducts, where they are fertilized by sperm. Fertilized eggs move into the uterus, where they attach to the uterine lining. The journey from fertilization in the oviducts to the uterus takes twelve to fourteen days from mating.

Male Reproductive System

The testes, which produce testosterone and sperm, are located beneath the anus in the scrotum. Sperm cells mature in the testes and the epididymis, which also acts as a storage reservoir. Sperm are transported through the vas deferens and mix with fluid produced by the prostate and bulbourethral glands (not pictured) to produce semen.

The feline penis is unique in having spines on its surface that probably provide additional stimulation to induce the female's ovaries to release eggs during mating. These spines develop at puberty and disappear once a cat is neutered.

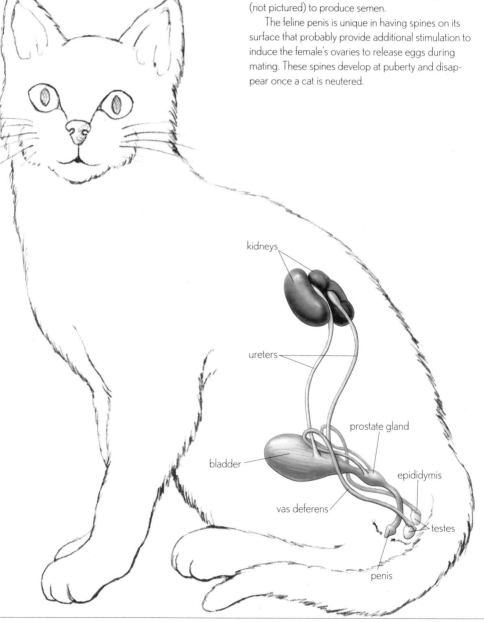

kidneys

ureters

prostate gland

bladder

epididymis

vas deferens

testes

penis

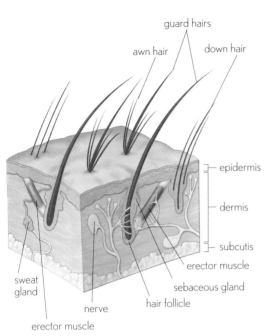

guard hairs

awn hair   down hair

epidermis

dermis

subcutis

erector muscle

sweat gland

sebaceous gland

nerve

hair follicle

erector muscle

the epidermis is the dermis, within which are sweat glands; sebaceous glands, which produce oils that coat the cat's skin and hair; and follicles, receptacles in which the hairs of the coat grow. Nerve endings in the dermis near the hair follicles assist in sensory perception, detecting pain as well as pressure on or movement of the fur.

Attached to each hair follicle of the top-coat is a tiny erector muscle that can pull the hair bolt upright. When a cat is cold, these muscles contract involuntarily, creating a thicker insulating layer of fur that can trap additional warm air close to the skin (the same action we experience as "goose bumps"). The erector muscles also spring into service when a cat is frightened, causing the hair on its neck, back, and tail to stand on end. This makes the cat look bigger, perhaps enough to discourage a potential aggressor.

"Fraidy" cats with their hair on end will stand sideways in an attempt to look larger and more threatening.

Skin and Coat

Although a cat's coat is a thing of beauty, it is also functional. The coat repels water, provides a layer of heat insulation, and helps protect the body from injury and disease. The skin underneath is quite elastic, allowing the cat to move with grace and fluidity. The skin is loosely attached to the trunk, able to stretch away from the body when the cat is grasped by an enemy, thus reducing the risk of serious injury.

The visible part of the skin is called the epidermis, the outermost layer of which is composed of dead cells. Beneath

The Himalayan has a long, dense coat that makes it the perfect cold-weather animal.

Rather than growing continuously, like human hair, cat hair grows in distinct cycles partly regulated by the amount of daylight. Once a hair has grown to its full length, it stops growing. It is eventually shed from the follicle and replaced by a new hair. Different hairs in the cat's coat are in different stages of the growth cycle at any given time—otherwise, the cat would spend portions of its life bald.

Most cats have a topcoat and an undercoat. In the topcoat are the primary hairs, which are of two types: coarse, relatively thick guard hairs and somewhat finer awn hairs. The undercoat is made up of secondary, or down, hairs.

Certain breeds of cats have variations on the basic coat composition. The Cornish Rex lacks guard hairs, while the Sphynx has almost no hair at all. The Devon Rex has all three hair types, but the hairs of the topcoat are very fine and resemble down hair. The British Shorthair has very few or no down hairs in the coat. The luxuriance of the Persian's coat is due to extraordinarily long and abundant guard and down hairs and an absence of awn hairs. "Double-coated" cats such as the Chartreux, the Manx, and the Russian Blue have a particularly thick, dense undercoat. "Single-coated" cats, including the Burmese, the Siamese, and the Oriental Shorthair, have a relatively thin undercoat. Nonpurebred cats run the gamut of coat types but rarely to the extremes that the purebreds have been bred for.

The Sphynx is not entirely hairless but is covered with nearly imperceptible down hairs.

Cats can move their whiskers freely according to the needs of the moment. When sniffing, cats pull their whiskers back against the face; when a cat is at rest or walking in the dark, his whiskers extend to the side; and when capturing prey, a cat extends his whiskers forward, helping direct his bite.

Whiskers

A cat's whiskers are superbly designed sensory tools that give the cat important information about the environment, especially during nocturnal expeditions. These stiff, tactile hairs are much thicker and longer than regular hairs, with follicles that extend about three times deeper into the dermis. At the base of each follicle are numerous nerve endings that make the tactile hairs exquisitely sensitive to the slightest movement—even a gentle breeze.

Contrary to popular myth, cats will not die if their whiskers are cut off, nor is it painful to have them cut, since they are composed of the same dead matter as hair and the outermost layer of the skin. But cats devoid of whiskers are less adept at getting around in the dark because they are less able to perceive obstacles in their path.

Whiskerlike tactile hairs may appear elsewhere on the cat's body but are concentrated on the upper lip near the nose, above the eyes, on the cheeks, and to a lesser extent on the chin and lower lip. Tactile hairs behind the cat's wrists probably come in handy when the cat is walking in the dark and might also help the cat determine the position of prey in its grasp.

Paws and Claws

Soft cushiony paw pads enable the cat to make its characteristically stealthy, nearly noiseless approach. When not in use, the cat's claws are hidden away and do not hit the ground when the cat walks.

The skin is thicker on the paw pads than elsewhere on the body to protect the cat's feet on hot, cold, or rough surfaces. A layer of fatty tissue within each pad serves as an excellent shock absorber, an important feature for an animal that often jumps from high places. The pad farther up toward the wrist is a non-weight-bearing carpal pad, perhaps an evolutionary remnant that might have once been larger and more functional but now serves no clear purpose.

Despite their thick skin, feline foot pads are highly sensitive information-gathering instruments that—along with the similarly hairless and supremely sensitive pad on the cat's nose—make contact with the environment before the rest of the cat's body does.

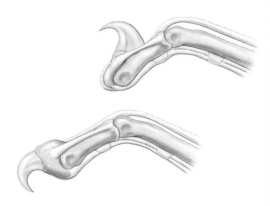

Top: The relaxed position of a cat's claws is retracted and enclosed within their protective skin sheath, where they are held by elastic bands of tissue. Bottom: The cat has to exert effort to unsheathe the claws for use.

The claws of the cat's rear feet are slightly less retractable than those of the forefeet.

Cats use their claws for climbing, marking, hunting, and protection.

Anyone who has engaged in rough-house play with his or her cat can attest to the fact that feline claws are formidable weapons. The outer layers of a cat's claws have to be constantly sloughed off to unsheathe the daggerlike points beneath.

When cats scratch rough surfaces, they are removing worn-down outer layers. Besides their obvious utility as hunting and defensive weapons, nails are important to cats for climbing.

Senses

The cat's quintessential swiftness and savviness have a great deal to do with their magnificent sensory powers: keen smelling ability, specialized sight, ultrasound hearing range, and uncanny balance.

The cat's sense of smell is much keener than a human's but far less acute than the dog's.

Smell

Unlike dogs, cats rarely depend upon their sense of smell for finding their dinner; hearing and vision are much more important to the feline hunter. Cats do, however, use the sense of smell as a means of communicating with other cats. Smell is also important for appetite

Facing page: The cat's expressiveness contributes to its natural charm and beauty, especially when its senses are aroused.

stimulation. Cats that can't smell their food because of a nasal obstruction often won't eat.

Like other carnivores, cats possess a vomeronasal organ, a pouchlike structure in the roof of the mouth, with openings just behind the incisor teeth. When a cat smells another cat—especially when a male smells a female in heat—he often lifts up his head, wrinkles his nose, partially opens his mouth, and curls his lips upward. This odd facial gesture, called the flehmen response, probably makes the odor more accessible to the openings in the vomeronasal organ, which then transmits the sensation to the brain for interpretation.

The flehmen response is often made by males reacting to females in heat.

Vision

Although the basic anatomy of their eyes is similar to that of humans and other mammals, cats see the world differently than we do. Humans can see the daytime world more clearly than cats, but cats can see objects in dim light much better than humans, requiring only one-sixth the amount of light we do to distinguish shapes and forms. Researchers have learned that, like us, cats can identify colors. The difference is that we see colors much more intensely. Cats have never needed good color vision to survive.

Feline eyes have special properties that human eyes lack. Cats can retract their eyes into the bony eye sockets of the skull for added protection against injury. Cats also have a nictitating membrane (sometimes referred to as a "third eyelid"). This opaque white membrane fans out from the inner corner of the eye to cover part of the delicate cornea for even greater protection. Usually a small part of the nictitating membrane is visible. (When the membrane protrudes continually, covering as much as three quarters of the eye surface, it often means the animal has a health problem—ranging from paralysis of a nerve to severe dehydration or a painful eye condition.)

The lenses of a cat's eye are not well equipped for bringing things into sharp focus, and the world in general probably looks somewhat blurry to cats. But they can focus very well on nearby objects within "pouncing range." Cats also have very good depth perception, thanks to the fact that their retina and nervous system are adapted to detect edges and movement. This helps them judge distances accurately and explains why a cat wanting to get from floor to tabletop

seems never to undershoot or overshoot his landing area by even an inch.

To regulate the amount of light entering the eye, a cat's pupils can expand or contract dramatically. At their widest, they can take up more than eighty-five percent of the eye area, allowing for excellent night vision. At their narrowest, they become vertical slits, shutting out all

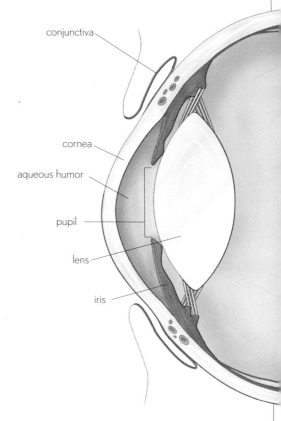

conjunctiva

cornea

aqueous humor

pupil

lens

iris

but a tiny amount of light. This leads to an extreme natural "squint" they share with many species of cats that sometimes chase prey while facing a low morning or evening sun. The pupils can also tip off a cat's intentions: when they become very wide in daylight or in a well-lit room, the cat is often planning to pounce on the object he is looking at. If your cat's pupils get big while he is staring at your hand, remove it from his line of sight—or accept the consequences.

Like humans, cats have two kinds of light-absorbing cells in their retinas: many rods (for black-and-white vision, especially in dim light) and very few

vitreous humor

choroid

sclera

retina

optic nerve

The feline cornea—the transparent, forward-facing surface of the eye—is relatively large in order to let in as much light as possible. Though the eyeball of the domestic cat is a bit smaller than ours, the area of a cat's pupil can increase three times more than a human's—another adaptation to nighttime activity.

cones (for color vision). Although scientists have trained cats—with food rewards and great patience—to distinguish between many different hues, outside the laboratory, a cat gets no benefit from interpreting colors. A mouse is a mouse, whether gray, green, or orange.

As predators, cats are much more interested in detecting movement. Serving them well in this is a portion of the retina called the *area centralis*. In humans, the *area centralis* is roughly circular in shape, enabling us to see objects in great detail. In the domestic cat, the *area centralis* lies in a broad horizontal band, an arrangement that makes moving objects easier to notice and track.

Like many other mammals, but unlike humans, the cat has a structure in its retina called the *tapetum lucidum*. This serves as a reflector, sending light back to the rods and cones of the retina, stimulating these light-sensitive cells a second time and enhancing the cat's night vision. When you see a cat's eyes apparently glowing in the dark, it is actually light reflected by the cat's *tapetum lucidum*.

Cats' eyes don't really glow in the dark; they merely reflect light that shines on a special structure at the back of the retina.

Hearing and Balance

To complement their excellent night vision and the keen tactile sense provided by their whiskers, cats possess an acute sense of hearing. While humans are able to detect sounds varying in frequency from roughly twenty vibrations per second up to about 20,000 vibrations per second, cats are less able to hear the bass frequencies but can easily sense sound some two octaves higher than a human's upper limit. Why is this important for cats? Ultrasound (sound at frequencies too high for human hearing) is very useful for short-range communication in dense habitats. Rodents communicate mostly in ultrasound—inaudible to us but well within feline listening capabilities. Cats hunting under cover of darkness are able to pick up these squeaks and, with their movable pinnae (outer ear flaps), efficiently zero in on prey.

The cat's pinnae can "swivel," enabling the cat to locate the source of a sound almost instantaneously and channel it down through the ear canal to the eardrum, which in turn vibrates from the sound waves striking it.

Also housed in the inner ear is the balance mechanism, which consists of the vestibule and the three semicircular canals. Functioning in a manner similar to a carpenter's level, these devices detect any change in motion of the head and evaluate the head's position relative to the ground. The data gathered by these structures is conveyed via the vestibulocochlear nerve to the brain, which then sends instructions to the muscles of the limbs and the eyes to help the cat stay coordinated and keep its eyes "on target" as it hunts.

The cat's finely tuned sense of balance (and to some extent its vision) works in conjunction with the flexible musculoskeletal system to allow it to right itself after a fall or jump. Although cats do not always land on their feet, they are remarkably adept at spinning around in midair—first the head, then the front feet, and finally the back feet—so they usually hit feet first. This has survival value for both the individual and the species: a tree-climbing cat has a much better chance of surviving to produce offspring if upon falling out of a tree he lands on his feet.

As in humans, the vibrations of the eardrum are picked up by a series of three interconnected bones in the middle ear: the malleus (hammer), the incus (anvil), and the stapes (stirrup), collectively known as the ossicles. These bones transmit the vibrations to the cochlea in the inner ear, which converts the vibrations into nerve impulses. These are then carried to the brain via the vestibulocochlear nerve.

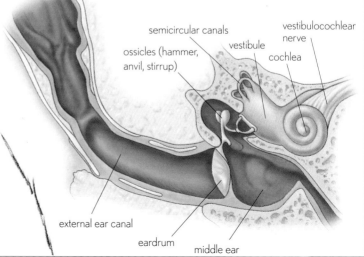

semicircular canals

vestibulocochlear nerve

vestibule

ossicles (hammer, anvil, stirrup)

cochlea

external ear canal

eardrum

middle ear

Cats owe their ability to survive falls from great heights partly to the fact that they can right themselves in midair.

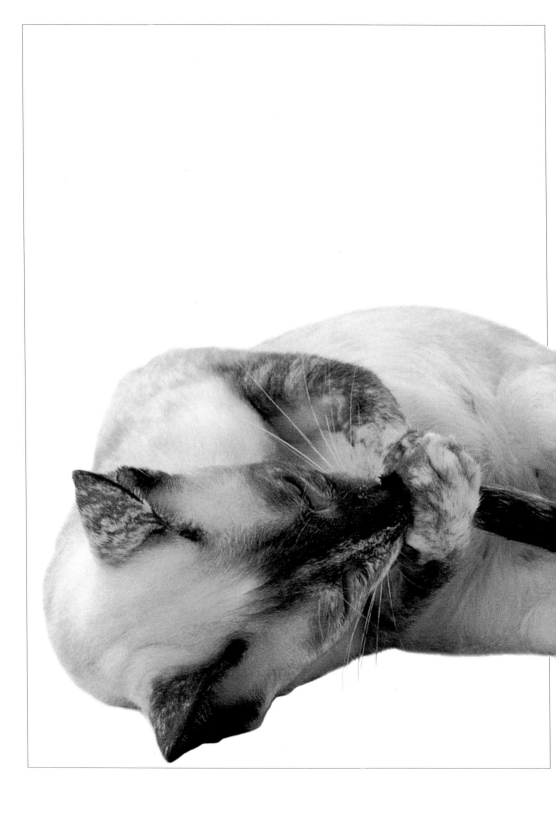

Understanding Your Cat

Living with cats gives us a chance to experience firsthand the behavior of domestic creatures that are by nature quite close to their wild relatives. Felines are much less dependent on humans for their livelihood than other domestic species—including dogs—and if forced by circumstances, they are better able to adapt to a self-sufficient lifestyle. Many cat behaviors can be explained in terms of how cats live in the wild: they need to be able to feed themselves and their kittens and to mate successfully. Other behaviors reflect the personality of the individual cat.

This chapter of the guide will provide some insight into just what your cat does all day—play, groom, "talk," sleep—and answer some common questions about why cats do these things in their uniquely feline way. Understanding "normal" feline behavior—and knowing in particular what is normal for your cat—will enrich your experience of sharing life with a cat and at the same time will make you a more responsible owner.

Cats have enchanted humans with their uniquely feline ways for thousands of years.

Pet owners persist in debating whether the dog or cat is the smarter species.

How Smart Are Cats?

It is difficult to assess the intelligence of animals. We can't sit them down with a standard IQ test or give them problems of logic to decipher. We can't judge them in human terms of intelligence at all, for they've got all kinds of smarts with which we can't begin to compete. A group of cats might judge human intelligence as mighty low indeed, given the slowness of our reflexes—we don't universally land on our feet when dropped head downward—and our lack of useful instincts.

It is natural for people to compare the intelligence of dogs and cats, as both are domestic animals that we have invited into our homes. Some pet owners claim that the dog's trainability is evidence of that animal's superior intelligence, but how easily a dog can learn to make the connection between a command, its action, and a reward has little to do with IQ. Canines have a highly developed social hierarchy in which subordinate members seek to placate dominant ones, so training a dog to respond to a dominant member of the "pack"—in this case the human trainer—taps into the dog's instincts.

Social hierarchy isn't as important to felines, so they are naturally much less motivated to respond to such training. But most cats can learn simple commands if their owners are patient and persistent enough. You can, for example, teach your cat to sit on command. Take your cat's favorite food treat, hold it in front of the cat's nose, and move it upward and backward. As the cat's nose follows the treat and points up toward the ceiling, the cat will naturally sit down.

Cats of Siamese lineage such as this Colorpoint are among the smartest of the breeds.

At that precise moment, say "sit" and quickly give the food treat. Practice this a few times a day, and soon your cat will sit on command. Eventually you won't need to use the food treat, but by occasionally giving one you'll reinforce the learning.

Some cat lovers assert that feline self-sufficiency proves that cats are more intelligent than dogs, but it is the cat's nature as a solitary hunter that has equipped it to find its own food. Innate behavior is also partly responsible for the relative ease with which a cat can be trained to use a litter box. Cats in the wild generally prefer to eliminate in loose soil, which is not too unlike litter box filler.

Cats are better than dogs at tasks that require manipulating a string or lever, and they can easily learn to pull open a door by using their paws as they would to scoop up a mouse. These talents do not prove that cats are more intelligent than dogs but simply that they are more dexterous with their paws.

Another test of intelligence, one less influenced by instinct and innate physical ability, measures how quickly an animal finds its way through a maze. Bad news for cat lovers: dogs, and even some farm animals, perform better than cats at mastering mazes. In intelligence tests that measure an animal's ability to remember which of several boxes contains food, or to recall which door allows escape, cats also tend to score lower than dogs, but they do perform better than farm animals.

Nonetheless it is clear that cats are careful observers and will remember things that have direct relevance to them. Many owners will recall that their cats go into hiding at the very sight of the carrier used to bring them to the vet, even if it has been more than a year since the last

Cats owe their ability to pry open a door to forearm bones that can rotate.

visit. And even subtle changes in your routine, to which cats get very accustomed, won't go unnoticed.

Cats most certainly have the capacity to learn. As with litter box training, it is easier for cats to learn actions that mimic ones in their natural behavioral repertoire. Cats also learn by observing other cats. Mother cats teach by example, demonstrating hunting behavior to their kittens. As a result, cats tend to seek the same kind of prey their mother brought home. Cats raised without the benefit of a mother's example often make poor hunters because they can't learn adequate hunting skills on their own (actually, it is the final kill that kittens really need mom's example for). Other research gives further evidence of cats' ability to learn by example: cats are quicker to learn to push down on a bar to receive a food reward if they've already observed another cat do the same.

Feral cats often form socially complex colonies based around a source of food.

grounds of other males. A male cat may defend a smaller territory against intruding cats, but he may share it—at least temporarily—with groups of related females, who often rear their kittens cooperatively.

Cats housed indoors tend to be able to coexist fairly peacefully as long as each cat can maintain some "personal space" for at least a part of the day. This can be a spot used exclusively by a certain individual or one shared with other individuals at different times in a sort of feline time-share. Kinship, gender, and food considerations also affect the relationships between cohabitating cats, as do individual personalities.

Cat-Friendly Cats

Most cats that were raised together in the same household will regularly play with each other, sleep together, and groom one another, especially if they were

How Sociable Are Cats?

Most cats do not live in groups with other adult cats unless they have to—to gather at a place where food is available, say—but cats are not simply solitary hunters that shun the company of others of their kind except to mate. Kittens and female adult cats are particularly willing to initiate physical contact with others.

Even feral cats—domestic cats that are not "owned" but subsist by scavenging, hunting, or eating food provided for them—often form relatively stable bonds with one another around common sources of food or shelter. Male outdoor or feral cats explore and hunt within an area that often overlaps with the hunting

Littermates that are raised together often continue to groom each other into adulthood.

Litters that stay together until eight to ten weeks of age tend to grow up to be cat-friendly adults.

neutered at an early age. Many of the factors that influence such cooperation are not well understood, but heredity and kittenhood experiences probably play important roles. Even in feral cat colonies, female littermates (as well as neutered males) raised together from birth tend to get along well as adults.

Although cats often seem to make an art of independence and nonchalance, there is no doubt that they come to cherish their companions. Some domestic cats even go through a kind of mourning period after the loss of a housemate. They may eat less, cry more, demand more affection from their owners, and spend time in their friend's favorite spot.

People-Friendly Cats

Some cats seem to truly enjoy humans, especially cats that have had a pleasant introduction to people as young kittens. In part, kittens learn how to behave with people by observing their mother interacting with humans, though there is probably a genetic influence on a cat's people-friendliness as well.

Kittens are most easily socialized with people from two to seven weeks after birth, though children shouldn't handle kittens younger than three weeks old. Those that have been handled by humans during this time are much more likely to be people-friendly as adults. Kittens that are handled by only one person during this period tend to be friendly with just that one person, and kittens that have contact with more people generally become adults that are friendly with everyone. Cats that have not been handled by

Socialization with children can begin when kittens are as young as three weeks of age.

humans during this initial period can still be socialized later, but the socialization requires much more time and effort for less return. Prospective owners should ask present owners how much they interacted with a kitten at this early stage.

Early handling does not always ensure that a kitten will become a friendly adult. Some kittens that resist handling continue to avoid human interaction as they mature.

How Do Cats Communicate?

For centuries people have realized that cats have a complex system of communication. They communicate successfully with each other in three basic ways: vocally, through body language, and with visual and scent markings. Because humans tend to focus on speech and more overt gestures, we can miss some of a cat's more subtle expressions.

Cat Talk

Sixteen different cat sounds have been identified. The sounds are generally divided into three categories: murmurs (including purring), vowel sounds (meowing), and high-intensity sounds.

Murmurs Most of the sounds cats make with their mouths closed are called murmurs. Purrs (see page 216) are probably the best recognized murmurs—they are surely among the more common of feline sounds—but murmurs include a variety of sounds, ranging from grunts to closed-mouth calls to brief utterances of acknowledgment.

Grunts are produced almost exclusively by kittens and are made even by kittens only a few minutes old. An adult cat will occasionally grunt, especially if confronted with an obstacle. Both females in heat and males use a call to notify the opposite sex of their readiness to mate. A short murmur of acknowledgment sometimes reflects a cat's anticipation of receiving something he wants.

Vowel Sounds Cartoonist Hank Ketchum says, "'Meow' is like 'Aloha'—it can mean anything." Subtle differences in sound project dramatic differences in meaning, and a cat can make demands, express bewilderment, complain, wail in anger, and sound a mating cry by opening his mouth and then gradually closing it while vocalizing. These vowel sounds are rarely produced by cats less than eleven or twelve weeks old, although younger cats can produce an anger wail.

Left: Cats begin to make sounds very soon after birth. By three months they have built up a repertoire that they will use throughout life.

Facing page: Cats hiss, snarl, and growl when fighting.

Demands vary quite a bit in intensity. A cat can even occasionally meow a demand with little or no sound. Owners often mistake this whisper as hoarseness, but this silent meow is perfectly normal. Many owners have seen their cat make another sort of demand when peering out a window at a bird, frantically swishing his tail and making short, open-mouthed chirping sounds. Still another common demand is the beg, a persistent meow commonly made by a cat asking to be fed.

Sounds of bewilderment and complaint are more prolonged, expressive meows; meows of bewilderment tend to contain a rising inflection that sounds more questioning. The mating cry, like the murmured call, is produced by females during mating season, but it expresses greater intensity and urgency. Young kittens first produce the anger wail as they compete during nursing. They later make this loud, intense two-part sound *(wa-ow)* during rough play with littermates.

High-Intensity Sounds These open-mouth sounds are usually made by cats during emotionally intense experiences. Cats most often growl during a fight with a rival, but a mother cat will also growl to warn her kittens of danger. Kittens will growl at littermates that attempt to run off with food brought by their mother. A snarl is an even louder and more abrupt sound made almost exclusively by rivals during fights.

Cats of all ages—even kittens that haven't yet opened their eyes—can make

Facts About Purring

- Cats first purr when they are about two days old. Purring is usually performed by both mother and kittens during nursing, and is thought to serve as a form of communication.
- Domestic cats are not the only feline species that purr; pumas, cheetahs, ocelots, and some other wildcats also purr.
- Purring is not only a sign of contentment; cats are also known to purr when sick, even during the terminal stages of illness.
- Cats do not purr when they are sound asleep.
- Although the sound changes from intake to outtake, cats purr as they both inhale and exhale.
- Cats are able to—and commonly do—meow while purring.

How cats purr remains a bit of a mystery. Most likely this unique sound is caused by the repeated, rapid opening and closing of structures in the voice box called vocal folds.

the familiar hissing sound. A variant of the hiss is the spit, a loud, short "pfft" sound.

Feline Body Language

The body language of cats is quite subtle and can be hard to interpret unless you consider the whole combination of the cat's features and gestures, including eyes, ears, tail, and body position. Most signals can be reduced to one of two basic types: either distance-reducing ("come closer") postures, which signal that the cat welcomes—or will at least tolerate—being approached, or distance-increasing ("go away") postures, adopted by cats who are feeling aggressive or defensive.

Leaning in for a head- or chin-scratch is a come-closer posture.

Distance-Reducing Postures Owners who are greeted by a cat with his tail held high are familiar with the friendly approach. The cat may also rub the side of his body along the owner's legs or arch his back against the owner's hand. The contented cat's whiskers point outward, the ears are upright and pointing forward, and the pupils are not overly dilated or constricted. Other friendly expressions are raising the hindquarters and sticking the tail even higher in the air when scratched above the pelvic area, and turning the head for a chin-scratch.

A friendly cat holds his tail high and his whiskers to the side, with the ears erect and swiveled forward.

Understanding Your Cat   **217**

Cats sometimes greet each other by touching noses.

Friendly felines will greet one another by gently touching noses, and if they know each other well, they may also rub heads. You can easily recognize distance-reducing play postures in the exuberant antics of kittens.

Distance-Increasing Postures

Sometimes it's hard (for a person, not for another cat) to tell what's motivating a cat that's saying "go away" through body language, because the defensive posture is really an act of bravado meant to obscure a cat's fear and can look like a posture of aggression.

A cat ready to attack will point the body and whiskers directly forward and twitch the tail (perhaps just the tip) back and forth while making direct eye contact with the other cat. The body is held erect, the head is held low, and the pupils are usually constricted. The ears will be perked up, but turned to the side or rear.

The familar "Halloween cat" look is a defensive threat posture assumed when a cat feels he has lost control of a situation and gets a surge of adrenaline as part of the "fight-or-flight" response. Rather than facing directly toward the enemy, these "fraidy" cats will stand sideways in an attempt to look larger by arching the back and bristling the fur. (This effect, called piloerection, is discussed further on page 197.) The ears are flattened backward, the pupils are dilated, the whiskers are pulled back against the face, and the teeth are bared.

Fearful cats may growl and hiss, and will attack if really provoked.

The pariah threat, another distance-increasing posture, is displayed by a low-ranking cat when approached by a higher-ranking one (in feral cat colonies, this is usually a territorial male). Instead of standing sideways, cats displaying the pariah threat assume a crouched position. As in the defensive threat posture, the pupils are dilated, the ears are flattened, and the teeth are often bared. If pushed far enough, these cats will attack to defend themselves.

The cat on the left is clearly the aggressor, while the one on the right is exhibiting the pariah threat, a submissive posture.

When a cat scratches, she leaves both a visual and an olfactory signal.

Marking Signals

Cats spend a fair amount of time sending signals, both visual and olfactory, that do not involve face-to-face encounters with other cats. These techniques not only help to prevent unwanted meetings but also announce a cat's presence and sexual status.

Visual Marking Cats leave visual markings for others not only to see but to smell. One common method of visual marking is the scratching of objects—usually wood in the wild and, to the dismay of owners, carpeting or furniture indoors. Scratching actually serves two purposes. The scratches and the scent left by sweat glands in the paw pad (the only place where a cat sweats) serve as a feline calling card, while the action of scratching removes the outer layers of the claws to reveal the sharper ones beneath.

Some cats develop a preference for certain textures, and apparently the longer a cat has scratched an object, the more important it becomes—and the more likely the scratching will continue. What's also important to cats is that the object be easily seen or encountered by others, which explains why they don't show much interest in a scratch post that is hidden away in a corner. (For advice on coping with a cat that is scratching inappropriately, see Furniture Scratching on page 255.)

Scent Marking A dominant tomcat may create a visual marker by leaving his feces uncovered around the perimeter of his territory, but the most common form of scent marking is urine spraying. With the tail up and twitching, a cat will back up near the object to be marked—usually a vertical surface—and expel a spray of urine rather than a stream. Sometimes cats will urinate in a squatting posture on a horizontal surface, like a bed or a

Unneutered male cats will urine mark to summon females for mating and to indicate the boundaries of their territory to rival males.

couch, for social or psychological reasons, but there may also be a physiological basis for this kind of behavior. (For advice on coping with problematic spraying, see page 253.)

Urine marking is a highly developed behavior that cats feel the need to perform routinely, particularly unneutered males. This kind of marking summons female cats to the male's territory during the breeding season. Some cats even seem to find spraying reassuring, a kind of anxiety release during times of stress.

Most people who live with cats are familiar with feline head-rubbing, or "bunting," whereby a cat rubs against the favored person with her cheek and then her body, often curling the tail around the person's hand or leg as if in a final embrace. Some cats even like to lick their owner's hands or face. Such a greeting is commonly interpreted as a sign of affection—and rightly so. But cats also use head rubbing as a form of scent marking. The rubbing allows odors from large sebaceous glands in the cat's skin around the mouth, chin, ears, anal area, and top of the base of the tail to come in contact with the rubbed object. Owners who enjoy this greeting should consider themselves "marked."

Cats that lick their owners or rub them with the top of their heads, the sides of their faces, or their chins are "marking" them.

Understanding Your Cat   **221**

Object Play

Kittens as young as two weeks old begin to engage in object play, which evolves into stalking, chasing, biting, or pawing at objects, whether animate, inanimate, or even imaginary. This type of play, in which adult cats also occasionally engage, is performed solo and almost certainly simulates predatory behavior. Kittens deprived of toys don't develop these predatory skills until much later than kittens that are given opportunity to engage in such play.

While the desire to pursue and capture prey is an inborn trait common to all cats, a cat's success as a hunter is believed to be influenced by early learning experiences. Hunting techniques, honed during kittenhood play sessions, are improved invaluably by the mother cat's instruction. The most successful hunters tend to be those raised by mothers who are good hunters themselves, and kittens generally grow up to hunt the same prey as their mothers.

Kittens raised outdoors begin to receive hunting instruction shortly before they are weaned. At first, the mother cat brings home dead prey and eats it in front of her litter. After a while, she brings home freshly killed prey and tries to entice her kittens to consume it. Eventually, she brings them live prey so they can try to capture, kill, and eat it themselves. Only about half the kittens that do not receive this important instruction manage to grow up to be efficient predators on their own.

Young kittens engaging in object play are simulating predatory behavior.

Playing and Preying

Cats are extremely skillful and efficient predators; ironically, one of their most charming traits is their expression of this incredibly strong and lethal instinct in playful ways. For felines, even play is serious business. It improves a kitten's physical conditioning, timing, and coordination and teaches social skills that are important later in life. In the wild, only kittens have the luxury to play. As adults they must worry about defending and providing for themselves, and those lighthearted antics give way to earnest hunting and survival.

A kitten's hunting technique is in part inborn but is also learned from the mother.

Often a cat that has caught a small rodent or bird will not kill it immediately, but will throw its victim into the air, bat it around with her paws, or allow it to escape temporarily—only to recapture it before it gets too far away. As long as the prey continues to move, the cat's instinctive predatory urge is stimulated. But this is not cruel so much as sloppy; it is likely that the cat just never learned from her mother how to kill quickly and efficiently and is simply at a loss as to what to do.

Social Play

The repertoire of social play includes wrestling, rolling about with, and biting an "opponent." Kittens usually begin to play with their mother and littermates at about three to four weeks of age; intensity of play increases until the kittens are about three and a half to four months old. Play can become quite rough, especially among older kittens. Biting and scratching can lead to squealing and screaming, but even this is a learning experience. The uncomfortable bite of others teaches kittens to reduce the intensity of their own attacks, a valuable lesson in social skills that reduces the chance of serious injury if engaged in a fight later in life. Kittens separated from their littermates at too young an age are more likely to bite during play because they did not learn to pull their punches as youngsters.

Social play is not restricted to youngsters. Adult cats are rarely interested in playing with other adults but will sometimes play if approached by an exuberant kitten—although an older cat that's not in the mood won't hesitate to reprimand a kitten for his presumption.

Kittens learn important social skills by playing, sometimes quite roughly, with littermates.

Unneutered male cats develop prominent jowls. They also develop unpleasant behavioral tendencies.

Courtship

Unneutered male cats naturally behave in ways that people find unpleasant. Urine spraying of territory—which may include furniture, stereo speakers, and walls—leaves an offensive odor that can persist for a long time, even with diligent use of cleansers and deodorizers. Intact males kept indoors are adamant about getting outside, and when they do, they tend to get in fights with other males. Fights can result in injuries, abscesses, and infection with deadly viruses and bacteria. The intact male's noisy mating behavior, which often seems to take place in the middle of the night, can disturb the slumber of even the deepest sleeper.

Neutering a cat is the only way to curtail his desire to roam, fight, and spray,

but the procedure is not reliably effective if performed on an adult cat. Tomcats are usually neutered at the onset of puberty (six to eight months) but can be neutered safely as early as two months of age, as can female cats.

When not in estrus, or heat, intact female cats act very much like neutered female cats. But the behavior of a female cat in heat—when she is fertile and will allow mating—changes dramatically. A few days before the onset of estrus, even the shyest female cat will be extremely affectionate. She may rub on objects more than usual, and the rubbing may progress to rolling about, purring, and "kneading" with the paws, in a display similar to that induced by catnip (page 228). She will become more vocal, and some cats, particularly those of Siamese lineage, will give the loud howling call almost continuously. She will urinate more during this period and may also spray.

As true estrus ensues, the female continually positions her chest and abdomen close to the ground and elevates her hindquarters, with her rear legs almost perpendicular to the ground. If rubbed, she will move into position to allow a male to mount and mate: with her tail sideways, treading with her rear legs. This dramatic behavior usually lasts for about seven days. Feline reproductive cycles, mating, pregnancy, and birth are all discussed in the chapter The Beginning and End of Life: Times for Special Care, beginning on page 333.

The behavior of female cats in heat is similar to that of cats aroused by catnip.

Are Cats Really That Clean?

Meticulous grooming, performed many times throughout the day and always after defecation or mating, consumes anywhere from 30 to 50 percent of a cat's waking hours. One of the major reasons a cat grooms himself is to help maintain healthy coat and skin. Licking the coat helps to keep it clean, untangled, and free of parasites and also removes loose hair. The stiff, backward-pointing barbs on a cat's famously rough tongue make the

Cats chew their rear nails to keep them trim and healthy.

perfect hairbrush. Licking also spreads oil from the skin to the fur to help water-proof the coat. Long-haired cats require additional brushing to prevent the coat from matting (see page 241 for advice on grooming your cat).

A cat can reach most of its body—from the neck backward—with its tongue, although some rather awkward-looking positions are required to reach all parts. The face presents a particular challenge, but by using the front paw as a washcloth—licking and moistening the paw first, then wiping it across the ears, head, and face—a cat can clean even this area fairly efficiently. Cats also use their incisor teeth for grooming, especially the areas between their toes.

Cats don't have sweat glands on most of the body, so they also lick their coats to keep cool. Some cats groom to release tension. Mutual grooming goes a long way in strengthening the bond between a mother and her kittens. This social grooming usually ends once a kitten is separated

Grooming serves to remove loose hair, distribute oils throughout the coat, control parasites, and release tension.

from the mother; adult cats rarely groom each other. There is one exception: Littermates that are neutered at an early age and that remain together will often continue the grooming and sleeping habits they had as kittens.

Feline claws grow continuously, so a cat must pay constant attention to keep them healthy. Scratching objects helps a cat groom the claws of the front feet, whereas chewing is the preferred method for removing dull old nail sheaths of the rear claws. (See page 243 for advice on trimming your cat's claws.)

the type of brain waves apparent during this phase; and rapid eye movement (REM) sleep, so-named because the muscles that control eye movement are active during this phase. A cat is in a phase of REM sleep when you see the tail, ears, or whiskers twitching as well as the eyes. As they sleep, cats often pass through several cycles of quiet sleep and REM sleep.

Humans dream during the REM phase of sleep, and it seems fair to assume that cats do as well—although the subject of their dreams is anybody's guess. REM sleep usually lasts for about six or seven minutes and alternates with twenty to thirty minutes of quiet sleep, but even this varies depending on age. Newborn kittens may spend more than three-quarters of their sleep time in REM sleep.

If your cat is keeping you up at night, see page 256 for suggestions on solving feline sleep problems.

Cats and Sleep

Cats spend an inordinate amount of time sleeping—up to eighteen hours a day, which is more than any other species that lives with humans. This slumber time is broken up into multiple cat naps throughout the day. The percentage of the day spent sleeping changes little from kittenhood through adulthood, but sleep periods tend to be shorter and more frequent in kittens.

There are two phases of cat sleep: quiet sleep, also called slow-wave sleep for

Felines spend most of the day sleeping.

Cats and Catnip

One-third to one-half of all domestic cats have unusual—and often zany—responses to catnip, a weed that grows wild in temperate parts of Europe and North America. A cat usually progresses from sniffing the catnip to licking and chewing it, rubbing her head, chin, and cheeks in it, and ultimately even somersaulting and writhing over it. Some cats may leap about, stretch, lick themselves, appear to hallucinate, and then get sleepy or hungry. Friendly, gregarious cats tend to have the most exuberant responses. The whole episode, which lasts about ten or fifteen minutes, is reminiscent of behavior just before and after mating. Afterwards, the cat is resistant to catnip for at least an hour.

We know that the catnip plant contains an unsaturated oil (nepetalactone) that elicits the antic response, triggered by the cat's sense of smell. It's not clear exactly why cats react to it. Some responsiveness is inherited and generally does not develop until two to three months of age. The only other animals known to respond are some wildcat species, including lions, leopards, jaguars, and bobcats.

There's no evidence of catnip being harmful, so if your cat does respond to it, there's no reason not to indulge him from time to time.

Most cats stimulated by catnip will lick and chew the plant leaves and then roll around in them, as shown here, while other cats have an even more dramatic response.

IV

Taking Care of
Your Cat

This section is a comprehensive reference guide to caring for your cat—in sickness and in health, in youth and in old age. The following pages take you through the everyday routines of feeding and grooming, the steps toward maintaining your cat's health, and the procedures of emergency care. Special features on household poisons and on caring for sick cats, pregnant cats, newborn kittens, and aging cats will keep you prepared for any eventuality. Within Section IV there are six chapters on caring for your cat:

Everyday Care for Your Cat

Domestic cats are generally robust creatures, but they depend on their owners to help keep them healthy and happy. This section guides you through the everyday essentials of caring for your cat: feeding, exercise, litter box maintenance, grooming, bathing, tooth brushing, and claw trimming. Here is also where you'll find help avoiding and solving feline behavior problems, including litter box lapses, furniture scratching, plant eating, sleep problems, and aggression toward people and other cats. And because cats often have a hard time dealing with major changes in the household—like moving to a new home or having to learn to share their home with a new baby—we offer instruction on how to ease potentially difficult transitions. Finally, we provide suggestions for making any travel experience with your cat as pleasant and safe as possible.

This section focuses mainly on the needs of the average healthy adult cat; for information on the specific requirements of newborn kittens, pregnant and nursing cats, and elderly cats, see The Beginning and End of Life: Times for Special Care, beginning on page 333.

Proper care from day one helps keep kittens like these playful and healthy.

Feeding Your Cat

Cats are carnivores. Their bodies require nutrients found only in meat, including certain amino acids, fats, and vitamins. They can't live on an exclusively vegetarian diet, but cats can take some nourishment from nonanimal sources. In fact, nutritionally balanced and complete commercial cat foods contain both animal and nonanimal ingredients. The next few pages offer you some help figuring out what to feed your cat and how often. Owners of overweight cats or cats with health problems that require special diets should, of course, consult with their veterinarian.

Choosing the Right Food

With few exceptions, commercially packaged cat foods are preferable to homemade diets, which are inconvenient to prepare and may not provide adequate nutrition. Should you choose to prepare your cat's food on your own, or should a medical condition require home-cooking, make sure your veterinarian provides you with a recipe for a nutritionally complete and balanced feline diet.

In general, if you stick with nationally marketed and recognized brands and steer clear of generic products, the food you purchase for your cat should be fine. Generic brands, whose formulas are inconsistent, may lack essential ingredients and cause serious nutritional deficits and can be difficult for cats to digest. The superiority of "premium" brands—those available at pet stores, pet food outlets, and veterinary offices—is

Reading Cat Food Labels

The most important information to look for on a cat food label is that the food you are considering meets the nutritional standards set in feeding trials by the Association of American Feed Control Officials (AAFCO). The label should also indicate if the product is nutritionally complete and balanced for all life stages or for a particular life stage, such as adult cat maintenance. Foods claiming nutritional completeness and balance must also provide suggested feeding instructions. If the food does not provide a complete and balanced feline ration, the label should say, "not to be fed as sole diet" or "for intermittent feeding only." The "guaranteed analysis" printed on most labels provides little guidance because it does not separate the digestible protein, fat, and fiber in the food from the indigestible; the percentages offered are for the crude protein, fat, and fiber, which means they are combinations of both digestible and indigestible. The ingredients in a cat food are listed in descending order of predominance by weight. Meat, fish, or poultry, as well as cereal grains and soybean meal, should be near the top of the list.

Overweight cats may need special diets.

under debate among veterinary nutritionists. An advantage of premium brands is that they are always made following the same recipe, whereas ingredients in some of the less expensive brands may change based on cost. Some cats' gastrointestinal tracts are sensitive to change. Also, the premium foods are more efficiently digested, produce less waste than some generic and supermarket brands, and are generally more palatable.

If you need to change your cat's diet for any reason, try to do so over the course of a week or so. Sudden changes in food can give a cat diarrhea. To introduce a new food, combine the new food and the old, then gradually decrease the amount of the old in proportion to the new.

A good-quality canned food is nutritionally equal to a good-quality dry or semi-moist one, but such factors as your cat's age, finickiness, and tendency to obesity and dental problems can make one type of food more suitable.

Dry foods are relatively inexpensive and can be left out for the cat to eat at will. (If you are leaving dry food out all day, be sure it's fresh and in a thoroughly cleaned bowl.) Cats fed dry foods tend to have less plaque and tartar buildup on their teeth than cats fed canned food, probably because dry food is more abrasive. Contrary to a common perception, there is no evidence that any of today's high-quality dry foods contributes to urinary tract disease, or any other recognized health problems. However, dry diets may be less palatable to some cats. If your cat is underweight, or if he is sick and has a reduced appetite, a canned diet may be the better option.

Canned foods are much more expensive than dry foods, especially considering that they are about 75 percent water. Because they spoil quickly, canned foods cannot be left out all day. Refrigerate any unused portion of the can (if your cat refuses to eat food straight from the refrigerator, let the food warm to room temperature). Canned foods are very palatable, which may be a problem if your cat is prone to obesity. But palatability is an advantage if your cat is sick and has a reduced appetite. You may need to experiment with different brands, but often the ones that people find smelliest and most offensive are the ones cats prefer.

Feeding a Kitten

By the time most cats have reached adulthood, their body weight has increased by as much as 50 times. Most of this growth occurs in the first six months of life. Make sure that the food you give your kitten is either a "growth formula," specially suited to the particular nutritional needs of developing kittens, or an all-purpose food nutritionally adequate at all stages of life. Between the ages of about three and a half months and five or six months old, kittens go through "teething," losing their baby teeth and gaining their permanent ones. There is no need to take any special feeding precautions at this time.

It is especially important to provide nutritionally balanced and complete food during the first six months of a kitten's life—a period of explosive growth.

Semi-moist foods contain 15 to 30 percent water and are usually priced somewhere between canned and dry. Semi-moist foods do not require refrigeration and can therefore be left out for the cat to eat at will, although they do tend to dry out. As with dry foods, provide fresh semi-moist foods daily after thoroughly cleaning the food bowl.

When to Feed

Is it better to leave food out for your cat to eat whenever she wants (free-choice feeding) or to feed your cat a specific ration at certain times of the day (meal feeding)? The answer depends on what kind of food you are serving and whether your cat is prone to obesity.

Scientific evidence suggests that allowing cats to eat multiple small meals throughout the day—as happens with cats fed free-choice—may help prevent certain types of urinary tract disorders. But many cats will overeat and become obese if food is available to them in unlimited quantities.

If you can feel your cat's ribs but cannot see them, she is probably the right weight.

Keep in mind that canned food may spoil if left out all day, so it can't be fed free-choice. Spoilage is rarely a problem in free-choice feeding of dry cat food as long as fresh food is provided daily and the feeding dish is cleaned frequently. Another concern with free-choice feeding is that you may not notice a subtle change in your cat's appetite, often an indication of illness, and you may miss an opportunity to diagnose a disease in its early stages.

Meal feeding involves dispensing food only at specific times of the day, usually two or three times daily. You can feed a specific amount, or you can provide unlimited food for a certain period of time. By feeding a set portion several times daily, you can monitor your cat's appetite; this is the best way to feed cats that are obesity-prone. If you have more than one cat, you may need to feed several small meals to each to ensure that everyone gets his fair share, especially if one cat is domineering. Cats that tend to eat their food too quickly and then vomit should also be fed multiple small meals throughout the day.

Too Fat or Too Thin?

Overweight cats are more likely than average-size cats to develop "sugar" diabetes (page 305), lameness problems, and certain types of skin disorders. Most at risk of becoming overweight are neutered cats with placid dispositions and those fed highly palatable cat foods. If you cannot easily feel your cat's ribs, she is too fat. On the other hand, if you can see the ribs through the fur, your cat is too skinny. To help your cat gain weight, provide four to six small meals a day or free-feed a high-calorie food such as a kitten food/feline growth formula. Consult with your veterinarian before adding any dietary supplements. Most healthy, newly adopted cats will have no problem gaining weight once they are comfortable in their new homes.

A recent survey found that about 25 percent of cats in the United States are overweight.

Water

Be sure to provide your cat with fresh water daily (many cats refuse to drink stagnant days-old water). Although cats don't gulp water by the gallon the way some dogs do, they still need to be properly hydrated. Cats that eat only dry food need more water than cats that eat moist (canned) food. In fact, some cats derive nearly all the water they need from canned food, but they should still be offered plenty of fresh water every day.

Treats

Giving your cat a little junk food—"people" food or commercial treats—now and then is okay if the cat is healthy and not overweight. Make sure that treats don't constitute more than five to ten percent of your cat's daily diet, and try to choose treats that are nutritious. Avoid table scraps that are overly processed, spicy, or fatty. There is no danger in feeding cats vegetable snacks such as lettuce or other green leafy vegetables. Some cats enjoy nibbling on "kitty gardens," little plots of grass that you can grow for them from kits available at pet supply stores. (Don't put out a garden until the grass is somewhat full or your cat may mistake it for litter.)

However picturesque the image of a cat contentedly lapping at a saucer of milk, it is not uncommon for older cats to lose the ability to digest the natural sugar in milk—and milk products such as ice

How Much to Feed

The suggested feeding amounts on cat food labels offer rough guidelines on how much to feed your cat. How many calories he needs depends on how active

Milk gives many cats diarrhea, but some felines can enjoy an occasional saucerful.

he is. A sedentary adult house cat may need no more than thirty calories per pound (sixty calories per kilogram) of body weight per day, whereas an active adult cat may require at least forty calories per pound. The correct meal size is that which maintains the cat's optimal body weight. A good rule of thumb is to follow the manufacturer's directions at first, and then add or subtract food by approximately 10 to 25 percent based on how your cat responds.

cream and yogurt—and to develop diarrhea if they drink it. While cats are not drawn to the majority of foods that are dangerous to them, some cats will readily eat chocolate. Chocolate can be fatally toxic, but cats rarely consume enough to kill them. (See the Household Poisons chart on page 330.)

Food and Water Dishes

You should provide a food dish for every cat in your household as well as one water dish on each floor of the home. Thoroughly clean all dishes daily. If you need to leave an adult cat alone for one or two days, you may want to invest in an automatic feeder, especially if your cat is the kind to gorge himself immediately if left with several days' worth of food. Introduce your cat to the feeder a few days before leaving to make sure that it works and that he will eat out of it. It's not a good idea to use automatic feeders on a daily basis, as doing so makes it difficult to monitor your cat's appetite, an important indicator of feline health.

The Litter Box Routine

Creating an environment that will encourage proper litter box behavior from the start is the best way for an owner to ensure that a cat will not take his business elsewhere. Maintaining good litter box habits is much easier than retraining a lapsed litter box user (page 254).

Which Type of Box Is Best?

There is a vast array of litter box types on the market, ranging from simple, inexpensive tray-like boxes to hooded affairs to sophisticated machines that automatically sift solid material from the litter and store it neatly in a plastic bag. When choosing a litter box, remember that what is convenient for you may not be desirable to a cat. Boxes that automatically sift litter may frighten some cats away. Hooded boxes designed to decrease odor may actually trap smells within, especially if the box is not cleaned frequently enough, and some cats find it difficult to assume a comfortable position in a covered box. On the other hand, some cats may appreciate the extra measure of privacy afforded by covered boxes, which also keep dogs and children out.

Simpler is better when it comes to choosing a litter box.

Location Is Everything

Some multicat households may need one litter box per cat on each floor of the home, but one for every two or three cats is often enough. Place the boxes in quiet locations that are easy for the cat to reach. Don't put them close to the feeding and drinking area. Not only do most cats dislike eliminating near where they eat, but doing so is unsanitary. Some cats prefer to have the box in a position that allows them to see in all directions; other cats prefer a sheltered area.

Litter Box Fillers and Liners

Of the many types of litter box fillers available, most cats seem to prefer the fine-grained, unscented clumping variety. In fact, many cats are repelled by any type of scented litter.

If you are adopting a new cat into a home with resident cats, provide the newcomer with the litter to which she is already accustomed. When she is relatively comfortable in her new surroundings, you can gradually switch her over to the resident cat's litter type. Two methods work well for changing the type of litter you use (whether you have a new cat or not). You can provide separate litter boxes containing the old and new types of litter, and when you see the cat reliably using the new litter, remove the old. Or, you can mix some of the new litter in with the old, and gradually increase the proportion of new to old (this doesn't work as well if clumping litter is mixed with another type of litter).

Plastic litter liners make cleaning the litter box much easier, but some cats avoid boxes with liners because the liners feel funny to their feet. Also, cats can scratch through the liners, allowing urine to seep under and odor to build up.

Keeping the Box Clean

Keeping your cat's litter box clean is perhaps the most important step you can take to ensure proper litter box behavior. It is much harder to retrain a lapsed litter box user than it is to maintain good habits.

With a clumping litter, place enough material (at least one inch, preferably more) in the box to prevent urine from leaching to the bottom and sticking. Scoop all waste every day and discard it in the garbage, or, if the litter is flushable, in the toilet. Add new litter as the level drops from scooping. Clumping litter may not need to be completely replaced for several weeks. Every time you replace the litter, wash the box with a mild dish detergent (avoid cleaning products that contain ammonia). You may also want to disinfect the box after cleaning (use a 1:32 dilution of household chlorine bleach in water; don't use disinfectants that contain pine oil or phenolic compounds). Make sure the box is dry before replacing the litter.

With a nonclumping litter, put enough in the box to prevent urine from seeping through to the bottom. Scoop solid material out daily, and dump and replace all the litter at least once a week (sooner if the bottom of the box has become damp). Boxes filled with nonclumping litter must be washed every week. Follow the cleaning instructions given above.

Keeping the box clean is vitally important in ensuring proper litter box behavior.

Grooming supplies, left to right: pin brush, narrow- and wide-toothed comb, scissors, flea comb, slicker brush, natural bristle brush, rubber brush

Grooming Your Cat

Brushing and Combing

All cats benefit from regular grooming sessions, and so do their owners. The pleasure a cat receives from routine brushing and combing sessions can strengthen his trust in you and make him more companionable. Loose hair removed with a brush or comb will not end up on the furniture, nor will it form a hairball for the cat to bring up. Owners who regularly comb or brush their cats often detect medical problems—such as fleas, mouth disease, and skin problems—in their early stages. For some longhaired breeds, daily grooming is essential to prevent matting, but grooming once a week is sufficient for most cats. It is best to get your cat accustomed to being groomed when she is a kitten. Always be gentle.

Grooming Equipment The tools needed to groom your cat are fairly basic and inexpensive. For a shorthaired cat you need a flea comb (a fine-toothed metal comb available at pet supply stores) and a natural bristle brush, a slicker brush, or a rubber brush. For a longhaired cat, you need a wide-toothed comb, a stiff natural bristle brush or pin brush, a flea comb (if your cat goes outside), and a pair of blunt-tipped scissors for removing hair mats. (All these tools are pictured above.)

Flea-Combing Your Cat Among the many compelling reasons for keeping your cat exclusively indoors is that indoor-only cats are much less likely to become infested with fleas than those allowed outside. If your cat does go outdoors, or if he is exposed to other animals that do, be on the lookout

Shorthaired cats should be groomed at least once a week with a fine-toothed comb and a brush.

for fleas. Cats at risk of exposure can be groomed with a flea comb as a regular part of their weekly grooming session. The coats of longhaired cats need to be tangle-free before you can run a flea comb through them. Look for flea debris, which looks like tiny black pepper flakes, in the teeth of the comb. Place a few flecks on a damp paper towel; if a red halo forms around the flecks, it is flea debris, not dirt. You can also look for the fleas themselves by parting your cat's fur and looking for small, wingless insects. For information on preventing, controlling, and treating flea infestation, see page 293.

Grooming a Shorthaired Cat

Shorthaired cats with single coats have fine under-coats and relatively short guard hairs (as in Burmese, Siamese, and most domestic shorthairs). They should be combed with a fine-toothed metal comb or flea comb along the nap and then given a final once-over with a natural bristle brush, slicker brush, or rubber curry brush.

Shorthaired cats with double coats have dense, downy undercoats and relatively long guard hairs (as in the American Shorthair, Manx, and Russian Blue). They require more frequent grooming than single-coated shorthairs—two or three times a week, depending on the individual. Don't use a rubber brush on these cats or you may damage the longer guard hairs.

Owners of Persians must make a serious commitment to grooming.

Grooming a Longhaired Cat For most longhaired breeds, brush along the nap of the coat with a natural bristle brush. Then use a wide-toothed comb to stroke against the nap, one small section at a time. Still using the wide-toothed comb, next stroke with the nap of the coat. Follow with the natural bristle brush, going with the nap.

Be aware that Himalayans and Persians require the most diligent coat care. If these cats are not groomed at least several times a week—daily grooming is often necessary—mats will form. Areas most prone to matting are behind the ears, under the chin, under the fore-limbs in the "armpit" area, under the hindlimbs in the groin area, and along the tail. Before getting a Himalayan or Persian cat, prospective owners should discuss the breed's special grooming needs with a professional groomer or an experienced breeder.

Hair mats may be gently teased apart (or carefully split perpendicular to the skin with blunt-tipped scissors), and then carefully pulled away from the skin. Never try to cut off a mat with scissors unless you are absolutely sure there is no skin between the blades. Large mats must be trimmed with an electric clipper, a task best handled by a veterinarian or professional groomer. For a severely matted cat, have a vet or professional groomer clip the entire coat.

Some breeds with special fur types, like the Rexes and the American Wirehair, have special grooming needs. Get instructions from an experienced professional groomer or the breeder from whom you obtained your cat.

Claw Trimming

Most cats are capable of keeping their claws the proper length, either by scratching an object (preferably a scratch post rather than the leg of your couch) or by chewing off the claw's outer layer (the usual technique for the rear claws). Only rarely does a cat—perhaps an old or debilitated cat, or one with extra toes—need human intervention to keep the claws from growing so long that they arc into the pad. Claw trimming is a matter less of length than of sharpness. The obvious advantage of keeping your cat's claws blunt is that any scratching will cause less damage.

Special claw trimmers (two types are shown above) are available from veterinarians or pet supply stores, but sharp nail clippers for humans work just as well. Keep a styptic (astringent) pencil or powder on hand in case you accidentally clip into the quick and bleeding hasn't stopped within a couple of minutes.

If possible, start training your cat to have her claws trimmed as a kitten. Be sure to reward your cat with a special food treat—one that she receives only during claw trimming or some other grooming procedure—during or immediately after trimming. The best time to trim your cat's claws is when she is relaxed or sleepy. Never try to give a pedicure right after a stressful experience or an energetic round of play.

Your cat should be resting comfortably on your lap, the floor, or a table. Hold a paw in one hand and press a toe pad gently to extend the claw. Notice the pink tissue (the quick) on the inside of the claw. Avoid the quick when you trim the claw; cutting into it will cause pain and bleeding. Remove the sharp tip below the quick (away from the toe), clipping about halfway between the end of the quick and the tip of

Gently press the cat's toe pads to reveal sharp claws in need of a trim.

the claw. If your cat becomes impatient, take a break and try again later. Even if you can clip only a claw or two a day, eventually you'll complete the task. (Because cats do little damage with their rear claws and do a good job of keeping them trim themselves—by chewing them—many cat owners never clip the rear claws. Others trim their cats' rear claws three or four times a year or have them done by their veterinarian or a professional groomer.)

If you accidentally clip into the quick, don't panic. The claw may bleed for a moment, but it will usually stop very quickly. Soothe your cat by speaking softly to her and stroking her head. If the bleeding hasn't stopped after a minute or so, touch a styptic pencil to the claw end or pat on styptic powder to help staunch the bleeding.

How often you need to clip your cat's claws depends somewhat on how much of the tip you remove, but usually a clipping every ten to fourteen days will suffice. If your cat absolutely refuses to allow you to clip her claws, get help from your veterinarian or a professional groomer.

Soft plastic covers that you can glue over your cats trimmed claws are available from veterinarians. These covers are well accepted by cats, further limit scratching damage, and also extend time between claw trimmings.

Hold your cat snugly against your body and extend one paw at a time for trimming.

Bathing

Pet cats rarely need to be bathed, unless they get very dirty or are infested with fleas. Show cats are bathed more often. If bathing is going to be part of your cat's routine, it's best to start when he is young.

In preparation for bathing, trim the cat's claws for your own protection (page 243). Then comb and brush your cat to remove loose hair; also remove any mats. Put some petrolatum-based artificial tears (available at pharmacies) in each eye to protect them from the shampoo. If your cat is prone to tear stains, gently clean the eye area with a cotton ball moistened in five percent hydrogen peroxide (being sure not to get any in his eyes). Finally, carefully place some cotton in each ear to keep water out.

As with any grooming routine, it's best to begin bathing your cat when he is young.

Most cats will resist being plunged into a tub of water, so it's best to use a hand-held spray attachment with the water turned on gently or to pour water from a cup.

Be sure to provide firm footing for the cat; a rubber mat or towel should suffice. Wet the coat thoroughly with warm water, avoiding the face, eyes, and ears. Once this is done, most cats will settle down.

Dilute one part cat shampoo with five parts water. Thoroughly work the solution into the coat. To avoid tangles, work only in the direction of hair growth. Avoid the face, eyes, and ears. Be sure to rinse completely—this step may take longer than you would expect, especially with long-haired cats—as shampoo residue can irritate the skin and attract dirt. Repeat the entire process if necessary. Conditioners designed for cats help avoid tangling in longer haired breeds. Work the solution completely through the cat's coat, then rinse thoroughly.

Clean the facial area with a washcloth. Unless the face is extremely soiled, plain water is fine. If shampoo is necessary, use an extra-diluted solution, then rinse gently but thoroughly, again avoiding the ears and eyes.

Take the cat from the tub or sink and wrap him in a large dry towel; cats can get chilled very quickly, so it's important to keep them warm. Remove the cotton from his ears and gently dry his coat. For long-haired cats, gently untangle the fur with a wide-toothed metal comb (always combing in the direction of hair growth). A hand-held hair dryer set on warm can be used at this stage (if it doesn't terrify the cat) along with the comb to part the hair and keep it free of tangles. Longhaired cats need to be brushed with a natural bristle brush once they are dry.

Tooth Brushing

By brushing your cat's teeth at home, you can reduce plaque and tartar buildup and thereby help keep your cat's mouth much healthier. (See page 295 for a discussion of disorders of the teeth and mouth.) Regular veterinary dental examinations are also essential, but brushing your cat's teeth on a regular basis can help limit the frequency of professional cleanings, which often require general anesthesia. It would be ideal to brush your cat's teeth every day, but once a week, or even twice a month, is very beneficial. It can be difficult to get your cat to cooperate. The younger your cat is when you begin tooth brushing, the better your chances are for success. Some adult cats can never be taught to accept tooth brushing. Don't force the issue or you may be bitten or scratched.

Brush your cat's teeth with a special cat toothbrush, or wipe them with a cotton swab, a gauze pad, or a soft cloth.

It may take several weeks for your cat to allow you to brush her teeth, so take your time and be patient. It's best to begin when your cat is relaxed or sleepy. To get your cat comfortable with having her head and mouth handled, make the procedure an extension of petting her head and scratching her chin, and move gradually through the following steps one at a time. Keep the sessions short, and if your cat starts to struggle, take a break and try again the next day. When you and your cat have succeeded with a step, reward her with a special food treat.

With your cat resting on your lap, a table, or the floor, and facing you, gently hold her head in your hand, with your palm on the top of her head and your thumb on her lower jaw. Move the forefinger of your free hand around and over her

lips, and then gently slide it between the cheek and the teeth and rub it in small circular motions over the outside of the teeth, especially the long canines, the pre-molars, and the molars. (See page 192 for a diagram of cat teeth.) The inner surfaces of the teeth are inaccessible and rarely have tartar buildup. Repeat the rubbing on the other side of the mouth; you may have to switch hands.

Once your cat is comfortable with having her teeth rubbed (a step that may take several days), you can introduce her to specially formulated pet toothpaste, available from your veterinarian. (Don't use people toothpaste—it contains detergents that can upset a cat's stomach.) Put a little bit on the tip of your finger before you rub the teeth. The final step is to use either a special brush that fits on your finger or a soft-bristled cat toothbrush, both available from your veterinarian or pet supply store. Alternatively, some cat owners find that a cotton swab, a gauze pad, or a soft cloth works just fine.

Playing with Your Cat

Take time to play with your cat every day—it's good for both of you. Interactive play sessions reduce feline and human stress levels and help keep neutered cats fit. Also, cats that are entertained regularly are less likely to become bored and occupy themselves in ways that owners find annoying. A round of play before bedtime can sufficiently tire out a nocturnal noise-maker to make him sleep through the night.

Some of the most popular commercially available cat toys are those that an owner can manipulate in a way that mimics the

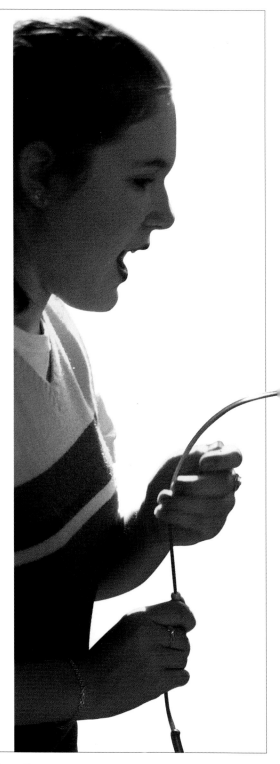

motions of prey. One such toy consists of a longish stiff wire with a few inch-long pieces of cardboard rope attached to one end and another piece at the other end for the owner to grip and twist. Even the most jaded and aloof of cats will be roused from her favorite resting spot at the sight of the paper "insect" flitting about her living room. Alternatively, you can make your own toy by stuffing an old sock with paper and some catnip, knotting the top, and attaching a piece of string for dragging the toy about (remove the string if you are leaving the cat alone with the sock).

Never allow your cat or kitten to play with yarn or string, rubber bands, ribbon, or Christmas tree tinsel, which can become lodged under the tongue or in the stomach or intestines, creating terrible problems and possibly leading to death.

Play Hazards

• Always put away interactive toys when playtime is over, for two reasons: they may have parts that are unsafe for cats to ingest, and toys are more exciting to cats when they disappear and then suddenly reappear at a future play session.
• Don't let a cat or kitten bite and scratch your hands and fingers, and don't play rough with your hands. Doing so teaches the cat that it is okay to bite and scratch people.

Kittens find amusement in just about anything—a paper shopping bag (without handles that can trap little heads), a pen lying on the floor. Keep in mind, however, that as kittens mature, they become less interested in objects that just lie around the house. Adult cats, especially those that are left alone a lot, appreciate play sessions with more mobile interactive toys.

Interactive toys are best for engaging your cat's attention and providing vigorous exercise.

Socialization to infants and young children should be continued throughout a cat's lifetime in preparation for the day a new baby may join the household.

Bringing Home a Baby

The arrival of a new baby is a very special time, but as with any other major changes in the household, it can be stressful for your cats. To express their anxiety, some cats, even those that have been neutered or spayed, will "spray" (see page 253 for further discussion of spraying).

It's best to have your cat examined by your veterinarian before bringing home a baby. Diseases transmittable from cats to people are not particularly common, but they do exist. Make sure your cat is not infected with ringworm and does not harbor any parasites that could be a potential health hazard to the baby.

Prepare your cat for the arrival of the new human member of the family by allowing her to explore the nursery a month or more before the baby's homecoming so she can get used to the new scents and sights. If there are areas that you don't want your cat to explore (such as the crib or changing table), now is the time to teach the cat to stay away. Set up traps that are startling but not harmful to the cat. For example, you can place five or ten upside-down mousetraps under some sheets of paper on the crib mattress; when your cat jumps in, she'll spring the traps without harming herself while being startled enough that she won't want to jump in again. You can similarly booby-trap a changing table by constructing a flimsy cardboard shelf along the top, then placing cans containing a few coins on it. When the cat jumps up, the shelf will collapse, bringing down the cans and making a lot of noise.

Be aware that especially shy, edgy cats may panic and strike out if they are startled in this way; if you have such a cat, you might instead place some double-sided tape, which feels unpleasant to feline feet, on a piece of cardboard and place the cardboard on the surfaces you want her to avoid. Of course, these contraptions won't be used when the baby is home, but by then your cat will have learned to steer clear of the baby's things.

If you are planning to make any changes in the cat's routine—for example, if her litter box is to be moved out of the room now being set up as the nursery—initiate them at least a month before the baby's arrival.

When the new baby arrives, if your cat is so inclined, let her see and sniff the newcomer, but don't force the issue. Do not hold your cat and force her on the baby; not only will you risk your cat scratching you or your baby, it may even make an eventual reconciliation less likely. Many cats just won't be interested. It is wise to keep the door to the nursery shut when possible to avoid inadvertent scratches (even though by now your cat should know to avoid certain areas in the baby's room). Make sure you spend some quality time with your cat during this time of adjustment.

Preventing and Solving Behavior Problems

Most cats have few behavioral glitches to tarnish the relationship with their human companions. Some of the behaviors that cat owners find irksome—for example, furniture scratching and urine spraying—are in fact perfectly normal feline activities. Fortunately, most feline behavior problems can be resolved or, better yet, avoided altogether.

It is wisest and easiest to prevent behavior problems from developing in the first place. Correcting undesirable behavior once it is established is much more difficult. The longer a behavior persists, the harder it is to correct. Just as it is much easier for kittens than for more mature cats to accept grooming procedures, it is also simpler to train younger cats to use scratching posts and a litter box. Teach and reinforce good habits early.

Seeking professional attention as soon as a behavior problem develops is one of the most important steps you can take to ensure a timely and successful resolution. Not only can your veterinarian look for any underlying physical abnormalities that may be causing or contributing to the problem, if necessary he can also refer you to a behavior consultant who can design behavior modification strategies. In some instances, your veterinarian may prescribe behavior-modifying medication (such as antidepressants, anxiety reducers, or mood stabilizers) to assist in the process. Though rarely successful by themselves, these drugs can sometimes be beneficial when integrated with other behavior-modifying strategies.

Never hit your cat. Physical punishment is not a positive solution to any cat's behavior problem. Striking can harm the cat or make him more aggressive, and the cat will usually associate the punishment with you, making him fearful of you or teaching him to avoid you altogether. Gentle "remote" methods are kinder and more effective. To interrupt destructive behaviors, spray the cat with a squirt gun or a can of compressed air. To keep a cat off of kitchen counters or certain pieces of furniture, put down some tin foil or double-sided masking tape on cardboard, which cats dislike walking on. Some cats will avoid areas containing lemon-scented air fresheners.

It is much easier to prevent undesirable habits from developing in the first place than it is to stop them once they've begun.

Inappropriate Elimination: Failure to Use the Litter Box

A recent survey of cat owners showed that about 10 percent of cats at least occasionally urinate and/or defecate outside the litter box. In fact, inappropriate elimination accounts for approximately two-thirds of all reported cat behavior problems. Persian cats seem especially prone to this behavior.

There are many possible medical and behavioral reasons for a cat to fail to use the litter box, so a veterinary examination is in order at the first display of such behavior. The veterinarian will ask you for the cat's behavioral history and will perform a physical examination and suitable diagnostic tests to identify any medical cause, such as bladder inflammation or disease of the large intestine.

Excluding medical causes, there are three major reasons that a cat will fail to use the litter box: aversion, preference, and urine marking. In cases of aversion, the cat dislikes the litter, the box, or the location of the box. In cases of preference, the cat prefers to eliminate in a place other than where the box is located, or prefers a different surface (such as carpet). In cases of urine marking, the cat is typically spraying to communicate with other cats or to express anxiety.

Aversion Probably the most common cause of litter box aversion is a dirty litter box, so the simple solution is to keep the box clean. Some cats are extremely picky about box cleanliness and will refuse to use the box if even a trace of urine or feces is present. Other cats have an aversion to a particular type of litter, often to scented ones, or to a particular type of litter box. It's a good bet that your cat dislikes the litter if he perches on the side of the box rather than stepping into it; if he quickly jumps out of the box after eliminating, and shakes his paws or runs away; or if he fails to cover his urine or feces.

Litter box location is very important. If the box is set up in a heavily trafficked or inconvenient site, the cat may use an area he finds more suitable. Common owner mistakes include positioning the box in a place that a kitten cannot get to easily and expecting an older cat to climb multiple flights of stairs to get to a box. Cats become accustomed to the litter box being in a certain spot. If the location of the box

Litter-Training a Stray Cat

Stray cats adopted into a home often fail to use the box. Strays and other cats that have been raised outside often prefer loose soil or leaves, materials that feel quite different than commercially available litter. These cats may also balk at stepping inside a box to eliminate. Owners can sometimes litter-train such cats by providing a litter material that is similar to what they were using before—try loose soil or sand—and confining the cat to a small room until he is using the box faithfully. (See also Retraining a Lapsed Litter Box User on page 254.) Providing several boxes with different litter types often helps, too, and can inform the owner of the cat's preferred material. Once the cat starts to use the litter box reliably, add some of the new litter material to the old, gradually increasing the proportion of new to old over the course of several weeks.

is suddenly changed, the cat may continue to eliminate in the former location.

If a cat associates a painful or unpleasant experience with the place where he eliminates, he can quickly learn to avoid the area altogether. Cats with a medical condition causing pain with urination or defecation will commonly associate their discomfort with the box and will eliminate elsewhere in an attempt to evade the pain.

You can inadvertently "teach" your cat to avoid the box if you use visits to the box as opportunities to grab him to administer medication, trim claws, or scold for an offense. If a dominant cat in the household takes advantage of another cat when he's eliminating, attacking him when he's vulnerable, this too will teach the cat to stay away.

Preference Most cats have a preference for one litter type over others. About 90 percent seem to prefer the feel of clumping types of litter. The smaller sandlike granules apparently feel better to their feet. If your cat shows an interest in soiling in a particular place, if possible, put a litter box in the desired spot. If the spot the cat has chosen is inconvenient for you, move the box a few inches a day to a more appropriate spot and make the original area less attractive to the cat by temporarily covering it with plastic, foil, or double-sided tape.

Urine Marking Cat urine found on a vertical surface is invariably due to marking behavior. Sometimes cats will urine mark or "spray" on a horizontal surface, but the volume of urine will be small; large puddles of urine found on a horizontal surface are never due to urine marking.

To determine whether urination on a horizontal surface outside the box is due

How to Avoid Inappropriate Elimination

Practicing the following steps can help prevent elimination problems from developing in the first place.

- Keep the litter box clean (page 240).
- Use unscented litter.
- Place the litter box away from the feeding area. Cats don't like to eliminate near where they eat.
- Place the box in an easy-to-reach yet out-of-the-way and quiet location.
- Avoid sudden changes in the location of the litter box.
- Avoid sudden changes in the type of litter, the kind of box, or the product used to clean the box.
- Limit the number of cats in the household. The likelihood of spraying increases to nearly 100 percent if there are too many cats in a given household.
- Be sure you have enough litter boxes for the number of cats in the household and/or the number of floors in your home (page 240).
- Clean the litter box with a mild cleaning product.

Know your cat. If he's sensitive or anxious, take care to insulate him from situations he is likely to find stressful and to prepare him well in advance of a change in routine.

Cats will spray on vertical surfaces to mark territory and notify other cats of their presence.

to marking behavior, litter aversion or preference, a physical disorder, or some other cause, you will have to observe the cat closely and also consult a veterinarian. Your veterinarian may be able to tell which is the case by discussing your observations with you, or she may need to run diagnostic tests. Virtually all unneutered male cats, and even some unspayed females, will urine mark as a sexually motivated behavior. Neutering almost always prevents this behavior, but "fixed" cats may also spray to communicate ownership of an area to other cats, to threaten other cats, to respond to a threat from other cats, or to express anxiety or stress.

Typical causes of feline stress include overcrowding, moving households, or the introduction of a new person or pet into the household. For advice on helping your cat cope with such stressful situations, see Moving with Your Cat on page 265,

Retraining a Lapsed Litter Box User

Before attempting to correct your cat's misuse of the litter box, bring her to the veterinarian for a full examination to rule out any medical conditions that may be contributing to the problem.

Once you are confident that your cat is in good health, confine her to a small room; a bathroom with a tile floor is a good choice. Remove any absorbent rugs and place a cat bed and some toys in the room as well as food and water dishes and, of course, a litter box. (It's a good idea to offer the cat a variety of boxes and litter types to choose from, if you have the room.) Put as much space as possible between the dishes and bedding and the litter boxes. Visit the cat three or four times a day, taking twenty minutes or so

each time for chatting, playing, or grooming. Keep track of when she uses the litter box. If she urinates on the bed, remove it.

After your cat has been using the box faithfully for two weeks, allow her access to the rest of the house one room at a time, preferably right after she's used the box. Keep a close watch to be sure she doesn't lapse into old bad habits, and don't let her roam when you are out of the house. When you observe her using the litter box reliably, you can allow her more time alone. If she doesn't soil out of the box at night, she need not be confined to her room overnight; if she does, confine her at night for two to four weeks, and then give her another try in the house at large.

Introducing a New Cat to a Resident Cat on page 60, and Bringing Home a Baby on page 250.

Plant Eating

A cat that eats houseplants not only destroys the plant but may harm himself if the plant is poisonous. (See the list of poisonous houseplants on page 328.) Try offering your cat alternatives, such as lettuce or other green leafy vegetables, or "kitty gardens" (plots of chewable grass available at pet supply stores). You can also make your houseplants less desirable to the cat by spraying the leaves with a commercial antichew spray (also available at pet supply stores), or make them inaccessible to the cat. If your cat is jumping into planters to chew plant leaves or eliminate in the soil, place an upside down mouse trap under a piece of paper in the pot so that when the cat climbs in, the trap springs shut, harmlessly scaring him away.

Kittenhood is the ideal time to introduce scratch posts.

Eating houseplants can be dangerous to your cat's health.

Furniture Scratching

Scratching is a normal and necessary activity that helps cats peel off old claw sheaths to expose new claws, mark their territory, and get a pleasant stretch. Unfortunately, the desired scratching object is often a stereo speaker or the side of an expensive couch or chair.

Prevention is the key. Provide a scratch post or, better yet, several scratch posts. Place one near where your cat sleeps, as most cats like to stretch and scratch upon waking up. A variety of scratching posts are available commercially; make sure to get ones that are sturdy and stable and tall enough to allow the cat to stretch with his legs fully extended (usually at least two to two and a half feet high). Cats tend to prefer certain textures; sisal rope, nubby fabric with a longitudinal weave, and tree trunks with bark are some favorites. A few prefer scratching horizontal rather than vertical surfaces. Keep the post interesting by sprinkling catnip on it once or twice a month. If you have a new cat or kitten that is not used to scratch posts, encourage him to use the post by placing a favorite toy on top or by having a post-using veteran cat around for him to observe. Some animal behaviorists advise that the sound of human nails scratching the post will stimulate some cats to scratch, while others suggest moving the cat's paws up and down on the post to give him the right idea.

If your cat has already begun scratching an inappropriate object, provide an acceptable alternative and at the same time make the scratched object less attractive to the cat. Temporarily cover the unsuitable object with plastic or aluminum foil, then place the preferred object in the same area. Once the cat is using the post, it can gradually be moved to a more suitable location.

Keeping the claws trimmed will not prevent or cure inappropriate scratching behavior, but it will minimize the damage. Another option is to acquire plastic nail covers from your veterinarian; these can be glued over the clipped claws to provide even more protection. (See Claw Trimming on page 243.)

Having your cat's front claws surgically removed is strictly a last resort. This procedure—in which not only the claws but part of the toe bones are severed or removed—is morally controversial. Recovery is painful, and cats frequently suffer postoperative complications (such as bleeding, infection, and claw regrowth). While all cats are safer indoors than out, cats without front claws are less able to defend themselves than cats with a full complement of claws. Their ability to escape danger by climbing trees is also hindered.

Sleep Problems

Cats tend to be most active at dawn and at dusk, but young, active cats who lack playmates are likely to get the feline "nighttime crazies" just at the owner's bedtime or in the middle of the night. The cat may run playfully around the house and perhaps become destructive—knocking over plants, tearing up paper, and making a general nuisance of herself.

This behavior can be disturbing, but it's quite normal for a cat who has been insufficiently stimulated during the day. The solution is simply to keep the cat as active as possible during daytime hours so she is more likely to sleep at night. In single-cat households where the owners are away during the day, this may require some creativity. Here are a few suggestions:

• Feed the cat just before bedtime to take advantage of the drowsiness that naturally occurs after eating.

• Play more with the cat during the day or when you get home from work. Interactive toys like cat "fishing poles" work best.

• Set up the cat in her own "bedroom" (the bathroom or a spare bedroom, perhaps) at bedtime, with a bed, a litter box, and a few toys, where she can't bother those who want to sleep.

• Consider getting another cat to serve as a companion, although this can unleash behavior problems (pages 30 and 31).

Young cats and kittens that are not stimulated enough during the day may keep their owners awake at night.

Signs of fear-induced aggression include flattened ears, a hunched body, and growling and hissing.

Aggression Toward People

Up to a third of feline behavior problems are related to aggression. Feline aggression is a serious matter. Equipped with very sharp teeth and claws, formidable strength, and lightning speed, an aggressive cat can inflict serious injuries within seconds.

Feline aggression toward humans can stem from physical causes (for example, pain or certain types of brain disease can cause aggression); as with other problem behaviors, it is important to consult with a veterinarian to rule out medical conditions. But feline aggression is usually a strictly behavioral problem. Aggression directed toward people can be induced by several sensations or stimuli, including pain, petting, fear, and play.

Pain-Induced Aggression Humans commonly encounter pain-induced aggression when trying to help an injured cat. Cats cannot comprehend a person's good intentions and will understandably strike out to protect themselves. (You must exercise much caution when handling an injured cat; see page 318.) Similarly, cats experiencing a painful medical condition may bite or scratch an owner who is unknowingly touching a sensitive area.

A young child may provoke pain-induced aggression by playing too roughly with a cat. For the cat's sake as well as the child's, do not allow young children to play unsupervised with cats until they are old enough to control themselves and treat animals compassionately.

Do not approach a fearful, aggressive cat unless it is absolutely necessary.

Petting-Induced Aggression Many cat owners are familiar with the singularly unpleasant behavior associated with petting-induced aggression, whereby a cat that seems to be enjoying being stroked suddenly lashes out at the bewildered bestower of affection, jumps down, and runs away. Sometimes a cat will tense her muscles or swish her tail in warning just before biting or scratching, but in other cases there is no signal whatsoever. No one knows for certain why cats do this, but some behaviorists believe that the cat initially likes being stroked but then, sometimes quite suddenly, decides that enough is enough and so reacts aggressively to get away.

The best way to prevent petting-induced aggression is to observe the cat carefully to determine his particular petting threshold and never exceed it. Watch the cat's signals. A cat that is twitching his tail or ears and tensing his muscles is telling you that his tolerance is near its limit—striking out is imminent. Stroking certain parts of the cat's body is more likely to evoke this reaction. Most cats do not like to be stroked on the stomach, hips, or feet. In severe cases, avoiding petting the cat altogether may be the safest resolution.

Fear-Induced Aggression A cat exhibiting fear-induced aggression will hunch down with his body close to the ground, his ears flattened and his tail held low, and will hiss or growl when approached. If pressed on the matter, the cat will strike out with exposed claws and bared teeth. Most cats will respond fearfully if sufficiently frightened, but some cats are by nature more fearful than others. Genetics may play some role, but cats not handled by humans when young, as well as those with a history of abuse, are particularly prone to fear-induced aggression. Do not approach a fearful, aggressive cat unless it is absolutely necessary.

If you must move a fearful cat, put on a long-sleeved shirt, long pants, and gloves, scoop up the cat in a thick blanket or towel (making sure his head and all four feet are covered), and place him in a carrier or a cardboard box with air holes.

Redirected Aggression Imagine the following: A normally calm and friendly cat is seated on his favorite window sill; upon seeing a strange cat outside, he becomes visibly upset and lashes out at his owner, who is trying to calm him, or at an "innocent bystander" feline housemate. This cat is demonstrating redirected aggression by taking out his aggression on something other than the actual stimulus. To avoid injury, refrain from handling your cat when he is visibly upset; this may take from thirty minutes to several hours in extreme cases. To deal with redirected aggression most effectively, the arousing stimulus must be identified and, if possible, avoided. For example, if the arousing stimulus is the sight of another cat outside, try to block the indoor cat's view by preventing access to the window.

Play Aggression Normal cat play—running, jumping, stalking, pouncing, scratching, and biting—often looks a lot like predatory behavior. Kittens and younger cats tend to engage regularly in this type of play activity, and even adult cats will occasionally succumb to temptation. If such behavior is directed at toys, it all seems in good fun; the acrobatic antics of playing cats are entertaining to watch. All is not so pleasant if the play-aggressor turns his attentions to a family member. Cats exhibiting play aggression will chase, bite, and claw a person or another animal; sometimes they may stalk, or hide around a corner with tail twitching, waiting for just the right moment to attack a passerby. Thankfully, most play aggression is fairly mild and doesn't result in severe scratching or biting, but at the extreme, the aggressive cat can inflict serious injury.

The most effective way to deal with a play-aggressive cat is to redirect his play to an appropriate object. See Playing with Your Cat on page 248 for suggestions of suitable toys for both kittens and cats. Many owners whose cats lie in wait to attack them as they round a corner carry a Ping-Pong ball or a favorite play object in their pockets, and toss it near the cat if ambush seems imminent.

Most of the time, the cat will redirect his energies to the object and will not attack the owner.

Don't allow your cat to bite and scratch your hands in play or she'll learn to think biting and scratching people is okay.

Cat Fights

There are many causes of aggressive interactions among cats; those most commonly encountered in a household are redirected aggression, aggression between males, and territorial aggression.

Redirected Aggression This form of aggression can occur between cats as well as between cats and humans. The causes and management of such behavior are described on page 258.

Fighting between unneutered male cats is very common. Neutering usually eliminates such behavior, but some neutered males will continue to fight with others if given the opportunity.

When a new cat is introduced into the household, it is common for the resident cat(s) to try to oust the newcomer. In many cases, this is a type of territorial aggression, a natural aspect of feline behavior designed to maintain social distance. It is crucial to make the introduction of a new cat as smooth as possible; follow the advice given on page 60.

Traveling with Your Cat

Going on vacation and thinking of taking your cat along? If they could speak, most cats would emphatically decline such an invitation. Traveling is always stressful to cats, and though they will probably miss you while you're away, letting them stay home will cause them less anxiety than bringing them along. There are some cats who seem to like trips, but they are exceptions that probably became accustomed to traveling when quite young.

Introducing a new cat to a household with resident cats is bound to incite antagonistic behavior, even among long-term housemates that previously got along well.

Pet Sitters and Boarding Facilities

Kittens under four months of age should not be left alone for more than four hours at a time, much less overnight. And adolescent cats (from six months to eighteen months of age) are more likely to become destructive if they are not sufficiently stimulated. If you'll be gone for only a couple of days, most healthy adult cats do fine if left alone with an automatic feeder (see Feeding Your Cat, beginning on page 234). Be aware, however, that cats with fastidious litter box habits may begin to eliminate inappropriately when the box becomes more soiled than usual. Asking a trustworthy friend, relative, or neighbor to care for your cat while you're away is best; a once- or twice-daily checking-in is sufficient for most cats.

If you can't find a friend or relative to care for your cat, ask your veterinarian for the name of a reliable pet sitter. Check the sitter's references and discuss his or her level of expertise. Find out if the sitter is bonded and insured and a member of any trade organizations (such as the National Association of Professional Pet Sitters; see below)—all these are signs of professionalism. You can contact the National Association of Professional Pet Sitters, 1-800-296-PETS, which maintains a list of sitters throughout the country.

Inform the sitter of your cat's feeding schedule; provide litter box instructions; discuss any health concerns, including medication and dosing schedule; explain your cat's likes and dislikes; and write a list of emergency phone numbers, including your veterinarian's as well as your own. And, of course, leave a supply of food and litter, and instruct the sitter to make plenty of fresh water available at all times.

Having a reliable friend, relative, or pet sitter check in on your cats a couple of times a day while you're away is sufficient for most healthy adult cats.

When you hire a pet sitter, you should feel completely confident that he or she will follow your directions and make your cat's well-being and safety a top priority. If you do not feel sure of this, work out other options, such as boarding your cat. Recommendations from your veterinarian or a fellow cat owner may help narrow the selection of boarding facilities. Before making any arrangements, visit the boarding facility to be sure it is clean, well-lit, well-ventilated, and free of offensive odors and noises. To lessen the chance that your cat will pick up a contagious disease, check that animals of different owners are housed individually, not allowed to run freely with others. Ask if a health certificate or certain vaccines are required and whether the facility operators are willing to feed a special diet or administer medication if necessary. When dropping off your cat, leave a familiar object, such as a favorite blanket or pillow, that can be placed in the cage to provide some comfort in your absence.

Car Travel

Most cats hate car rides. For some, even a short trip strikes enough terror to cause yowling, panting, vomiting, or even diarrhea. For most, though, the occasional short trip to the veterinarian is inevitable. Try to accustom your cat to the car by taking her on frequent short rides with pleasant endings. Most cats eventually lose

their fear of the car, and some even start to enjoy the ride.

Always keep your cat confined to the carrier to keep her from getting in the way of the brake and accelerator pedal, and to prevent her from getting out of the car. Line the bottom of the carrier with a towel in case your cat vomits or has diarrhea, and label the carrier with your name, address, and telephone number. If possible, fasten the carrier with a seat belt; if you cannot do so, place the carrier on the floor of the car.

For longer trips, take along your cat's litter box, food (and a spoon and can opener if necessary) and bottled water, and food and water dishes. Allow access to these in the car at rest areas (most cats probably won't partake). Be sure the doors and windows are closed and that someone is in the car with the cat when she's out of the carrier. If your cat is already harness-trained and used to walks in strange places, short walks on a leash can be a pleasant break; just make sure that your cat wears some kind of identification in case she manages to escape (page 56). If you're traveling during the warmer months, do not allow your cat to get overheated in a parked car. It's always a good idea to travel with a feline first aid kit. Be sure it includes a current photo of your cat that could be photocopied for Lost Cat posters, just in case. (See the checklist at left for a list of other items you should bring along when traveling. See page

---

Travel Checklist

- ✓ feline first aid kit
- ✓ paper towels
- ✓ cat food and water from home
- ✓ litter box, litter, and scoop
- ✓ plastic bags for cleaning up litter box
- ✓ food and water bowls
- ✓ soap for cleaning bowls
- ✓ can opener and spoon (if food is canned)
- ✓ break-away collar
- ✓ identification tags and/or microchip (page 56)
- ✓ harness and leash (if cat is harness-trained)
- ✓ crate lined with absorbent material
- ✓ toys and familiar bedding or blankets
- ✓ your veterinarian's phone number
- ✓ health and vaccination certificates and records

Whether you're traveling by car or by plane, a cat carrier is essential.

319 for a list of things to keep in a feline first aid kit.)

Most cats travel better on an empty stomach; by not feeding for three to four hours prior to the trip, you can avoid much of the expected car sickness. Tranquilizers, some of which help prevent motion sickness, are sometimes suggested for cats that must travel. Unfortunately, the results are not always reliable, with some cats becoming either too sedated or not sedated enough. Consult with your veterinarian for more information.

Air Travel

If you have the option, carry your cat onboard and keep him under the seat in an airline-approved cat carrier. The Federal Aviation Administration requires that cats be kept in their carriers and stowed under a seat while onboard. If for some reason your cat cannot fly in the cabin with you (this can depend on how busy the flight is, or on how many other animals are in the cabin; call the airline ahead of time to confirm), he can be checked as "baggage." However, it is much safer and more comfortable for your cat in the cabin, where there is less jostling and the temperatures remain much more constant.

If your cat must travel in the baggage compartment (a pressurized compartment beneath the passenger cabin), the cat carrier you choose must comply with airline standards.

Be sure the crate has the words "live animal" written on it in letters at least one inch tall, and prominent arrows that indicate the upright position of the carrier. Your cat should wear identification on an elastic or break-away collar, and your name, address, telephone number, and destination should be clearly visible on the top of the carrier (make sure this information is written in waterproof ink). You should also note who is traveling with the cat or whether someone will pick him up at the destination point.

Line the crate with an absorbent layer, and firmly attach two bowls—one each for food and water—to the inside of the carrier (position the bowls so that airline personnel can fill them without opening the door). Close the carrier door securely but leave it unlocked so that airline personnel can open it if necessary. Finally, if your flight will last more than twelve hours, fasten a container of dry food with feeding instructions to the top of the carrier. Animals are fed during layovers.

The United States Department of Agriculture (through the Animal Welfare Act) oversees the way all animals are handled when traveling by plane out of their owner's custody. Mishaps are uncommon these days, but you should still take precautions. Fly nonstop or direct when you can (less chance for delays and lost luggage) and avoid weekends and the busy seasons. Contact the airline well in advance of the anticipated voyage to be sure your cat will be welcome. Be prepared for airline security to ask you to take your cat out of the carrier so that the carrier can be inspected. If this is required, insist that it be done in a small, enclosed space. Find out the required check-in time, which health documents you'll need, and whether your cat can travel in the passenger compartment with you.

Ask the airline about its policy on unsafe conditions for animal transport. For example, if the temperature is too hot (above 85°F or 30°C) or too cold (below 45°F or 7°C) at the point of departure or the destination, the airline may restrict the times when you and your cat can fly. Try to avoid traveling in extremely hot or cold weather conditions; late morning or early evening flights are best if you are flying through hot states.

As in travel by car, tranquilizers should be avoided. Not only are the results unreliable, but sedated cats may not be able to adequately maintain their body temperature and may become too cool while awaiting loading into the baggage compartment on cold days. Also, to help avoid travel sickness, don't feed your cat for three to four hours before a flight.

Before putting your cat on a plane, schedule an appointment with your veterinarian to make sure your cat is healthy enough for the trip and to secure any necessary health certificates. Many states require that an official health certificate

(USDA/APHIS Form 7001 entitled "United States Interstate and International Certificate of Health Examination for Small Animals") and/or a rabies vaccination be completed by an accredited veterinarian in order for a cat to enter. In most cases, the certificate must be completed within ten days of your journey, and rabies vaccination will likely be required if your cat is over twelve weeks of age. The requirements vary from state to state; your veterinarian should have a copy of the regulations in her office. Also, the United States Department of Agriculture Animal and Plant Health Inspection Service (USDA/APHIS) maintains a site on the World Wide Web (http://www.aphis.usda.gov/vs/sregs) that details health requirements governing the admission of cats for each state.

The requirements for travel abroad are usually considerably more complex; quarantine may even be necessary. You can obtain pertinent information from the Office of the State Veterinarian, Division of Animal Industry, in your state. The consulate of the country you are visiting is an additional source of information.

Lodging with Your Cat

When making lodging reservations, ask whether cats are welcome; when checking in, let the receptionist know that your cat is accompanying you. If you must leave your cat in the room while you're out, keep her in the bathroom with the door shut, provide a litter box and plenty of food and water, and put a "do not disturb" sign on your door. If you must be out while your room is being cleaned, place your cat safely back in her carrier.

Moving with Your Cat

If you and your cat are moving to a new home, there are a number of things you can do to make the move safer and less stressful for everyone. On moving day, confine your cat to her carrier in the bathroom and put a "do not disturb" sign on the door. Place the cat in the car at the last possible moment. Then, before unloading in the new place, bring your cat into an isolation room (such as a second bathroom) and leave her in the carrier until the movers are gone and the litter box and food and water dishes are set up. At that point, allow the cat out of the carrier and leave her alone. Check back in thirty to sixty minutes to see how she's doing. If she seems anxious, keep her in the isolation room until she seems relaxed enough to explore her new home at her own pace.

Keeping Your Cat Healthy

The old saying aside, cats only have one life, and they are afflicted by injury and disease just like all other living beings. One of the best ways to safeguard feline health is to know what is normal for your cat, and to be on the lookout for physical and behavioral changes at all times. You can do this by incorporating a mini–physical exam into your grooming routine; by keeping track of how much your cat eats and drinks and how often she visits the litter box; and by noticing if her demeanor changes. Taking these simple steps will enable you to catch most illnesses in their early stages, when they may be most curable.

In addition, schedule regular veterinary checkups. Your veterinarian will tell you how often your cat needs to come in for well-pet visits, which will include vaccinations, based upon your cat's age and state of health. Of course your vet will also see your cat when any medical problems arise. The more observant you are and the better your communication with your veterinarian, the healthier your pet is likely to be.

Cats may seem independent, but they rely on humans to keep them healthy.

The Mini-Physical Exam

It's a good idea to give your cat a mini–physical examination as part of the weekly grooming session. Make the home checkup an extension of the normal physical attention you pay your cat and he will not even know that he is being "examined." It doesn't matter where you perform the exam, as long as both you and your cat are comfortable. If your cat usually isn't allowed on the kitchen table or counter, don't examine him there, as it may be confusing and stressful.

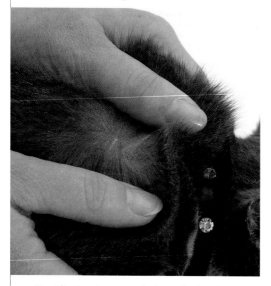

Check for fleas by parting the fur and looking for the small wingless insects or by using a flea comb to detect flea dirt. (See also Skin Problems on page 290.)

Skin and Coat

Weekly grooming provides a good opportunity for evaluating the health of the skin and hair. Pass your hands over your cat's body, feeling for swelling, asymmetry, or sensitive areas. Call the veterinarian if you discover patches of hair loss, the black flecks that signal the presence of fleas (see page 292 for more about fleas), scabby areas, or skin bumps.

With your cat facing away from you, gently lift the tail and take a quick peek at his rear end. If you see tan-colored, rice-size objects, you are probably looking at packets of tapeworm eggs (page 299), which require veterinary treatment. Next, use a moist paper towel to clean away any feces. In longhaired cats in particular, feces can get caught in the fur and, if trapped against the skin, can cause serious problems. If the hair has become matted, you will need to use blunt-tipped scissors. Be very careful cutting out mats or, better yet, take your cat to a veterinarian or professional groomer, who can use clippers to remove the mats.

Eyes

Face your cat head-on and examine the eyes. They should be bright, and the pupils should be of equal size. There should be little if any tearing at the corners of the

The tissue lining a cat's eyelids should be pink and there should be no discharge. (See also Eye Problems on page 286.)

eyes, and the nictitating membrane (page 204) should not protrude. Gently roll down the lower eyelid with your thumb; the tissue lining the lid should be pink, not white or red. Be sure your cat is not squinting with either eye.

Ears

With your cat facing you, gently pull up on the ear flap and look at the inner surface and down into the ear canal. The ears should be clean and light pink in color. Any discharge, redness, swelling, or odor is abnormal. Do not attempt to clean your cat's ears; probing into the ear canal can aggravate an ear condition or even cause trauma or infection.

Discharge of any sort in a cat's ear is abnormal. (See also Ear Problems on page 288.)

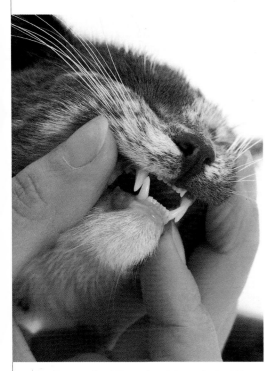

A cat's gums should be pink and the teeth should be clean and free of tartar. (See also Mouth Problems on page 295.)

Mouth and Nose

With your cat facing you, push back the lips to examine the gums and teeth. The gums should be pink, not white or red, and should show no signs of swelling. The teeth should be clean, without any brownish tartar. Sniff your cat's breath; while a cat's breath is never pleasant, a strong, fetid odor is abnormal and may indicate a problem. Excessive drooling can also be a sign of oral disease. Unless it is normally colored or marked with color, the nose should be pink, and there should be no nasal discharge.

Subtle Signs of Illness

Cats are notorious for their ability to appear healthy when they are actually sick. How can owners detect illness early? Get in the habit of giving your cat a weekly mini–physical examination, and always be on the lookout for the following, often subtle, signs of illness.

Lethargy or excessive sleepiness

This common sign of sickness is sometimes difficult for owners to recognize, as healthy adult cats may sleep up to 16 or 18 hours a day. Get to know how much sleep is normal for your cat.

Change in appetite or water consumption

Keep track of how much your cat normally eats and drinks so that any variation can be detected easily and early.

Change in grooming behavior

An ill-kempt, oily coat can indicate illness. Conversely, cats that groom too often may have a nervous or itchy skin condition.

Weight loss

This sign often goes unnoticed, especially in long-haired cats. Owners who regularly groom their cats may notice the ribs and backbone becoming more prominent. Those who regularly weigh their cats are sure to see a change. A sudden loss of one pound in a cat that normally weighs ten pounds is cause for concern.

Change in litter box habits

Cats that start visiting the litter box more frequently, or that repeatedly urinate or defecate outside the box, may be suffering from a disease of the lower urinary tract or large intestine. Cats that strain to urinate may have a urethral obstruction; such cats are in grave danger and need immediate veterinary attention.

Change in behavior

House soiling and aggression are both behavioral problems that can sometimes be prompted by a physical illness.

The Cornish Rex is a naturally svelte cat. By knowing what is normal for your cat you will be better able to detect even a subtle loss of weight.

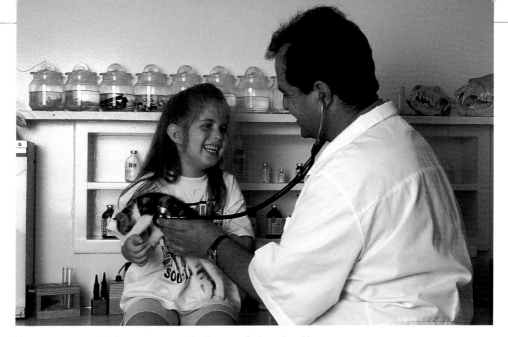

It's very important to find a veterinarian with whom you feel comfortable.

You and Your Veterinarian

Your veterinarian will be your ally throughout the life of your cat, someone you'll depend on to help maintain your cat's health from kittenhood through old age. As your cat matures, your veterinarian can serve as both knowledgeable advisor and compassionate friend, helping you to understand how your cat is aging and eventually to come to terms with his death. The following pages provide advice on finding and choosing the right veterinarian for you and your cat and on establishing a good working relationship with that veterinarian. Also included is a brief overview of what to expect from a routine veterinary examination.

Finding a Veterinarian

Finding and choosing the right veterinarian for your cat is extremely important. But how do you go about it? Cat-owning friends are a good source, and the shelter or person from whom you adopted or purchased your cat may also be able to recommend someone. If you are moving, you can narrow the search by seeking the advice of your present veterinarian. You can also contact the American Association of Feline Practitioners (AAFP) and ask for a referral (tel.: 800-204-3514 or 505-888-2424; Web site address: http://www.avma.org/aafp). While there are plenty of highly capable vets who are not members of the AAFP, you can be assured that member veterinarians take particular interest in cats. Some even have cat-only practices designed to cater specifically to the needs of felines, and their offices will not have barking dogs, which can be stressful to cats. Within the last several years, the American Board of Veterinary Practitioners has begun recognizing feline specialists. There are just a few board-certified feline specialists at this time, but the numbers are growing.

In your search for a veterinarian, you may come across different types of practices. Some owners prefer solo practitioners to a group practice because they like the consistency of care and the familiarity that the vet develops with each pet's case. Veterinarians in a group practice regularly consult with one another about their patients and are also able to cover for each other during vacations and other times.

Referral hospitals are staffed by board-certified veterinarians with extra training in specific specialties, such as internal medicine, dermatology, or surgery. Referral hospitals typically treat patients referred to them by general practitioners.

Pet health insurance is a fairly recent development. Some policies require owners to use only participating veterinarians; others allow owners to use their veterinarian of choice. When shopping around for pet insurance, check references, read policies carefully, and ask your veterinarian to review any policies you are seriously considering. Make sure you understand the range of services covered. Some, for example, do not cover well-pet visits.

A veterinarian should be as gentle as possible, even with her more fractious patients.

Evaluating a Veterinarian

Once you have narrowed down your choices in veterinarians, arrange to visit the facilities that interest you. Schedule such visits during relatively quiet times, and keep the following factors in mind.

A veterinary clinic should be neat, clean, and well equipped and should not have any unpleasant odors. The condition of the office and examining rooms will give you a good indication of the conscientiousness of the doctors and staff.

Good communication is important. The doctors and staff should encourage you to ask questions, and they should answer them in an understandable way, without using excessive medical jargon. Lack of communication is the most common problem in the veterinarian–owner relationship.

Doctors and staff should always treat the pets in their care as gently as possible. Some cats, being the independent creatures they are, may resist a veterinarian's attempts to help them and require firm restraint. However, a vet should never be overly rough or aggressive.

Find out whether there are veterinary specialists or referral centers in the area and if your veterinarian utilizes them. It is impossible to be proficient and up-to-date in all areas of veterinary medicine; a good veterinarian should not be reluctant to seek the advice of other veterinarians or to refer difficult cases to a specialty center if necessary.

When an emergency happens, every second counts. Find out how after-hours emergencies are handled. Some hospitals prefer to attend to their own emergencies, while others may refer them to a special emergency facility in the area.

Don't be afraid to talk about rates, fees, and accepted methods of payment. The veterinarian should be willing to provide running estimates on all services provided.

Working with Your Veterinarian

Keeping your cat healthy is much easier if you and your veterinarian have a cooperative relationship. Following are some ways that you can help your veterinarian to give your cat the best care possible.

If you have adopted a new cat or kitten, schedule an appointment for a physical examination within twenty-four hours after purchase or adoption. Give the veterinarian as much information as possible about the new cat, including date of birth and medical record.

A kitten needs his first visit to the vet at about six to eight weeks of age. At this time he should be given a complete physical and initial vaccinations (see the vaccination chart on page 279). Bring along a fresh stool sample so that your vet can check for internal parasites.

If your cat is sick, use the checklist at right to keep track of all the problems so you won't forget them when you are speaking with the doctor. If the cat has diarrhea or is vomiting, the doctor will want to know whether it happens at certain times of day,

Checklist for Veterinary Visits

Present Medical Problem(s)

If you think your cat might be sick, make a list of the following information so that you can provide your vet with a full account of the cat's condition.

✓ date of onset
✓ changes in behavior, appetite, water intake, activity level, or litter box habits
✓ medication(s) the cat was taking before illness began
✓ medication(s) the cat is now taking
✓ current diet, including any changes

Past Medical Problems

If you are seeing a new veterinarian, either obtain your cat's records from previous care providers or make a list of the following information for all of your cat's past health problems.

✓ date
✓ tests administered
✓ diagnosis
✓ treatment

Also include the cat's complete vaccination history and the type and date of any surgery the cat has had.

Remember to ask the vet the following questions: What is wrong with my cat? What tests are needed for diagnosis? How will the condition be treated? Are there alternative treatments? Will hospitalization be necessary? What will the cost be? What is the expected outcome? Do you have any literature on this subject?

New cats should be taken to the veterinarian within twenty-four hours of purchase or adoption.

and what the cat's normal diet consists of. If your cat is urinating outside the box, the veterinarian may ask where specifically the cat is taking her business. Be prepared to discuss how long the problem has been going on and how often it occurs. It's best if the cat's primary caregiver takes her to the veterinarian, especially if she's sick. Otherwise, be sure that whoever brings the cat in has a complete history of the cat's problem and can make prompt decisions about the cat's medical care.

Bring your cat to the veterinarian's office in a carrier (page 54), and unless you are instructed to do otherwise, keep him there until you are in the examination room. Your cat will remain much calmer and so will be easier for your veterinarian to examine.

Bring a paper and pen with you and write down (or have the veterinarian write down) all important information and instructions. If you must administer medication or other treatments at home, make sure you understand how to do so. Ask the veterinarian or a staff member to show you, then have them observe while you perform the procedure to make sure you are doing it correctly.

Follow the doctor's instructions carefully, and faithfully return for any recommended follow-up visits. If you don't understand something, ask questions. Veterinarians like to know that pet owners are interested and concerned. If you are uncomfortable speaking with your veterinarian, it may be a good idea to try to find another with whom you can communicate better.

The Veterinary Examination

Your cat should be given a complete physical examination whenever he goes in for a well-cat visit. Through annual or semi-annual exams, many problems can be detected before they start to cause obvious disease. Some veterinarians prefer taking a complete medical history before even touching the cat, while others prefer to ask questions during the examination. Each veterinarian has his own order for performing an examination—some start by taking the temperature, others by evaluating the coat—but the typical complete physical exam should include at least the components listed below.

Observation Veterinarians make an initial "hands off" observation of the cat's demeanor, posture, gait, and general physical condition.

Weights and Measures A physical exam includes a recording of body temperature, weight (using a scale sensitive enough to register small gains or losses), pulse rate, respiratory rate, and state of hydration.

Skin and Coat Veterinarians examine the skin and coat on all parts of the body; this includes a thorough evaluation of the mammary area. They check for parasites as well as for changes in the skin and coat that might warn of illness.

Head and Neck The vet palpates (examines by touch) the neck and throat to evaluate symmetry and to check the salivary glands, lymph nodes, and thyroid gland for nodules or swelling.

Face Veterinarians make an evaluation of facial symmetry by sight and by touch.

Eyes Examination of the eyes includes checking pupil size, response to light, clarity, color, and condition of tissues; checking the eyelids for swelling, squinting, and discoloration; and looking for masses. An ophthalmoscope is used to view the inside of the eye.

Weight loss in cats can easily go unnoticed, so it's important to have your cat weighed regularly on a sensitive scale—preferably the same one each time.

Nose The nose is examined for swelling, discharge, and color.

Ears The ears are examined for discharge, odors, masses, color, and pain. The ear canal is examined with an otoscope; if a thorough ear examination is necessary, the cat may have to be sedated.

Mouth Examining the lips and mouth for tooth and gum health includes an open-mouth check for foreign bodies, growths, disease, or gum discoloration.

Limbs The paws and limbs are examined for symmetry, muscle tone, and joint flexibility, and painful areas or swelling. The lymph nodes are palpated for enlargement.

Chest Examination of the chest includes palpation for symmetry, a chest auscultation (listening with a stethoscope) to evaluate heart and lung sounds, and sometimes a chest percussion (sharp taps on the chest to detect areas of increased or decreased resonance).

Abdomen Palpation of all parts of the cat's abdomen enables the vet to evaluate internal organs.

Rear End Examination of the pelvis, back, and tail includes palpation for symmetry, swelling, pain, and flexibility. The rectal and external genital area is also inspected.

Vaccination

Vaccines are indispensable weapons in the battle against infectious disease for animals as well as humans. Vaccines contain antigens that "look" like the disease-causing organism to the immune system but that don't cause disease. When a vaccine is given to a healthy animal, the immune system mounts a protective response to fight the disease. If the cat is then exposed to the disease-causing virus or bacteria, the immune system is prepared and either prevents infection or reduces the severity of the disease.

Vaccinations for Kittens

Colostrum, the first milk a mother cat produces, contains antibodies that help protect kittens from infectious disease

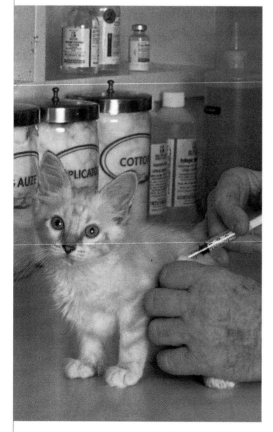

Most kittens should receive their first series of vaccinations when they are six to eight weeks old.

until their own immune systems are more mature. These antibodies also interfere with a vaccine's ability to stimulate the kitten's immune system. Therefore, veterinarians administer vaccines every three or four weeks beginning when the kitten is around six to eight weeks of age (see the vaccination chart on page 279). Vaccinations continue until maternal antibodies have waned, usually when the kitten is a little over twelve weeks old. In some cases, as with the rabies vaccine, the initial vaccine is not given until kittens are twelve weeks old.

Vaccinations for Adult Cats

Adult cats need boosters of vaccines to maintain sufficient protection from disease. Some feline rabies vaccines provide protection for three years. Recent research suggests that panleukopenia/rhinotracheitis/calicivirus vaccines provide adequate protection for several years, so many veterinarians are now recommending that this vaccine be boosted at three-year intervals. Because far less is known about the duration of protection provided by other vaccines, annual vaccination with those products is a reasonable course of action if your cat is at risk of exposure. If you have questions about other vaccines, or how often they need to be administered, be sure to ask your veterinarian for details. Your veterinarian will probably send you reminders, but it is a good idea to mark your calendar ahead of time to remind you when the boosters are due.

Safety Factors

Your veterinarian will help you decide which vaccines are appropriate for your cat. The choice depends on a number of factors, including:

- your cat's risk of exposure to the disease-causing organism (depends in part on the health of other cats to which yours is exposed and the environment in which your cat lives)
- the consequence of infection
- the risk an infected cat poses to human health
- the protective ability of the vaccine
- the frequency or severity of reactions the vaccine may produce
- the age and health of your cat
- reactions to vaccines that your cat may have experienced in the past.

Your veterinarian will help you determine which booster vaccinations your adult cat should receive.

Serious reactions to vaccinations are quite rare; it's much safer to vaccinate most kittens and cats than it is to leave them unprotected.

Generally speaking, vaccines are very safe. In most cases, the risk of vaccination is much smaller than the risk of the cat contracting disease if vaccines are not given. But to minimize the risk, before your cat is vaccinated, inform your veterinarian of any health problems she is experiencing, any medication she is receiving, and any reaction she has experienced in the past.

Following is a brief list of reactions that may occur after vaccination. If you think your cat is experiencing a problem associated with her vaccines, call your veterinarian right away.

Mild Reactions The following reactions are fairly common. They may appear within hours to several days after vaccination and should last no more than several days:

- discomfort at the site where the vaccine was given
- mild fever
- diminished appetite and activity
- sneezing (about four to seven days after administration of an intranasal vaccine)
- development of a small, firm, non-painful swelling under the skin at the site where the vaccine was given. The swelling usually goes away after several weeks, but if you notice such a swelling, contact your veterinarian.

Serious Reactions These reactions occur very rarely:

- a serious and potentially life-threatening allergic reaction within several minutes to an hour after vaccination, manifested as hives, severe vomiting and diarrhea, and/or collapse and death
- a kind of tumor, called a sarcoma, developing at the vaccine site several weeks, months, or even longer after vaccination. (Vaccination-induced sarcomas are discussed further on page 286.)

Vaccination Chart

Core vaccines are highly recommended for all cats. Noncore vaccines are required only by some cats, depending in part on the cat's risk of exposure. Your veterinarian will help you decide which of the non-core vaccines your cat should receive.

Core Vaccines	Kitten Series	Boosters
Feline panleukopenia virus (FPV) Feline herpesvirus 1 (FHV-1) Feline calcivirus (FCV)	Usually combined into one vaccine—the "three-way" vaccine. First vaccine at 6 to 8 weeks of age, then repeated every 3 to 4 weeks until over 12 weeks of age*	1 year later, then every 1 to 3 years
Rabies virus (RV)	First vaccine at 12 weeks of age or over	1 year later, then every 3 years (if local law permits and a 3-year–approved vaccine is used)

Noncore Vaccines	Kitten Series	Boosters
Feline leukemia virus (FeLV)	2 doses 3 to 4 weeks apart; first dose given when kitten is over 8 weeks of age, second when over 12 weeks of age	1 year later, then annually
Feline infectious peritonitis virus (FIPV)	2 doses 3 to 4 weeks apart beginning when kitten is over 16 weeks of age	1 year later, then annually
Chlamydia	If a live vaccine: 1 dose between 6 and 12 weeks of age. If a killed vaccine: 2 doses at 3- to 4-week intervals between 6 and 12 weeks of age	1 year later, then annually

*For kittens at high risk of exposure (such as kittens in some catteries and shelter kittens), a special three-way vaccine given as nose and eye drops beginning as early as 2 to 3 weeks of age may be necessary. Vaccines given by injection may commence 3 to 4 weeks later.

Common Feline Health Problems

The following pages present basic information on a wide selection of common feline health problems. A few uncommon conditions, such as toxoplasmosis, are included because they are important for cat owners to know about. Also, although rabies is uncommon, it is covered here because it is a significant public health concern. (For more extensive coverage of feline diseases, consult the Recommended Reading appendix.)

Most of the conditions are grouped according to the anatomical system that they tend to affect most directly; for example, conjunctivitis, inflammation of the tissue lining the eyelid, is discussed under Eye Problems, even though sneezing and a runny nose may accompany conjunctivitis. Diseases that tend to affect a wide variety of body systems and display a wide range of signs are covered separately, in the categories Viral Diseases and Cancer.

Cats are complex creatures and, like all mammals, can be afflicted with a number of diseases.

Viral Diseases

Viruses cause disease in many different ways: by damaging or killing cells in organs, by changing normal cells into cancerous ones, or by stimulating a severe immune response that harms the cat. The signs of viral disease vary tremendously. Covered here are some of the most significant feline viral diseases.

Feline leukemia virus (FeLV) is the leading viral killer of cats. The virus is spread from cat to cat in saliva, through bite wounds, by prolonged casual contact (mutual grooming and sharing of food and water dishes and litter boxes), and from infected mothers to their kittens. Most at risk of infection are cats that spend time outdoors and have contact with other cats that may already be infected. Young cats are especially vulnerable to infection.

Feline leukemia virus can adversely affect the cat in many ways. It is by far the leading cause of cancer in cats (see *lymphosarcoma* on page 285); it can cause severe anemia; and it incapacitates the immune system, making the cat susceptible to a variety of secondary infections. Although statistics vary, the long-term outlook is grim: less than 20 percent of infected cats survive for more than three years.

FeLV vaccination is recommended for all cats at risk of exposure to the virus (see the vaccination chart on page 279). Sadly, the vaccine does not protect all cats; the best way to avoid infection is to prevent exposure to infected cats. Chemotherapy (if the infected cat develops cancer) and other treatments may extend an infected cat's life, but there is still no cure. Blood tests are available to determine if a cat is infected with the virus. Infected cats may appear to be healthy, so always have any new cats tested before bringing them home.

Feline immunodeficiency virus (FIV) is related to the human immunodeficiency virus (HIV) and causes a similar type of disease. It is not, however, the same virus: HIV is not contagious to cats, nor is FIV contagious to people. FIV is transmitted mainly through bite wounds.

The gravest danger posed by FIV is suppression of the immune system. It may take years for an infected cat to show any sign of illness, but as the immune system becomes more and more compromised, the cat begins to develop infections. These secondary infections are the major cause of sickness and death in cats infected with FIV.

There are no vaccines to protect cats from FIV infection, nor is there a cure. Treatment for secondary infections may be successful initially, but as the immune system deteriorates, animals ultimately succumb to these other diseases. Prevention is best. Keep your cats indoors and away from FIV-infected cats with which they may fight.

Feline infectious peritonitis (FIP) is a routinely fatal disease that sometimes develops as a result of infection with a coronavirus, an extremely contagious virus shed in saliva and feces. FIP usually affects many different organ systems, so the symptoms are extremely variable. Common signs are intermittent loss of appetite, lethargy, a rough unkempt coat, weight loss, and fever. Generally speaking, there are two forms of the disease: the wet form and the dry form. Cats with wet FIP develop a thick yellow fluid in the chest and/or abdomen. Those with the dry form of FIP may experience organ failure, seizures, paralysis, and a host of other maladies.

FIP is relatively uncommon in the general cat population, affecting less than 1 percent of cats presented to veterinarians for treatment. However, in multiple-cat environments—such as breeding catteries or shelters—the disease rate can be much higher. Cats less than two years of age, cats in overcrowded environments, and cats infected with feline leukemia virus are most likely to contract FIP.

There is a vaccine to protect cats from FIP (see the vaccination chart on page 279), but there is no effective treatment for cats once they have developed the disease.

Feline calicivirus and feline herpesvirus type 1 (also called feline rhinotracheitis virus) are responsible for 80 to 90 percent of infectious feline upper respiratory diseases. Most cats are exposed to either or both of these viruses at some time in their lives. Once infected, many cats never completely rid themselves of the virus; they become "carrier" cats that may not show any clinical signs of the disease but continue to infect other cats indefinitely. Carriers of herpesvirus will often "shed" the virus and exhibit mild cold symptoms (sneezing, runny nose, and sometimes also conjunctivitis) after a physically or psychologically stressful experience. In such cases, no treatment is necessary, and the signs go away after a few days.

All cats are susceptible to infection, but as with most other infectious diseases, youngsters tend to get the sickest. Sneezing, runny eyes and nose, fever, and loss of appetite are typical symptoms. Rarely, an infected cat will come down with pneumonia, and some cats develop ulcers in the mouth or nose or even on the eye.

Most cats weather the infection if given proper supportive care (fluids, forced feeding, and antibiotics), but in some cases the runny nose may persist for years after the initial infection.

Vaccinations minimize the severity of upper respiratory infections, although none will prevent disease in all situations.

Cats with FIP commonly experience weight loss, lethargy, and fever.

Viral upper respiratory infections are still a major health risk to any cat, especially those residing in multicat environments. Vaccination is highly recommended for all cats (see the vaccination chart on page 279).

Feline panleukopenia, also called feline distemper or feline infectious enteritis, is a highly contagious and deadly viral disease. Although uncommon, panleukopenia outbreaks still occur, especially where groups of cats and kittens are housed together. The disease is spread by direct contact with infected saliva, urine, vomit, or feces, or indirectly through contact with contaminated objects.

The virus causes two distinct forms of illness, depending on the age of the cat when infected. *Classic panleukopenia* affects the white blood cells and the intestinal tract, causing severe vomiting and diarrhea, fever, and extreme dehydration. The death rate among kittens is quite high, while adult cats may not show any signs of illness at all. Treatment consists of fluid therapy, antibiotics, and supportive nursing care. *Cerebellar hypoplasia* afflicts kittens born to mother cats infected while pregnant, or kittens infected very early in life. In these kittens, the virus destroys some of the cells responsible for forming the cerebellum, the part of the brain responsible for coordination. Although such kittens remain uncoordinated throughout their lives, those that are not too severely affected can make fine pets. Vaccination is highly recommended for all cats (see the vaccination chart on page 279).

Rabies (Latin for "to do violence"), a deadly viral disease that affects the brain and spinal cord, is a major public health concern; a rabid animal can easily pass the infection to any other warm-blooded animal, including humans. Worldwide, close to 30,000 cases of rabies in animals are reported each year, but the true number is probably much higher. And the threat of feline rabies is increasing; currently in the United States, rabies is reported in cats far more than in all other domestic animals.

The rabies virus is present in the saliva of infected animals and is usually transmitted through bite wounds. Rabies can also be transmitted if the infected saliva contacts a fresh, preexisting wound or mucus membrane, such as the lining of the mouth or nose, though transmission this way is rare.

Once signs of the disease are apparent—the most common in felines being behavior changes (such as aggression or lethargy), a blank stare, increased vocalization, appetite loss, seizures, and/or weakness in the rear legs—most cats die within four to seven days. If you think your cat may have been bitten by a rabid animal, see your veterinarian right away. If you have not had your cat vaccinated for rabies, or if you do not have the proper documentation to prove it, your cat may be quarantined for up to six months, or he may be euthanized immediately. There is no accurate test to diagnose rabies in living animals and no treatment or cure once your cat has been infected with the rabies virus.

If you are bitten by an animal that you suspect may be rabid, see a doctor immediately. You may need to get a series of injections that will save your life. There is no treatment or cure once symptoms appear. If you see an animal that is acting strangely—a wild animal may act tame, a previously friendly animal may act fearful, and a nocturnal animal may be out and about in the daytime—stay away from it and report it to animal-control officers as soon as possible.

Because of the routinely fatal outcome of infection in cats and the terrible potential for human exposure, rabies vaccination is highly recommended for all cats and is required by law in many parts of North America. Nevertheless, it is estimated that less than 4 percent of pet cats in the United States are currently vaccinated against rabies.

Cancer

Cancer, the uncontrolled growth of cells, may be confined to a single area or may spread throughout the body. As a cat ages, her chances of developing cancer increase. Signs of cancer vary according to the organ affected, but evidence of a lump or swelling, persistent sores, abnormal discharge from any body opening, foul breath, lack of energy, or weight loss should prompt you to have your cat examined by a veterinarian. Diagnosis usually involves a biopsy, in which a small piece of tissue is removed for examination under a microscope. (Insist that any lump or nonhealing wound be biopsied no matter how small or insignificant.)

Unfortunately, because the cause of most cancers is unknown, prevention is difficult. An exception is mammary cancer. Spaying your cat before her first heat will greatly reduce her chance of developing this type of cancer. Many cancers are treatable, however. Treatment depends on the type of cancer but may include surgery, chemotherapy, radiation, or cryosurgery (freezing) or hyperthermia (heating) of the cancerous cells. Your cat will have a much better chance of survival if the cancer is detected and treated early.

Lymphosarcoma, the most common form of cancer in cats, is caused by the feline leukemia virus (page 282). The disease is often characterized by enlarged lymph nodes, the location of which determines the signs of illness. Enlarged lymph nodes in the chest frequently cause difficulty breathing, while enlargement of abdominal lymph nodes may cause intestinal obstruction or weight loss. Cats with lymphosarcoma are usually anemic and lethargic, and typically they lose their appetite. Lymphosarcoma may be treated, though never completely cured, by chemotherapy. To prevent the development of lymphosarcoma, prevent your cat's exposure to the feline leukemia virus.

Squamous cell carcinoma is a skin cancer caused by repeated sunburning of facial areas unprotected by pigment and hair. Cats with white ears are particulary prone to this disease. Before the cancer develops, the edges of the ear just look red, but as the disease progresses over several years, the edges of the ear lose hair, become scaly,

Cats with white ears are particularly susceptible to developing skin cancer on their ears.

and curl. Once tumors develop, the outsides of the ear become ulcerated, scabby, and often bloody; surgical removal of the ear flaps is the only course of action. Sunblock lotions applied to the ears every three to four hours can provide some protection, but keeping your cat indoors and out of direct sunlight is the best way to prevent this disease.

Vaccination-induced sarcomas are very rare tumors that can develop over the course of several months or longer at the site where a cat has received a vaccination. Their exact cause is unknown. For most cats, the benefits of vaccination far outweigh the risks of developing these rare tumors (see the vaccination chart on page 279). When your cat is vaccinated, ask your veterinarian to show you exactly where the vaccines have been injected, and have your cat examined if you notice any swellings at these sites. Surgery is the treatment of choice for these tumors.

Cancer of the mouth occasionally afflicts cats. Warning signs include foul mouth odor, bleeding from the mouth, difficulty eating, and a mass on the gums or elsewhere in the mouth. Treatment usually involves surgery.

Eye Problems

Signs of feline eye disease include squinting, pawing or rubbing of the eye, redness of the tissue lining the eyelid, excessive

The Persian's shortened face can cause tears to drain over the edges of the lower eyelid and irritate the skin below, as in these kittens. See Excessive Tearing and Tear Overflow on page 287.

tearing, unequal pupil sizes, a visible third eyelid (a white membrane that fans out from the inner corner of the eye), cloudiness or color changes in the eye, and, of course, blindness. If you need to administer eye drops or ointment to your cat, see page 314.

Conjunctivitis, inflammation of the conjunctiva, the tissue lining the eyelid and covering part of the surface of the eyeball, is common in cats. It is usually caused by a viral or bacterial infection spread either by direct contact with an infected cat, through the air over short distances, or by contact with contaminated surfaces. The conjunctiva may also become aggravated in dusty conditions, and some veterinarians believe conjunctivitis can be caused by allergies.

Cats with conjunctivitis usually have excessive discharge at the inner corner of the eye. The discharge may be watery initially, but as the condition advances, it often becomes thick and cloudy and may flow over the edges of the eyelids. The conjunctiva is red instead of a healthy light pink, and may be swollen. Conjunctivitis is uncomfortable, and most afflicted cats will squint. The third eyelid sometimes moves up and covers the inner and lower part of the eye. Sneezing and a runny nose often accompany the kind of conjunctivitis caused by infection. Feline herpesvirus type 1 is the leading infectious cause of conjunctivitis. Chlamydia is a bacterial cause of conjunctivitis. Some bacterial causes of conjunctivitis may be contagious to humans, so always wash your hands after handling a cat with the infection.

Vaccines against feline herpesvirus and chlamydia will not protect cats from infection, but vaccinated cats get less sick if they do become infected. Infected cats are treated with antibacterial and/or antiviral medication administered orally or as eye drops or ointment.

Excessive Tearing and Tear Overflow

Excessive tearing can result from inflammation of the eye and its surrounding structures; there is a multitude of causes, including irritation, injury, or infection. However, what sometimes appears to be excessive tearing is not really overproduction of tears, but tear overflow. In cats with very short muzzles, such as Persians, Exotic Shorthairs, and Himalayans, tears may not exit the eye as they should but rather drain over the edges of the lid, usually near the inner corner of the eye, and continually moisten the areas of the face below. The fur on the wet areas becomes discolored, and the underlying skin can become irritated from the constant moisture. It may be impossible to correct the overflowing tear condition, but keeping the wet area as clean and dry as possible can prevent skin irritation.

Exotic Shorthairs are susceptible to tear overflow. This one has healthy eyes.

Cherry Eye

Cherry eye is a condition in which the gland at the base of the third eyelid protrudes and sometimes becomes quite irritated. This is not a particularly common disorder in most cats but occurs with some frequency in Burmese and Persians. Cherry eye is probably associated with the inherited short facial conformation of these breeds and must be corrected surgically.

Burmese are more prone to developing cherry eye than most other breeds. The one shown here has healthy eyes.

Keratitis, inflammation of the cornea (the transparent front surface of the eyeball), has many causes but is most often a consequence of feline herpesvirus type 1 infection and frequently occurs along with conjunctivitis (described immediately above). Squinting, tearing, and cloudiness of the cornea are typical signs. Particularly severe inflammation can result in a corneal ulcer, which, if deep enough, can actually perforate the cornea. In some purebred cats, most notably Persians, Exotic Shorthairs, Himalayans, and Bengals, keratitis can be caused by an abnormality called *entropion,* an inward rolling of the eyelid, usually the lower one; the hair on the lid rubs against the cornea, creating irritation. Entropion must be corrected surgically.

Retinal diseases (the retina is the light-sensitive layer of cells in the back of the eye) are fairly common in cats, and may result from infections, inherited disorders, physical trauma, nutritional inadequacies, or hypertension or other diseases. Retinal disease may not be apparent to an owner, but the consequences can range from minor vision impairment to blindness.

One of the most common manifestations of retinal disease is *retinal detachment,* a condition in which the retina either partially or completely loses its attachment to the back of the eye. High blood pressure is a major cause of retinal detachment in cats. Treatment of retinal detachment due to hypertension relies on controlling the high blood pressure; even if the hypertension can be managed successfully, vision often cannot be restored.

Ear Problems

A healthy feline ear flap (pinna) has a fine layer of hair on its outer surface, with no bald spots, and its inner surface is clean and pink (except in cats with pigmented skin inside the ear flaps). Any discharge, redness, swelling, or odor is abnormal, as is a great deal of ear-scratching or head-shaking. Unless otherwise directed by your veterinarian, do not attempt to clean your cat's ears on your own; probing the ear canal can aggravate an ear condition or even cause trauma or infection. Disease deep within the ear may cause your cat to become uncoordinated, to tilt the head, and to walk in circles. If your cat exhibits any of these signs, schedule an appointment with your veterinarian as soon as possible.

Ear mites (Otodectes cynotis) are the most common cause of external ear canal inflammation in cats; kittens in particular seem to be prone to infestation. Cats with ear mites have itchy ears (and sometimes an itchy rash on other parts of their bodies), and as a result frequently shake their heads and scratch their ears. A glance down into the ear canal usually reveals a blackish-brown material; microscopic examination of the ear debris reveals the mites or their eggs. Treatment involves cleaning out the debris (your veterinarian should do this or should show you exactly how to clean the ears at home), administering a miticide in the ears (see Ear Drops or Ointment on page 314), and applying a topical insecticide to kill mites on the skin and hair.

Otitis externa, inflammation of the external ear canal, is most commonly caused by ear mites and clears up when infestation is eradicated. Other infectious agents (bacteria and fungus) and foreign bodies (usually plant material) can also cause this condition. Cats with otitis externa tend to shake their heads and scratch their ears, and discharge is frequently visible in the ear canal. Treatment depends on the cause but usually includes a thorough cleansing by a veterinarian and administration of medicine into the ear several times a day by the owner (see Ear Drops or Ointment on page 314).

Otitis media, inflammation of the middle ear, and *otitis interna,* inflammation of the inner ear, are both fairly uncommon in cats; they usually result from an

Cats that shake their heads and scratch their ears excessively may have ear mites.

Veterinarians and owners can part a cat's hair to evaluate the health of the skin, though diagnostic tests are usually required to confirm the cause of an abnormal condition.

extension of disease occurring in the external ear canal.

Aural hematomas, accumulations of blood between the cartilage and skin that appear as soft swellings in the ear flaps, may result from the scratching and head shaking associated with ear mites and otitis externa (both described on page 289). In the most serious cases, surgical draining is recommended in addition to treating the underlying cause.

Deafness may be congenital (many white cats with blue eyes are born deaf) or may occur as a side effect of certain drugs—aminoglycoside antibiotics (given to treat serious infections) and diuretics (administered to remove excessive fluid buildup, which most commonly occurs with heart failure), for example. Deafness may also occur as a consequence of aging.

Skin Problems

There are just a few ways that feline skin responds to disease: by getting red and/or itchy, by developing scabby bumps, by losing hair, and by flaking. In some severe skin disorders, lumps or open sores may develop. Because the repertoire of signs is so limited, different skin diseases often look exactly the same. On the other hand, the same disease may manifest itself completely differently from cat to cat. This situation presents a diagnostic challenge. Only rarely can veterinarians ascertain the cause of a skin condition by just looking at the cat; diagnostic tests are almost always necessary.

Cat bite infections are probably the most common form of feline bacterial disease. An infected cat bite often forms an abscess, a collection of pus and dead tissue. Fortunately, veterinary treatment of these painful and destructive infections is fairly simple if begun promptly. Surgically draining the abscess and starting the cat on appropriate antimicrobial medication usually eliminates the infection. You can prevent your cat from getting these infections by keeping him indoors.

Atopy, also called allergic inhalant dermatitis, is caused by an allergic reaction to inhaled particles: pollens, house dust, and mold spores, to name a few. In most cats the mainstays of therapy are avoidance of the allergen when possible, anti-inflammatory medication, antihistamines, and/or medications that contain special fatty acids. Itchiness is one of the main signs of atopic skin disease, but owners may not realize that their cats are grooming or scratching excessively. Sometimes bald spots are the only sign. Remember that the signs of atopy can resemble those of flea-bite hypersensitivity (page 292), which can be confused with those of a food allergy, and so on.

Food allergies usually develop in response to foods the cat has been consuming for a while, not to something new. A typical sign is itchiness, particularly of the facial area, the feet, and the ears, but symptoms vary. The only way to diagnose a food allergy is to feed the cat completely different food for approximately six to eight weeks. A homemade diet using only ingredients that the cat has never eaten is usually best. The best way to manage a diagnosed food allergy is, of course, to avoid feeding your cat the foods in question.

Ringworm (dermatophytosis) is a contagious fungal skin disease most often caused by the fungus *Microsporum canis*. It often appears as expanding circular, red, flaky, bald patches, but some infected cats have little or no skin condition at all, so diagnosis rarely can be made simply by looking at the skin.

Cats are infected by fungal spores directly from an infected cat or from spores persisting in the environment. In a multicat household, it's a good bet that if one cat is infected, most of the others are as well. Ringworm spores are extremely hardy and resistant to disinfection; indeed, any spores in the environment retain the capacity to cause infection for well over a year. As if this were not bad enough, *Microsporum canis* can cause skin disease in people too; it is not uncommon for owners to become infected from their cats.

A vaccine for *Microsporum canis* is available commercially, but it is not widely used. While it shows some ability to prevent or cure the skin condition in some cats, it does not prevent or eliminate infection itself. Elimination of infection from a household of cats is very time consuming, labor intensive, and expensive. Treatment—antifungal dips or baths, oral medication, and topical antifungal medications applied to the skin lesions—may have to be given for several months or more, and the environment must be cleaned thoroughly and treated periodically with antifungal disinfectants (such as household bleach) to kill lingering spores. Prevention is the key; take any new cat for a veterinary exam before introducing her to your household.

External Parasites

Fleas are without question the most significant external parasites afflicting cats. Fleas can cause life-endangering anemia, particularly in severely infested kittens, and host one of the major tapeworms that infect cats. Fleas can also transmit plague, a potentially fatal infection caused by the bacteria *Yersinia pestis,* most commonly from infected rodents and rabbits to cats and humans. Rarely, fleas transmit the disease from cat to cat or from cats to other species, including humans and dogs. Although plague is not common in cats, numbers of feline cases, as well as cat-associated human cases, have been on the rise since 1977 in the western United States.

Fleas can cause potentially fatal anemia in severely infested kittens.

But as far as the cat is concerned, probably the most bothersome problem associated with fleas is *flea-bite hypersensitivity,* an allergic reaction to flea saliva. For the unfortunate cat that suffers from this disorder, just a few flea bites are often enough to cause a severe skin reaction. Common signs of flea-bite hypersensitivity are itchy skin, scabby bumps, and hair loss—but these signs are not always exhibited, and other diseases can have the same symptoms. The only solution for such cats is to prevent fleas from coming near them. This is usually a simple matter if your only pets are cats—keep them indoors—but can be a difficult task for many households with dogs. Anti-inflammatory medications can be very helpful, but they are not a cure. They must be given as long as the cat is exposed to fleas,

The Life Cycle of the Flea

Fleas have complex life cycles and pass through several stages of development as they mature from egg to adult. A female flea will lay up to 20 eggs at a time, which hatch after several days to a couple of weeks. The larvae that emerge continue to grow and molt a couple of times over the next two weeks to six months. After the final molt, the larvae spin cocoons around themselves in which they metamorphose into adult fleas. If necessary, the cocoon can protect the flea for many months, but at just the right time—usually determined by temperature and physical pressure or motion—the flea emerges from the cocoon, ready to jump on your cat or you. It then feeds on the blood of its host. Warmth (temperatures between 60°F and 90°F or 15°C and 32°C) and relative humidity (between 65 and 85 percent) favor the flea life cycle; warm, humid areas such as the southern United States are notorious for the severity of their flea problem.

Flea (magnified)

and they can sometimes produce harmful side effects when used long-term.

By parting the fur, you may be able to see these small, brownish, wingless insects running about. If the infestation is fairly light, fleas may be impossible to spot on the coat, but flea dirt (droppings)—which looks like tiny black pepper flakes—confirms their presence. To find flea dirt, thoroughly comb the coat with a flea comb and look for black flecks entrapped in the teeth of the comb. If you can't tell if the black material is flea dirt or just debris, take a fleck or two and place it on a damp paper towel; if a red halo forms around the fleck, it is flea dirt.

To control flea infestation, you must treat the environment as well as all the animals in the household. There are many safe, effective, and easily administered flea products available from veterinarians. Convenient monthly treatments given orally or applied to a small area of the skin are a boon to pet owners because they eliminate fleas not only from their pets for a month at a time but from the indoor environment as well. This is especially important in households where family members (often children) have an allergic reaction to flea bites.

Make certain that any over-the-counter products you use are labeled specifically for use in cats, as some dog products may not be safe for cats, and follow the directions carefully. Never apply a flea product unless you can monitor the cat closely for at least several hours after administration, and do not use more than one product at a time (see Household Poisons on page 330 for signs of poisoning by flea products).

Ticks are small parasites that bury their heads in the skin of their hosts and suck blood until they look like fat, gray or brown beans. When the ticks can't hold any more blood, they fall off the host and lay thousands of eggs. Heavy tick infestations, rare in cats, can cause anemia as well as skin irritations and infections. It has not been proven that cats can get Lyme disease from ticks.

Other external parasites that can cause skin disease in cats are several species of *Cheyletiella mites* (large, oval, blimplike parasites visible as small white specks that cause an itchy skin disease known as cheyletiellosis, or "walking dandruff"), plus a number of other species of mites (ear mites are discussed on page 289) and *lice* (small, flat, wingless biting parasites that cause itchiness, hair loss, and dandruff). Correct diagnosis and treatment ensure successful management of problems from external parasites.

Skeletal Problems

Aside from disorders caused by injury, diseases of the bones, joints, and muscles of cats are fairly uncommon. Dogs are more prone to such diseases, partly because some of the most severe canine joint problems are hereditary, and selective breeding is much more common with dogs than with cats. Also, the physical size and structure of the domestic cat is fairly uniform and not too unlike that of its closest,wild relatives, so unusual stresses and strains are not placed on structures ill-equipped to handle them. The signs of musculoskeletal disease can be obvious, such as swelling or lameness, but they can also be quite subtle. Elderly cats with degenerative arthritis may simply become less active or use the litter box less faithfully because of difficulty getting to the box or climbing in.

Patellar Luxation

Patellar luxation, dislocation of the kneecap, is sometimes associated with hip dysplasia (page 295) but sometimes occurs by itself in the Abyssinian, the Devon Rex, and the Chartreux. Patellar luxation is a rather uncommon hereditary condition in the general domestic cat population, but it is becoming more prevalent in purebred cats. Surgery may help alleviate the discomfort associated with patellar luxation and may also reduce the cat's likelihood of developing arthritis in the affected limb.

Devon Rexes such as this (healthy) one are becoming more susceptible to patellar luxation.

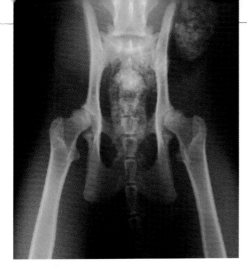

This X ray of a cat's pelvis shows signs of hip dysplasia, an abnormal looseness of the hip joint.

Mouth Problems

Maintaining your cat's oral health can go a long way toward upholding her overall well-being. Problems in the mouth can not only be quite painful, causing some cats to refuse to eat, but oral infections can also "seed" other parts of the body with harmful microorganisms and cause life-threatening infections. Most problems in the mouth can be managed successfully if they are caught early enough. Signs of oral disease, which may include particularly bad breath, drooling, and difficulty eating, should prompt a visit to your veterinarian.

Owners can play an important role in maintaining their cats' oral health by cleaning their teeth regularly (see page 247 for advice on tooth brushing) and by faithfully examining their mouths during the routine mini–physical exam (described on page 268). In addition, your veterinarian should perform a thorough dental examination at least once a year. You might also consider feeding your cat dry food; some veterinarians believe dry food's abrasive action helps delay the formation of plaque.

Tooth and gum disease in cats, like in humans, is brought on by the accumulation of plaque, a soft, pastelike substance composed of bacteria and organic material that, over time, mineralizes to become dental tartar. Tartar can build up on any of the teeth but is most commonly found on the outer surfaces of the canine teeth, especially near the gum line, and on the outer surfaces of the upper premolars (see page 192 for an illustration of feline teeth). Early tartar buildup may cause no apparent problems for the cat, and may go unnoticed unless the owner faithfully

Hip dysplasia begins as an abnormal looseness of the hip joint and may ultimately lead to severe and painful arthritis. Most cats with hip dysplasia experience no problems, but a few may intermittently become stiff or lame and may be reluctant to jump. Medication can help reduce inflammation, while surgery can bring relief for cats that seem to be in great pain. Overweight cats often benefit from losing weight.

Arthritis in cats often affects the elbow joint, though it can afflict many joints, and usually strikes older cats as their joints degenerate with age. Overall stiffness, lameness in one or more limbs, reluctance to move, lethargy, and impaired litter box habits are all signs of arthritis. Treatment involves weight reduction, if necessary, and anti-inflammatory medication. Various pain medications may be helpful if used judiciously, but owners should not treat their cats with human medications. Acetaminophen and many other drugs for humans are very poisonous to cats. Your veterinarian will tell you which medications are safe and effective.

examines the mouth. As this brownish, bacteria-rich material continues to form, it extends below the gum line, eventually causing the gums to become red and inflamed. If this inflammation, termed **gingivitis**, remains untreated, it eventually affects the periodontal tissues, supportive tissues surrounding the teeth.

Gingivitis is reversible with regular annual or biannual tooth cleaning by a veterinarian and daily brushing at home. If not treated in time, periodontal disease eventually leads to tooth loss, and can even make the cat more susceptible to other diseases as well. Telltale signs of gingivitis or periodontal disease include foul-smelling breath, drooling, and oral discomfort, depending on the severity of the condition.

Inflammation of the mouth (stomatitis) and/or *inflammation of the pharynx* (pharyngitis) sometimes develop as a result of severe periodontal disease, though some cats develop these conditions independent of any dental disease. Often the cause is not known. Cats whose immune systems have been suppressed by infection with FeLV or FIV may develop stomatitis or pharyngitis as secondary infections. The inflamed areas are red, swollen, and painful, and affected cats may drool or have difficulty eating; in particularly severe cases the afflicted areas bleed. As the cause of inflammation cannot always be determined, successful management is difficult. Long-term use of medications that suppress inflammation can sometimes make afflicted cats feel more comfortable.

Cervical line lesions, pitlike areas very commonly found in the teeth of cats, are similar to cavities in people, but in cats their cause is unknown. The lesions tend to form near the gum line, and as they grow, the tooth becomes weaker and weaker and may eventually break off. Such lesions can be quite painful; cats experiencing discomfort may grind their teeth, chatter while eating, chew on only one side of the mouth, or suddenly drop food from the mouth. Some veterinarians recommend placing "fillings" into the pitted areas before they penetrate into the pulp cavity, temporarily delaying growth of the lesion. Unfortunately, the lesions invariably progress; once they invade the pulp cavity, extraction is the only option.

Digestive Problems

The feline digestive system is affected by many disorders, signs of which include weight loss, vomiting, diarrhea, and/or loss of appetite. Thankfully, because the quality of commercial cat foods today is generally high, nutritional problems in cats are becoming increasingly rare. Following is a discussion of common or significant disorders that specifically involve the stomach and intestinal tract, including those caused by internal parasites.

Diarrhea and vomiting can happen occasionally without any major disease being involved—say, if the cat has hairballs or has been fed a new diet—but you should take your cat to the vet if either symptom occurs frequently, lasts more than a day or two, or is accompanied by any other signs, such as lethargy, fever, or weight loss.

Diarrhea may be a sign of one of the following serious conditions: internal parasites (page 298), a food intolerance, bacterial infection (salmonellosis, for example, a potentially fatal disease that is transmitted through contaminated food, feces, or water), viral infections (such as feline panleukopenia; page 284), inflammatory bowel disease (IBD; page 298), and hyperthyroidism (page 304). Vomiting also may accompany infectious disease, IBD, kidney failure (which more commonly afflicts older cats; page 308), and intestinal obstructions caused by swallowed foreign objects (discussed next).

Swallowed foreign objects are a less common cause of vomiting in cats than in dogs because cats tend to be much choosier about what they eat. Unfortunately, certain types of linear objects, such as yarn, string, thread, and Christmas tree tinsel, tempt even the most discriminating cat to chew them. Ill-equipped to pull the object out of his mouth, the cat swallows it;

a wad or loop can then become lodged under the tongue or in the stomach or intestines. As the intestine attempts to work the material through the tract, it saws back and forth over the lodged string, which eventually cuts through the intestinal wall and creates terrible problems for the cat. In most cases, the only remedy is to remove the offending object surgically. *Do not try to pull the object out of the mouth or anus, as doing so may cut through delicate tissues and further threaten the life of the cat.*

Hairballs are clumps of hair that cats ingest during grooming and subsequently cough up. If your cat vomits and you notice hair in the vomit, consult with your veterinarian, who may recommend daily brushing to remove loose hair and the

Never allow your cat to play with string, yarn, Christmas tree tinsel, or other linear objects, which are potentially fatal if swallowed.

regular use of a cat laxative to prevent hairballs from forming. Usually, hairballs are not serious; if your cat is vomiting frequently, another condition is probably to blame. In rare cases, hairballs can cause blockages that require surgical removal.

Inflammatory bowel disease (IBD) is a gastrointestinal condition that in some cases may be caused by an abnormal response of the immune system. Chronic or intermittent vomiting or diarrhea results, and if the disease is severe or long-lasting, afflicted cats may eventually lose considerable weight or even die. A few cases of IBD progress to intestinal cancer. Middle-aged and older cats are more prone to develop this condition, but cats of any age can be affected. There is no cure for IBD, but most cases can be satisfactorily treated with dietary management and anti-inflammatory medication or drugs that suppress the immune system.

Idiopathic megacolon is one of the leading causes of chronic constipation in older cats. For reasons that are not completely understood, the muscles in the colon of cats with this condition become progressively weaker, and ultimately lose the ability to move stool out of the body. Newly introduced medications called prokinetic agents offer some promise, although they are not effective for all cats. A surgical procedure called subtotal colectomy (removal of most of the colon) can save the lives of cats that do not respond to treatment with medication.

Internal Parasites

A parasite is an organism that lives and feeds within or upon another organism or host at the host's expense, sometimes causing disease or even death. Internal parasites afflicting cats may be one-celled organisms called protozoa or multiple-celled wormlike creatures. Because many internal parasites spend a portion of their life cycles within the cat's digestive tract, they are discussed here along with other digestive problems that afflict cats. However, the disease they cause may affect other parts of the body as well.

Roundworms are a common problem in cats; in fact, most cats are infected with roundworms at some point in their lives, usually as kittens. The adult worms that reside in the small intestine usually do not cause many problems for the cat, but if the concentration is large, especially in kittens, vomiting or diarrhea, and a scrawny, potbellied appearance can result. Roundworms, which resemble three- to four-inch-long pieces of spaghetti, are sometimes visible in a cat's vomit or stool.

Cats can be infected by ingesting roundworm eggs that have been shed in the feces of an infected cat (the eggs can last for years); by eating a rodent carrying the parasite; or, most commonly, by ingesting milk from an infected mother. Diagnosis and treatment are simple; many safe, effective, and inexpensive oral medications are available.

A word of caution to cat owners with young children: By ingesting roundworm eggs, humans can acquire a condition called visceral larva migrans, which sometimes leads to muscle or joint pain, abdominal pain, coughing, skin rashes, or seizures; if the larvae reach the eye, vision may be impaired. Keep toddlers away from the litter box, and prevent children from playing outside in soil that may be contaminated with dog or cat feces. Timely and routine treatment of all kittens and new cats with medications that kill roundworms is a crucial preventative measure.

Hookworms enter their host in the larval stage through the mouth—in contaminated feces or in the milk of an infected mother—or by penetrating the skin. Some infected cats develop diarrhea, but the major problem caused by this intestinal parasite is anemia. Adult worms residing in the intestine survive by sucking blood from their host, and if there are enough worms, there can be significant blood loss; kittens tend to be most severely affected. Your veterinarian can easily diagnose and treat hookworm infections with orally administered medications.

Hookworm larvae can tunnel through human skin and cause a condition called cutaneous larva migrans, which causes extreme itchiness. Avoid close contact with soil or litter contaminated by the feces of hookworm-infected cats.

Tapeworms are segmented worms that commonly afflict cats but rarely cause them problems. Owners, however, may be quite alarmed by the sight of the rice-size tapeworm segments crawling near their cat's rear end. Dried segments that look much like large sesame seeds can be seen clinging to the fur around the anus. Cats are infected by ingesting a flea or rodent carrying the immature stage of the parasite. Treatment is simply and effectively carried out by administering medication either by injection or by mouth, but unless owners control fleas and prevent their cats from hunting, reinfection will occur.

Coccidia are single-celled parasites that commonly afflict kittens and young cats through contact with infected feces. Most of the time the infection causes no particular health problems, although diarrhea can occasionally result. Treatment with oral medication is usually simple and straightforward.

Giardia are another group of protozoan parasites spread by the ingestion of contaminated water or feces. Infection may cause diarrhea, or it may cause no disease at all. Simultaneous treatment of all cats in the household with oral medication is usually necessary to eliminate the infection, and treatment must sometimes be repeated several times. Litter boxes should be changed and disinfected more frequently. It is not certain whether giardia infections can be transmitted from cats to humans. People who are living with or treating infected cats should wash their hands thoroughly after handling the cat or the litter box.

Toxoplasmosis afflicts cats that either ingest raw meat or prey that contains the microscopic parasite *Toxoplasma gondii* or that ingest material contaminated with the stool of an infected cat. Kittens can become infected in the womb and die before birth. The stage of the parasite shed in the feces of infected cats is very hardy and can survive outdoors in soil for many months.

Although infection is fairly common in felines, most cats do not get sick. Young cats are at the highest risk; symptoms include fever, loss of appetite, lethargy, diarrhea, and weight loss. Pneumonia, liver disease, and infection of the central nervous system are more devastating possibilities; many afflicted cats do not survive. However, infection involving just the eyes often can be managed successfully.

Toxoplasmosis also poses a serious health risk for people. Infection is especially dangerous and sometimes fatal for developing fetuses and individuals whose immune systems are compromised. The good news is that prevention is fairly simple. Pregnant women and people with suppressed immune systems should heed the following recommendations (the first six apply to all pregnant women, not just those with cats):

- Do not eat raw or undercooked (rare) meat. Cook all meat to an internal temperature of at least 158°F (69°C) for at least fifteen minutes.
- Avoid eating unpasteurized dairy products.
- Wash raw vegetables thoroughly before consumption to cleanse them of any possibly contaminated soil.
- Wash hands thoroughly in soap and water after handling raw meat, raw vegetables, or unpasteurized dairy products.
- Avoid contact with soil in which cats may have defecated. Wear rubber gloves when gardening, and wash your hands thoroughly afterward.
- Avoid handling free-roaming cats or any that show signs of illness.
- Protect your cats from infection by keeping them indoors, and do not feed them raw meat or unpasteurized dairy products.
- Change your cat's litter every day; it takes at least a day for any organisms passed in the stool to become capable of causing infection, so by changing the litter daily you dramatically reduce the chance of infection. For additional security, wear rubber gloves or have someone else change the litter.

If you are contemplating becoming pregnant, have your blood tested to determine whether you have toxoplasma antibodies (these would have formed as a result of prior exposure to the parasite). If you have antibodies and are accidentally exposed to the parasite during pregnancy,

the likelihood of transmission to the baby in your womb is dramatically reduced. If you don't have antibodies, then you should be especially cautious to avoid exposure, as you and your developing baby are more susceptible to infection. Cats that will be living in households with pregnant women should also be tested for the presence of toxoplasma antibodies. A positive-testing cat is probably immune to infection. A negative-testing cat is susceptible to infection, and if exposed might shed the organism in the feces for a week or two afterward. In either case, be sure to reduce your cats' chance of exposure by following the list of recommendations on the left.

Liver Problems

The liver is integrally involved with countless vital body functions, so it's not surprising that this organ is commonly affected by a number of diseases, even some that begin elsewhere in the body. Here we focus on a few diseases that originate in the liver.

Hepatic lipidosis is a very serious disorder in which the cells of the liver become engorged with fat, severely compromising liver function. Fat can accumulate in the liver as a result of such diseases as hyperthyroidism and diabetes mellitus (both described on pages 304 and 305, respectively), but when an underlying cause cannot be found, veterinarians label the condition idiopathic (meaning "of unknown cause") hepatic lipidosis. The disease occurs most commonly in overweight cats but can also afflict cats that are average in weight. Typical signs are prolonged loss of appetite, dehydration, weight loss, liver enlargement, and jaundice. With aggressive therapy (including intravenous fluids and forced feedings) and long-term hospitalization, about 60 percent of cats with idiopathic hepatic lipidosis survive. Take care if you are trying to slim down an overweight cat; diet changes must be performed gradually, as a too-rapid weight loss predisposes a cat to developing hepatic lipidosis.

Cholangitis/cholangiohepatitis complex, one of the more common liver disorders in adult cats, is actually a spectrum of liver diseases characterized by inflammation of the vessels that carry bile within the liver, and sometimes inflammation of the liver tissue itself. Its cause is not known, but evidence suggests that some cases may be linked to inflammatory bowel disease (page 298). There are at least three different forms of the disease, each requiring different treatments; hospitalization is routinely required. The signs of all forms are similar, commonly including loss of appetite, fever, listlessness, jaundice, and liver enlargement. While long-term survival can be expected in cats suffering from milder forms of the disease, the outlook is much bleaker for those afflicted with more severe forms, and rarely can a cure be expected.

Congenital portosystemic vascular anomalies are birth defects in kittens whereby blood carrying "toxins" from the intestine goes directly into the circulation via a shunting vessel, rather than passing through the liver, where toxins are filtered out. Signs may include stunted growth, loss of appetite, vomiting, diarrhea, and a variety of neurologic and behavior problems. Surgery to close the shunt is the best treatment in most cases, but medical management alone may suffice.

Respiratory Problems

The signs of problems in the respiratory tract vary depending on the cause and location of the problem. For example, such coldlike symptoms as sneezing and/or nasal discharge are common signs of disease in the nasal passages; gagging may be associated with disease in the nasal part of the pharynx; while coughing and/or labored breathing characterize disorders of the larynx, the trachea (the windpipe), and the lungs (see page 189 for a diagram of the respiratory system).

Foreign objects, cancer, and fungal infections occasionally cause disease in the upper respiratory tract (the nasal cavity and the nasal part of the pharynx), but by far the major causes of problems here are viral in origin. (See page 283 for a discussion of feline calcivirus and feline herpesvirus type 1, major causes of upper respiratory tract disease in cats.) The lower respiratory tract (the trachea, the bronchial tubes, and the lungs) of the cat is most commonly affected by diseases such as asthma and chronic bronchitis, though viral, bacterial, parasitic, and fungal infections, as well as cancer, can all create disease in the airways and lungs.

Bronchial disease is quite common in cats, and takes many forms; two of the most significant are *chronic bronchitis* and *bronchial asthma.* Coughing is the hallmark of bronchial disease; episodes of severe breathing difficulty may punctuate periods of relatively normal breathing. The cause of chronic bronchitis and bronchial asthma often remains unknown, but an underlying allergic condition is suspected in some cases, and feline heartworm disease (page 302) has been found to produce asthma-like symptoms.

Treatment of both chronic bronchitis and bronchial asthma aims to control the cough and breathing difficulty with anti-inflammatory medication, drugs to help dilate the bronchial tubes, and antibacterial medication if a bacterial component is suspected. An asthma attack—a sudden onset of severe breathing difficulty—requires immediate veterinary attention.

Pneumonitis (inflammation of the lungs) and *pneumonia* (inflammation as well as pus and cellular debris in the lungs) are among the most serious respiratory diseases caused by viral, bacterial, parasitic, or fungal infection. Depending on the severity of the infection, cats with infectious pneumonitis or pneumonia experience breathing difficulty, coughing, listlessness, loss of appetite, and sometimes fever. Treatment and outcome depend upon cause and severity.

Heart Problems

A diseased heart is less able to pump blood, and may deprive the body of life-giving oxygen and nutrients and/or allow fluid to "back up" in various parts of the body. Major signs of oxygen deprivation are weakness, perhaps most noticeable after exercise, and fainting, which may look like a seizure, while fluid in or around the lungs usually causes breathing difficulty. Almost any form of heart disease in cats can cause sudden death.

Congenital heart defects (which the animal is born with) in cats are usually "plumbing problems" that either disrupt or divert the normal flow of blood through the heart. Possible defects include openings where there should be none, openings that are too small, valves that leak, blood

vessels that are in the wrong place or are too narrow, and vessels that are supposed to shut down at birth but that fail to do so. Weakness, fainting, breathing difficulty, or stunted growth are often seen in cats with congenital heart defects. With few exceptions, the end result is heart failure. Treatment and outcome depend upon the nature of the defect.

Hypertrophic cardiomyopathy is a disease of the heart muscles whereby, for unknown reasons, the muscle walls of the left ventricle become thickened and ultimately compromise the heart's ability to pump blood. Congestive heart failure with pulmonary edema (fluid in the lungs) is a common consequence. In addition, blood clots tend to form within a chamber of the heart. If one breaks free, it circulates rapidly and lodges in an artery, commonly one supplying blood to the rear legs; sudden paralysis of the rear limb(s) is the repercussion.

Some cases of hypertrophic cardiomyopathy can be diagnosed early if the veterinarian detects abnormal heart sounds during a routine physical examination; ultrasonic examination of the heart confirms the diagnosis. If treatment is started early enough, the prognosis for long-term survival is guarded to fair for most cats. Medications are given to control pulmonary edema, the strength of heart muscle contractions, and the formation of blood clots.

Heartworm disease is commonly considered a disease of dogs, but the offending parasite (a worm called *Dirofilaria immitis* that is transmitted in its larval stage by mosquitoes) can infect cats as well. Some heartworm-infected cats have no problems at all; some just act lethargic or lose appetite and weight; some suffer temporary or intermittent vomiting, coughing, or breathing difficulty; others die suddenly. Fortunately, many cats are able to fight off infection by themselves.

When a cat is bitten by a mosquito carrying the larval parasites, the larvae are carried along with mosquito saliva through the bite hole into the cat's body and continue to mature as they migrate through the tissues. Eventually, they reach the heart and pulmonary vessels, stimulating an intense inflammatory reaction in the lungs that often results in rapid breathing, coughing, or vomiting. These signs usually abate after several weeks, but in some cases they may persist. After the initial episode, mature worms usually cause few signs of disease. But it is after about two years, when the worms die, that a cat exhibits some of the most severe signs of heartworm infection—very severe coughing, marked breathing difficulty, or sudden death.

There is no safe way to kill the worms, but they do not live as long in cats as they do in dogs, so many cats that experience problems as a result of infection may be free of disease after a period of time. Coughing and vomiting caused by the parasite usually can be controlled by an oral cortisone-like medication. A preventive medication that kills the larvae before they reach the heart is recommended for routine use in areas where heartworm disease exists. Heartworm has

Congenital heart defects are reported more often in Siamese cats than in any other breed.

been seen in almost all parts of the United States and southern Canada, but it is most prevalent on the east coast of North America, in the southern United States, and in the Mississippi River valley.

High blood pressure (systemic hypertension) is common in elderly cats. It is almost always secondary to some other disease, especially kidney disease and hyperthyroidism. Left untreated, hypertension can cause enlargement of the heart, worsening of kidney disease, seizures, and sudden blindness. Treatment of the condition primarily relies on managing the underlying condition; if necessary, antihypertensive medications similar to those used in people are given orally.

Blood Disorders

Aside from liquid, the major components of blood are red blood cells, white blood cells, and platelets. This guide focuses on disorders involving the red blood cells, which carry oxygen to body tissues. Some of the most serious disorders of the white blood cells often result from infection with feline leukemia virus or feline immunodeficiency virus (both discussed on page 282), or from cancer in the bone marrow. Disorders of the platelets, which are involved with the blood's clotting mechanism, are uncommon in cats.

Anemia, which results from a diminished number of red blood cells, is a fairly common condition in cats, and can take one of two forms: *regenerative anemia* is caused by blood loss or by premature destruction of red cells; *nonregenerative anemia* is caused by inadequate production of red blood cells by the bone marrow. In addition to blood loss (such as may occur

with injury, severe flea infestation, or poisoning with certain types of rodent poisons), other causes of regenerative anemia are destruction of red cells by a malfunctioning immune system and loss of cells due to damage caused by the blood parasite *Hemobartonella felis,* which causes feline infectious anemia. The most common causes of nonregenerative anemia are FeLV infection (see page 282) and cancer in the bone marrow (usually caused by FeLV). Whatever the cause, a cat with severe anemia is very listless and weak, and the gums, ear flaps, and nose may be quite pale instead of pink.

Regenerative anemia can often be cured by treating the underlying cause; blood transfusions are sometimes necessary as well. Most cats suffering from nonregenerative anemia have a much poorer outlook because the underlying cause— FeLV infection or cancer—is often progressive and incurable.

Endocrine System Disorders

The endocrine system is composed of tissues that secrete hormones, chemical substances that regulate the activity of certain organs. Some of the most important organs in the endocrine system are the thyroid glands, the parathyroid glands, the pancreas, the adrenal glands, the pituitary gland, and the ovaries and testes. Hyperthyroidism and diabetes mellitus are by far the leading hormonal abnormalities afflicting cats.

Hyperthyroidism, which most commonly afflicts middle-aged to older cats, results from excessive production of thyroid hormone. Although somewhat variable, the signs seen in most cats are fairly dramatic:

a marked increase in appetite, weight loss, increased thirst and urination, occasional vomiting and diarrhea, an unkempt, greasy appearance, and hyperactivity. The disease is easy to diagnose in most cases, and treatment—antithyroid medication, surgical removal of the thyroid glands, or administration of radioactive iodine—is very effective.

Diabetes mellitus ("sugar" diabetes) causes signs that are often remarkably similar to those seen in hyperthyroidism: weight loss despite a ravenous appetite, and increased thirst and urination. Middle-aged and older cats (especially overweight ones) are more prone to the condition. Diabetes mellitus is caused either by inadequate insulin production by the pancreas, or by an abnormal response of the body's cells to insulin. Among other functions, insulin enables glucose in the bloodstream to enter the cells that need it. In diabetic cats, blood sugar rises, but the cells of the body are not able to utilize it—the cells are surrounded by a nutrient they need but cannot acquire.

Diabetes mellitus is a serious disorder, but properly regulated cats can often live

Diabetic cats usually require daily or twice-daily insulin injections.

long lives. Dietary management is a crucial component of diabetic cat care. High-fiber diets, available by prescription from veterinarians, may delay the absorption of sugar from the intestine, as well as help reduce a cat's weight to normal. In addition to managing their cats' diets, owners of diabetic felines usually must administer medication once or twice a day. Insulin injections are the answer for most cats, but some cats respond well to an orally administered medication. (Oral medication seems like an attractive alternative, but in most cats it's harder to give pills than it is to give shots. See pages 312 and 315 for instructions on performing these procedures.)

Urinary Tract Disorders

The urinary tract is composed of two kidneys (which filter blood and eliminate waste products via the urine), the ureters (tubes that carry urine from the kidneys into the bladder), the bladder, and the urethra (a tube from the bladder through which urine exits the body). Congenital abnormalities (which the cat is born with), inflammation, infection, cancer, and deterioration can all affect the various components of the urinary tract. By far the most common urinary tract disorders in cats are feline lower urinary tract disease and chronic kidney disease. Although both of these disorders may result in frequent urination (sometimes outside the litter box), your veterinarian will need to examine your cat and perform tests in order to properly diagnose and treat the condition.

There is no way to prevent most urinary tract diseases, but it is always wise to provide plenty of fresh water to drink. Although feeding dry foods exclusively has been cited as a cause of bladder disease in the past, there is little evidence that

Polycystic Kidney Disease

Initially, cats with polycystic kidney disease (PKD) show no signs of disease, but progressively enlarging fluid-filled cysts within the kidney gradually crowd out the tissue, ultimately leading to kidney failure with the typical associated signs (see chronic kidney disease on page 308). Failure may occur within the first year of life, or it may not become evident for years. There is no cure for the condition, but medical management of chronic renal failure often helps improve the cat's quality of life.

Polycystic kidney disease afflicts certain lines of Persian cats and cats with Persian heritage.

today's high-quality commercial dry diets contribute to bladder disease.

Bladder or urethral disease afflicts many cats at some point in their lives. The most common form of the disease is actually a spectrum of disorders given the name **idiopathic feline lower urinary tract disease,** or FLUTD. Cats experiencing idiopathic FLUTD commonly suffer from **cystitis** (inflammation of the bladder) and/or **urethritis** (inflammation of the urethra). Afflicted cats usually make frequent and/or strained attempts to urinate, passing only a small amount of urine (and sometimes blood) at a time, and lick the genital area often. They may urinate outside the litter box simply because the pain makes them feel that they suddenly have to relieve themselves. FLUTD may also cause litter box aversion; a cat experiencing pain during urination may avoid going to the box that he now associates with that pain. Cats that are urine marking may act similarly to cats urinating outside the box due to bladder or urethral disease; a veterinary consultation may be the only way to determine the cat's motivation.

Even with extensive diagnostic tests, the actual cause of many cases of FLUTD may not be determined. Many types of treatment have been attempted, but the results have been inconsistent. Fortunately, whether treated or not, many cats recover from the condition within several days or weeks.

The formation of mineral deposits within the bladder or urethra is also frequently associated with idiopathic FLUTD. A particularly dangerous consequence is obstruction of the urethra, with sandlike mineral deposits, thick mucuslike material, or a combination of both. Males are much more likely to become obstructed than females simply because the male urethra is smaller

Renal Amyloidosis

In most cases, renal amyloidosis, an inherited kidney disease, ultimately leads to kidney failure, which may take a number of years. Once renal failure develops, few cats survive more than a year, though some are so mildly affected that their life span may be normal. The mode of inheritance is not completely understood, and diagnosis of the condition is usually not possible until after affected cats have reproduced. These difficulties make eliminating the condition from affected lines of cats impossible at this time. There is no reliable treatment for renal amyloidosis.

Renal amyloidosis affects some lines of Abyssinian (shown here) and Somali cats.

in diameter. Early signs that a cat's urethra is obstructed are essentially the same as those seen with cystitis (straining, licking, etc.), but they tend to be more pronounced. Within a short period of time, obstructed cats experience more and more pain; if not treated quickly, they will lapse into a coma and die within forty-eight to seventy-two hours. *If you have any question regarding your cat's ability to urinate, seek veterinary attention immediately.*

Chronic kidney disease is so common in cats that it is, at present, almost an expected consequence of aging; the kidney failure that ultimately results is the leading cause of death in old cats. There are many possible causes—infectious agents and high blood pressure are a couple—but the end result is the same: kidneys that are no longer able to function adequately.

Cats with kidney disease may experience pain in the kidney area, drink excessively, produce greater quantities of urine (evidenced by urinating more frequently and by passing a large quantity each time—and sometimes by urinating outside the litter box), and in some cases have blood in the urine. Cats with failing kidneys may become quite ill; they typically lose their appetite and weight, become dehydrated, and vomit.

Finding a treatable cause of kidney failure is rare, so medical management relies on slowing the progression of the disease when possible and providing supportive care. "Kidney diets" that are lower in protein levels and that have modified amounts of various minerals are helpful for some cats with kidney failure, but there is no evidence that feeding such diets prevents kidney disease.

Nervous System Disorders

The delicate structures of the nervous system—the brain, the spinal cord, and the sensory and motor nerves that carry messages between the spinal cord or brain and the rest of the body—are prone to disease from many different sources. And even though the brain and spinal cord are well protected by bony armor, they can be seriously injured by automobiles, falls, animal bites, and other traumatic encounters. Because the tissues of the brain and spinal cord have a limited ability to heal, the consequences of disease and injury can be profound. The signs of nervous system disorders vary depending on the disease and the location, but seizures, behavior problems, weakness, and paralysis are some of the most common.

Epilepsy is defined as recurring seizures of any kind. (Seizures, and what to do if your cat has them, are discussed on page 323.) The term idiopathic epilepsy is used when a cause cannot be identified, and symptomatic epilepsy when a cause has been identified either in the brain (tumors, trauma, infection) or elsewhere in the body (liver disease, low blood sugar, poisoning). The long-term outlook for cats with symptomatic epilepsy mostly depends on the severity and treatability of the underlying disease. For example, if the cause is feline infectious peritonitis (page 282), the outlook is grim, as FIP is invariably fatal; if the cause is low blood sugar in a diabetic cat given too much insulin, the outcome is potentially much better. Cats with idiopathic epilepsy may live relatively normal lives depending on the frequency and severity of their seizures, and on how well the seizures can be controlled with anticonvulsant medications.

Feline hyperesthesia syndrome makes cats act as though their skin is extremely irritated. The cause is unknown, but cats with this condition typically twitch the skin on the back; frantically bite or lick the skin on the back, sides, or tail; flick the tail; and make loud hysterical sounds. They often act as if they are hallucinating, madly dashing about with wide eyes and dilated pupils. They may even attack objects, including their owners, without provocation. The frequency of this bizarre behavior varies and may last anywhere from a few seconds to a few minutes or longer. Most cats behave perfectly normally between episodes.

Some of these signs sound remarkably like normal feline play behavior, but owners of affected cats remark that their cats' actions seem much more accentuated. The condition can develop at any age but most commonly begins between the ages of one to four years. Several other conditions may cause similar signs; very itchy skin or pain must be considered. If diagnostic tests fail to reveal a cause that can be treated, anticonvulsant medication sometimes helps control the behavior.

Any type of cat can acquire feline hyperesthesia syndrome, but it seems to be more common in Abyssinian, Burmese, Himalayan (left), and Siamese cats.

Home Nursing

This chapter is designed to be used in combination with directions from your veterinarian, reminding you how to administer eye drops, eye ointment, pills, liquid medication, ear drops or ointment, and injections, and to take your cat's temperature. When medication is prescribed, ask your veterinarian or a member of the hospital's staff to show you exactly how to give it to your cat. If possible, have them observe you administering the medication, just to make sure you have it right. If you have problems medicating your cat or taking his temperature, ask your veterinarian for assistance; the techniques described here work in most situations, but sometimes other approaches might be called for.

Ill or elderly cats sometimes need to be nursed at home.

Medicating Your Cat

Regardless of the procedure you need to perform, make sure your cat is as relaxed as possible, and find a comfortable position for both of you. Sometimes placing your cat on the floor next to you works well; in other cases it's better for the cat to be on a table. (However, if your cat generally is not allowed on the kitchen table or counter, administering medications there may cause confusion and stress.) Trial and error will show what's best. If possible, have someone assist you. Your partner can hold your cat from behind, gently but firmly grasping the shoulders with each hand, cradling the cat along either side. If you are working alone, you might want to place the cat with his rear end facing into a corner so he can't back away from you. You can also try kneeling down over the cat with your legs on either side and with his head facing in the same direction you are.

Particularly difficult patients may need to be wrapped in a towel before being medicated.

Restraining a cat to give medication is a serious undertaking. Cats are very strong, quick, and flexible. To protect yourself from a particularly resistant patient, you might roll the cat tightly in a towel, leaving just the head exposed. Unfortunately, such forms of restraint may be only temporarily useful—most cats resent the procedure so much that they will hide the next time they see you coming. It is best to use the least amount of restraint necessary to get the job done. Smoothness and speed are your best allies; if you are struggling with your cat, take a break and try again later.

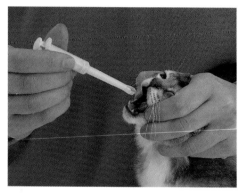

It's easier to give pills to some cats using a pill popper. With or without such a device, the procedure is basically the same.

Pills

Place one hand (if you're right-handed, use your left hand) on top of your cat's head. Reach your thumb down to one corner of his mouth and your fingers to the other corner. Tilt the cat's head back until his nose is pointing upward; this will cause him to open his mouth slightly. Place the pill between the thumb and forefinger of your other hand and, while gently lifting his head, open his mouth with the middle finger of your hand holding the pill. As his mouth opens, move the thumb and forefinger of the hand holding his head a little way into the corners of his mouth. Make

When giving a cat liquid medication, be sure to squirt it in slowly so the cat has a chance to swallow the medicine and does not spit it out.

sure the cat's lips are between your fingers and his teeth so you don't get bitten. Drop or place the pill at the center of the back of your cat's throat, aiming for the V-shaped area at the back of the tongue, and quickly but gently push it as far back as you can. Hold the cat's mouth closed. To be sure he swallows the pill, rub his throat or gently blow in his face. If he licks his lips, it's a pretty good indication that he's swallowed the pill.

It's a good idea to offer your cat a favorite treat as a reward after successfully getting the pill down, but don't be surprised if he's not interested.

Your veterinarian or local pet supply store can sell you a "pill popper" (pictured on page 312) that comes with instructions. Some cats are easier to medicate this way.

Liquid Medication

Hold your cat's head with one hand as described above for pills or cradle his head with your hand placed under his neck (as pictured above). Place the dropper or syringe containing the medicine into the cat's mouth, preferably in the pocket between the cheek and gums at the corner of the mouth. Slowly squirt in the medicine, giving your cat a chance to swallow.

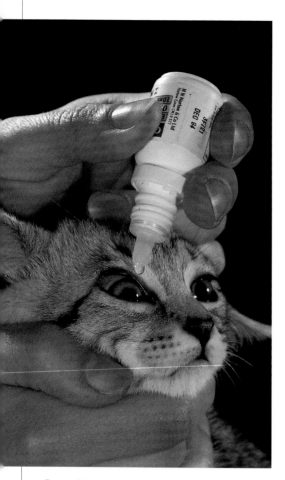

Be careful not to touch the bottle to the cat's eye when administering eye drops.

Eye Drops

Place one hand on your cat's chin, lift his head, and gently pull down the lower eyelid with your thumb. Hold the bottle between the thumb and forefinger of your other hand and gently hold the upper eyelid open with the heel of your hand. Squeeze one or two drops out of the bottle onto the surface of the eye. Try to apply the drops onto the white of the eye rather than the colored part, as this is more comfortable for the cat.

Eye Ointment

Hold the cat the same way as for giving eye drops. Place a strip of ointment about an eighth to a quarter of an inch long directly on the white of the eye or in the pocket between the eyelid and the eye. Be careful not to poke the eye with the tip of the container.

Ear Drops or Ointment

Place your thumb and forefinger on either side of the cat's ear flap and lift it up so you can see down into the ear canal. Squeeze the drops or ointment into the ear opening, making sure that the medicine goes down into the canal. Gently massage the base of the ear to distribute the medicine. It is normal for your cat to shake his head after you've administered ear drops.

Taking Your Cat's Temperature

A veterinarian may instruct an owner to take a cat's temperature to determine whether the cat is sick enough to be taken to the vet, or to monitor the effectiveness of treatment. Do not assume that your cat has a fever if his nose feels warm or dry. Instead take his temperature with a rectal thermometer. If you have the standard glass variety, shake it down to 96°F (35°C) or below. Lubricate the tip with petroleum jelly or mineral oil.

Place your cat facing away from you on a table or kneel down next to him on the floor and have a partner hold the cat between the neck and shoulders. If you are alone, turn the cat so his rear end is facing forward and hold him firmly against your left side (if you are right-handed) with your left arm. You may need to roll the cat in a towel, leaving just the head and rear exposed.

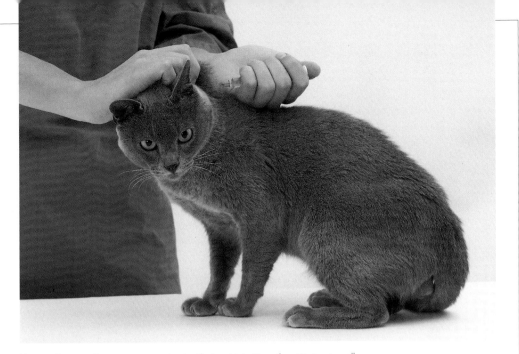

It's actually easier for many owners to give their cat injections than it is to give pills.

Gently lift the tail (with the hand of the arm restraining the cat if you are alone) and insert the thermometer into the anus using a slight twisting motion. Expect some initial resistance from the anal muscles, but with continued gentle pressure, they will eventually relax. Do not hurriedly force the thermometer into the anus or you may injure your cat. Insert the thermometer about an inch, and leave it in place for about two minutes; digital thermometers will give a signal letting you know when the reading is done. The normal feline body temperature ranges from 100.4° to 102.5°F (37.6° to 38.8°C) but can be as high as 103°F (39°C) if the cat is excited.

Injections

Most pet owners will never have to give their cat an injection, but most diabetic cats need daily or twice-daily injections of insulin. To give a shot, draw the medicine into the syringe, then hold the syringe with the needle pointed upward. Flick it a few times so any bubbles will rise to the top, then push the plunger to expel any air. Injections are easiest to give in the loose skin anywhere along the upper back avoiding the spine.

Lift a "tent" of skin and part the hair at the base of the tent (it is not necessary to clean the surface with alcohol, but avoid any visibly dirty areas). Push the needle into the skin where the hair is parted, and gently pull back on the plunger. If blood comes back into the syringe, move to a different site because you may have hit a blood vessel. If air comes in (if you see air bubbles or if the plunger is too easily pulled back, indicating a syringe filled with air, not medicine), you've pushed the needle in one side and out the other. If no air or blood comes back, push the plunger to administer the medication.

First Aid

When an emergency occurs, reason does not always prevail. Panic, fear, and confusion can hinder your ability to think clearly and act appropriately, so it is very important to have an emergency plan. If your cat has suffered a traumatic injury—if he's been struck by a car or mauled by a dog, for instance—the first priority is to protect yourself. A cat that is hurt and frightened can suddenly and seriously injure a person who is simply trying to help.

Your next priority should be to transport a seriously injured or ill cat to a veterinarian immediately. If possible, have someone call the veterinarian to warn the vet of the emergency case en route. Although there are ways that you can help your cat on the spot if immediate transport is not available, don't lose precious time—first aid delivered at the scene is rarely as effective as seeking professional help as quickly as possible.

Know your veterinarian's office hours and emergency procedures. Some veterinarians work with a team of doctors, one of whom is always on call and will meet you at the office. Others are associated with emergency care facilities that are open when the veterinarian's office is closed. If your veterinarian works with a separate emergency care facility, make sure you know the phone number, address, and how to get there. Post the name and phone number of your veterinarian and, if applicable, emergency facility in the same places in your home that you post other important numbers, such as those of the fire and police departments.

It's a good idea to practice techniques for checking heartbeat and other vital signs on a well cat so that you can cope more easily in an emergency.

Emergency cases such as broken limbs are best handled by professionals.

Handling an Injured Cat

Approach an injured cat slowly while speaking to her in a calm voice. Before attempting to touch the cat, cover her head with a thick blanket or heavy towel to protect yourself from being bitten. Gently lift the cat and place her, without force, into a box or carrier with the top open. If you suspect the cat has suffered spinal injuries—if the rear legs are flaccid, if the cat is dragging her legs, or if there are visible wounds over the back—support the cat's head while lifting and be careful not to twist the neck or spine.

Cats that are struggling can be restrained in the following way: firmly grasp the skin at the back of the neck as far forward as possible and gently lift the cat while supporting her body with your hand. Try to keep her feet pointing away from you as you gently place her into the box or carrier.

If you need to restrain the cat in order to perform a procedure, such as applying a bandage or putting pressure on a wound, grasp the skin at the back of the neck and lay the cat on her side with her feet facing away from you; lay the arm that is grasping the neck alongside the cat's back. Restrain the hindquarters by placing your other hand between the rear legs, being careful not to get scratched. If you need the cat to be on her left side, grasp the neck skin with your left hand; if you need her on her right side, grasp the neck with your right hand.

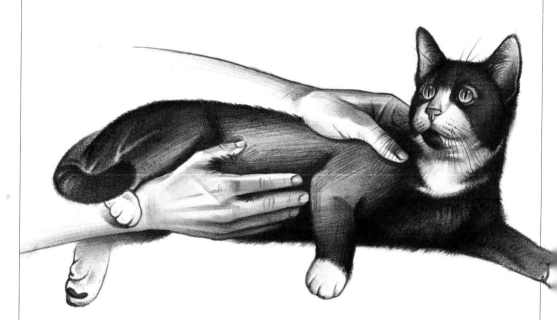

To restrain and treat an injured cat that is struggling, grasp the skin at the back of the neck and lay the cat on her side with her feet facing away from you. Support her back with the arm that is grasping the scruff of her neck and restrain her hindquarters by placing your other hand between her hindlegs.

Home First Aid Kit for Cats

- Your veterinarian's office phone number and after-hours emergency number

- ASPCA National Animal Poison Control Center number (888-426-4435, 800-548-2423, or 900-680-0000)

- Clean, heavy towels or thick blankets to protect yourself from injury, and to protect the cat from further injury

- Sterile nonstick bandaging material (such as Telfa pads) to put directly on an open wound

- Absorbent cotton or gauze pads to place over nonstick pad

- Roll of gauze bandaging material to wrap around nonstick or gauze pad

- One-inch adhesive medical (not masking) tape to hold bandages in place

- Cotton-tipped swabs

- Rubbing alcohol

- Antiseptic solution, such as povidone iodine (Betadine), to clean wounds

- Masking tape to secure a cat with spinal injuries to a stretcher

- A cat-length board to use as a stretcher. A large aluminum baking pan can also serve this purpose and can be used to store the other materials in the kit.

- Eye wash for flushing eyes

- Styptic pencil or powder to stop bleeding from claws if they are cut too short

- Syrup of ipecac or 3 percent hydrogen peroxide to be given orally to induce vomiting; never induce vomiting without first consulting with your veterinarian or poison control center (see What to Do If Your Cat Is Poisoned, page 324, and Household Poisons, page 330)

- A syringe obtained from your vet or, if necessary, an eye dropper to administer liquid (e.g., hydrogen peroxide, syrup of ipecac) by mouth

- Pair of thick gloves to protect yourself

- Flashlight or penlight

- A pencil to tighten a tourniquet

- Antibiotic ointment

- Scissors with rounded tips to remove bandages

- Tweezers to remove thorns

- A cat carrier with a removable top to transport cat

- Rectal thermometer for taking your cat's temperature (see page 314)

- Current photograph of your cat to put on posters in case your cat gets lost

- Copy of your cat's medical records

Lifesaving ABCs

If your cat has been injured and does not respond to you when you speak to him or stroke his head, he may be unconscious. If he is breathing, gently place him in a blanket-lined box, cover him with another blanket, leaving his head uncovered, and transport him to a veterinarian as quickly as possible. If he is not breathing, the next steps you take—the ABCs—may spell the difference between life and death. Your cat can die or suffer permanent brain damage if his brain is deprived of oxygen, which happens if the heart stops beating or breathing stops for four to five minutes.

Perform the ABCs described below as someone else prepares for immediate transport to a veterinarian; you can also perform these steps during transport if someone else is driving.

A. Check the Airway

Extend the cat's head and neck, open the mouth, pull the tongue forward, and, using a flashlight, look as far back into the throat as possible. Clean away any vomit or debris, and check for foreign objects at the back of the throat that might be obstructing breathing. If one is present, remove it; a sharp rap to the chest may help dislodge the object.

If a cat is not breathing despite a clear airway (see A. Check the Airway, above), perform artificial respiration. Rest the cat on his side, extend his head and neck, hold his mouth and lips closed, and blow into his nostrils once every three seconds for fifteen minutes or until he resumes breathing.

B. Check for Breathing

If the cat has not resumed breathing once you've removed any obstructions at the back of the throat, place him on an elevated surface with his head facing you. Position him on his side and perform artificial respiration. (Now is a good time to feel for a heartbeat as well; see "C," next, and follow the instructions.) Extend the head and neck, hold the mouth and lips closed, and blow into the nostrils once every three seconds for fifteen minutes or until the cat breathes on his own. Don't blow too hard—just enough to cause the cat's chest to expand.

C. Check Circulation (Heartbeat)

Place your hand around the lower part of the cat's chest about an inch or so behind either elbow. You should feel a heartbeat. (You can also check for a pulse by feeling the inner part of the rear leg up near the groin area, but finding a pulse even in a normal, healthy cat is difficult for most owners.) If you don't feel a heartbeat, you'll need to perform cardiac massage while also giving the cat artificial respiration. Together these two procedures are called cardiopulmonary resuscitation, or CPR.

With your hand in the same position used for checking heartbeat, compress the chest between your thumb and four fingers at a rate of about one or two compressions per second. Ideally, one person should provide artificial respiration while another massages the heart. One person can do both if necessary: after five chest compressions, blow once into the nostrils, then compress the chest five times, and so on. Continue chest massage until you detect a heartbeat and artificial respiration until the cat begins to breathe. If heartbeat and breathing have not returned within twenty minutes, the cat cannot be revived.

Feel for a cat's heartbeat by placing your hand on the cat's chest about an inch behind either elbow. If there is no heartbeat, perform cardiac massage while also giving the cat artificial respiration. To massage the heart, keep your hand in the same position as for checking heartbeat and compress the chest between your thumb and four fingers at a rate of one or two compressions per second. For instructions on performing artificial respiration at the same time, see C., above.

How to Tell If Your Cat Is in Shock

When a cat is in a serious accident, the amount of fluid moving through her blood vessels may be decreased. As a result, the heart and blood vessels are unable to deliver nutrients and oxygen to vital organs such as the brain or heart, and the cat may go into shock. Other potential causes of shock include heatstroke (see page 324), severe infection, and heart failure.

Signs of Shock

- Pale or muddy (brown) gums

- Gums that do not return to a normal pink color from white within two seconds of being pressed by your finger

- A weak and rapid pulse. (Check the pulse by feeling the inner part of the rear leg near the groin area. Count the beats for fifteen seconds, then multiply by four. A normal feline pulse rate is 110 to 240 beats per minute.)

- Rapid breathing (more than 60 breaths per minute)

- A low rectal temperature (below 100°F/ 37.4°C), with the skin and legs cool to the touch

- Difficulty standing

- Loss of consciousness

If you suspect that your cat is in shock, cover him with a blanket or coat to keep him warm, lift him gently and place him in a box or carrier, and transport him to the veterinary hospital immediately.

How to Stop Bleeding from a Wound

To stop bleeding, firmly press a clean cloth directly on the wound (if possible, put a nonstick pad on the wound first) and apply pressure for three to five minutes. Do not remove a blood-soaked pad from the wound or you may disturb the clot; instead, place another pad over the old one.

If bleeding persists, you'll need to apply pressure to the major artery supplying the area. For a wound on a front leg, press on the inside of the limb a couple of inches above the elbow. For a wound on a hindleg, press on the inner thigh. For a tail wound, press on the middle of the underside of the tail. If the wound is on a front paw, press on the inside of the leg just above the foot. If the wound is on a rear paw, press the bottom part of the foot between the ankle and paw.

Consider applying a tourniquet to a limb only as a last resort when all other efforts at stopping the bleeding have failed. A tourniquet may cut off circulation and necessitate amputation. First, tie a strip of gauze around the limb between the wound and the body. Next, tie a pencil or short stick over the knot. Now twist the pencil around in a circle to tighten the tourniquet until the bleeding stops. Tie the pencil in place with another strip of gauze. Loosen the tourniquet every five minutes to see if the bleeding has stopped and to allow blood to flow back to the limb.

Bandaging a Wounded Limb
Bandages can be applied at home to stop bleeding, to keep wounds clean, to support an injured area, and to deter a cat from scratching or excessively licking a wound until the cat can be taken to your veterinarian.

How to Handle a Broken Limb

If a limb is obviously fractured, do not try to splint it. You will only cause the cat a lot of pain and further damage the soft tissues around the fracture. If the fracture is accompanied by an open wound, gently cleanse the area with warm tap water and remove as much hair and debris from the wound as possible, dry the area with a clean towel, then apply a small amount of antibiotic ointment. Carefully cover the wound with a sterile nonstick pad and wrap lightly. Place the cat in a box and seek veterinary attention as soon as possible.

Signs of a possible fracture include a crooked limb, pain in and/or swelling of the limb, a piece of bone protruding through the skin, and reluctance to use the limb.

After cleaning and drying a wound on a limb, cover the wound with a clean nonstick bandage or pad and wrap it with adhesive tape in overlapping bands.

First, clean away any dirt in the wound with warm tap water or antiseptic solution. Carefully dry the area with a towel and apply a small amount of antibiotic ointment to the wound. Wrap the cleaned wound with a nonstick pad, gauze bandage, or a clean cloth. Securely (but not too tightly) wrap adhesive tape around the covering in overlapping bands, including hair on both sides of the bandage so it won't slip.

To avoid having the whole lower leg, paw, or tail end swell, the bandage must include all of the extremity. For example, if the wound is located on the ankle, apply a bandage from the ankle to the bottom of the paw.

What to Do If Your Cat Has a Seizure

Seizures, also called convulsions or fits, are caused by electrical malfunctions in the brain. They have a multitude of causes, among them poisoning, low blood sugar, infection, epilepsy, trauma, and tumors. Their potential for harm depends to a great extent on the underlying cause.

If your cat has a seizure, bear in mind that he is totally unaware of what he is doing. *Do not restrain your cat or put your finger in his mouth*; you may inadvertently injure your cat, and you are sure to be injured yourself. Move away any objects that may injure your cat during the convulsion. If necessary, carefully push the cat away from the edge of any surface he might fall from; use a broom, your hand wrapped in a towel, or even your foot. Seek immediate veterinary attention, especially if the seizure lasts more than a few minutes or if multiple seizures follow one after the other.

Reviving a Drowning Cat

Feline drowning is uncommon. Cats are cautious, sure-footed creatures and are not likely to end up in a body of water. (Kittens, though, have been known to climb up shower curtains and then fall off into toilet bowls; if you have a kitten, keep all toilet bowl lids down.) And though most cats don't particularly care to swim, they are actually adept at it. However, if a cat accidentally slips into water and is unable to get out, he can drown.

There is no need to try to resuscitate the cat if he is conscious. If he is unconscious, before performing CPR (see pages 320 and 321), water must be removed from the airways. Grasp the cat by both rear legs and hold him upside down to let the water drain out. If this does not work, swing the cat outward several times in a large circle; centrifugal force will move water trapped in the cat's airways out through his mouth. Be careful not to strike the cat on a nearby object or let him slip from your hands. Then make sure the mouth is cleared of debris and proceed with CPR.

What to Do If Your Cat Has Heatstroke

Heatstroke, a condition marked by extremely high body temperature, can occur when a cat is in a very hot environment, perhaps without access to water and/or a cool spot (such as in a hot parked car), and is unable to regulate his body temperature by panting. Shock, organ failure, a swelling of the brain, and death are possible consequences.

Signs of heatstroke include a rectal temperature over 105°F (40°C), excessive panting, a fast-pounding pulse, vomiting, seizure-like tremors, weakness, and collapse.

To treat heatstroke, try one or a combination of the following techniques until the cat's body temperature lowers and other signs of heatstroke abate:

- Pour cool water on the cat or apply a cool, wet rag.
- Apply ice to the head and between the thighs.
- Move the cat to an air-conditioned room or to a room with a fan.
- Monitor your cat's temperature (see page 314) when treating for heatstroke.

Overly aggressive treatment can result in hypothermia (excessively low body temperature); stop cooling methods when the cat's temperature reaches 103°F (39°C). Normal feline body temperature ranges from 100.4°F to 102.5°F (37.6° to 38.8°C) but can be as high as 103°F (39°C) if the cat is excited. See a veterinarian as soon as possible, even if the cat responds. Additional treatment, such as intravenous fluids, may be needed to prevent permanent organ damage.

What to Do If Your Cat Is Poisoned

If you suspect that your cat has ingested something poisonous, contact your veterinarian immediately. Signs of poisoning are extremely variable depending upon the poison ingested but may include vomiting, diarrhea, drooling, difficulty breathing, seizures, coma, and death. If possible, provide your vet with the following information: the full name of the product; the ingredients and their concentrations; the amount and dilution of the product ingested; the route of exposure (for example, did the cat eat the poison, drink it, or perhaps lick it off the fur?); the timing of the incident; the cat's behavior, including the progression of any signs exhibited by the cat; and a list of any treatments you have given the cat.

If your cat requires examination by your veterinarian, be sure to take along the container that held the toxic substance. If you do not know what kind of poison your cat ingested, save any vomitus for examination by your veterinarian.

When and How to Induce Vomiting

Although in some cases of poisoning it can help to induce vomiting, in others doing so can worsen the situation, so it is always best to speak to a veterinarian or poison control center—such as the ASPCA National Animal Poison Control Center, at 888-426-4435, 800-548-2423 (a per-case fee is charged to your credit card at these numbers), or 900-680-0000 (a per-minute fee is billed to your phone) before taking action. If more than several hours have elapsed since the poison was consumed, inducing vomiting is generally of no benefit.

• Never induce vomiting if the cat is unconscious because the vomit may

Preventing Poisoning

Hundreds of household products are potentially poisonous to animals—everything from various household cleansers to car-, lawn-, and garden-care products to human medication to some houseplants. Even chocolate is poisonous to cats. As a precaution, keep all potentially poisonous products out of the reach of your cat, do not leave open containers unattended, and make sure that containers are tightly sealed and properly labeled.

Cats are most likely to ingest household detergents and disinfectants by licking the substance off their fur or feet during grooming. Make sure that any surface that has been cleaned and/or disinfected is completely dry before a cat is allowed back on it. *Never use a detergent or disinfectant with pine oil or phenol on the list of ingredients around cats.* One of the safest, most effective, and most inexpensive disinfectants is a 1:32 dilution of household chlorine bleach in water (one-half cup of bleach per gallon of water). Mix a fresh batch of solution prior to each use, and do not mix it with any

ammonia-containing products. If your cat gets a toxic or irritating substance on his fur, rinse him with lukewarm water for 10 to 15 minutes.

If you have your lawn commercially treated with fertilizer, keep your cat indoors during application of the product, and for 24 hours afterward; water the lawn before allowing your cat to walk on it; and discourage your cat from eating the treated grass.

Make sure any flea product you apply is designed for use in cats. Some dog products are not safe for cats. Do not apply a flea product to a sick or debilitated cat without first checking with your veterinarian. Follow the label instructions scrupulously; resist the urge to over-apply the product. Do not apply a flea product unless you can monitor the cat closely for at least several hours after administration, as cats will usually exhibit a problem within hours after the product has been applied.

Cats can be poisoned by eating poisoned rodents or insects; use rodenticides and insecticides with caution, if at all.

run down into the lungs or obstruct the airways.

- Never induce vomiting if the cat has swallowed a corrosive substance (like strong acids or bases, and certain household detergents such as toilet bowl cleaner, lye, or dishwasher detergent) because it will damage tissue coming up just as it did going down.
- Never induce vomiting if the cat has consumed a petroleum distillate (like gasoline, kerosene, or paint thinner) because the consistency of the product may allow it to run backwards into the lungs and cause severe damage.
- Never induce vomiting if the cat has consumed a plant from the arum family (see Poisonous Plants on page 328).

It may be difficult to induce a cat to vomit; the methods and medications that are quite successful in other animals often don't work for cats. Try the following methods:

- Administer one to two teaspoons of a 1:1 mixture of 3 percent hydrogen peroxide and water by mouth; repeat once or twice at intervals of fifteen to twenty minutes if necessary. Do not administer more than three times.
- Administer one to two teaspoons of syrup of ipecac by mouth; repeat once after fifteen to twenty minutes if necessary.

If you don't have any of the above products to induce vomiting and your cat is conscious, give him milk (preferably) or water by mouth to dilute the ingested poison and take him to the veterinarian. Even if you succeed in getting the cat to vomit, you should still consult with your veterinarian.

Bites and Stings

Although venomous insects, snakes, and toads account for a smaller percentage of cat poisonings than household products, it's important to know what to do, just in case.

Yellow Jacket

Stinging Insects

Stinging insects such as bees, yellow jackets, wasps, and hornets inject a painful toxin into the skin. Cats are often stung on a paw or in the mouth as they try to bat or catch the insect. Pain and swelling at the site of the sting, the most common outcome, is rarely life-threatening, but severe swelling caused by a sting on the face or mouth may impede, or even obstruct, breathing. Some cats develop severe generalized reactions causing rapid breathing, rapid heart rate, and loss of balance regardless of where they were stung.

If your cat is stung, remove the stinger (if it is still there) by gently scraping it off with a stiff object such as a credit card or a thumb nail. (It's not a good idea to use tweezers or your fingers because if you squeeze the venom sac attached to the stinger, you may inject more toxin into the cat's skin.) Apply a cold pack to the site for ten to fifteen minutes; to be on the safe side, watch your cat closely for several hours afterward.

Call a veterinarian if the cat's face or mouth has been stung. Antihistamines and cortisone-like drugs prescribed by a veterinarian may help reduce swelling. Rarely, intravenous fluids, oxygen, or even an emergency tracheostomy are required.

Snakebites

If your cat is bitten by a nonpoisonous snake, clean the wound with an antiseptic solution and call a veterinarian. If your cat is bitten by a coral snake or pit viper (rattlesnakes, cottonmouths, and copperheads are in the pit viper family), *do not attempt any first aid at home;* keep the cat still and take him to a veterinarian as quickly as possible. Treatment must be aggressive, and usually involves IV fluids and antivenin, if available. Survival depends to a great extent on the size of the cat (bigger is better), the location of the bite (on the tongue or body is worse than on a limb), and the amount of venom injected into the wound.

The first sign of a bite by a snake in the pit viper family is swelling and redness that begins at the bite wound and progresses to surrounding areas. The tissue around the wound may actually die and slough away over time. Excessive bleeding, lethargy, rapid breathing, a rapid and irregular heartbeat, and/or death may

occur within a few hours. Over the course of a few days after the bite, a host of serious disorders may develop. Coral snake bites cause little pain or swelling at the bite wound. Instead, paralysis develops, resulting in death if the muscles responsible for breathing are profoundly affected.

Cane Toad

Toad Poisoning

The Colorado River Toad (*Bufo alvarius*), which is found in the Colorado Sonoran desert, and the Cane Toad (*Bufo marinus*), which lives along the Gulf Coast from Texas to Florida as well as in central Florida and the Caribbean, contain poisonous glands in their skin. Cats that pick up these toads in their mouths may become poisoned. Depending on the amount of toxin that gets in the mouth, poisoned cats will salivate profusely, collapse, and possibly die—all within fifteen minutes. Rinsing the mouth with water for five to ten minutes helps wash away the poison. Poisoned cats should be taken to a veterinarian immediately.

Poisonous Plants

Almost any plant can adversely affect a cat if sufficient quantities are ingested, but certain plants contain substances that can poison a cat even in small doses. Poisonous substances may be present in only certain parts of the plant, or only during certain seasons or stages of growth.

Fortunately, cases of plant poisoning in cats are fairly rare, at least partly because cats don't normally consume large amounts of plant matter. Kittens are more prone to plant poisoning; their natural curiosity and inclination to chew on things tend to get them in trouble. But even mature cats will sometimes eat houseplants, especially if they are bored or if there is a change in daily routine. A cat is most likely to eat a plant shortly after it has been brought into the home.

Learn the names of your houseplants and the plants in your yard—preferably both the common (English) and scientific (Latin) names—so that if your cat eats one of your plants, you can tell your veterinarian what it is (keep the labels from plants you buy). Bear in mind that it is common for cats to vomit after chewing on any plant, poisonous or not. If you suspect that your cat has eaten a poisonous plant, contact a veterinarian or poison control center immediately. The ASPCA National Animal Poison Control Center telephone number is 888-426-4435, 800-548-2423 (a per-case fee is charged to your credit card), or 900-680-0000 (a per-minute fee is billed to your phone).

Hundreds of plants are potentially poisonous to cats. Following is a brief list of some of the more common ones.

Amaryllis family
Hippeastrum species (e.g., amaryllis)
Narcissus species (e.g., daffodil)

Arum family
Alocasia antiquorum (Elephant's Ear)
Caladium species (e.g., Angel's Wings)
Dieffenbachia species (e.g., Dumb Cane)
Epipremnum aureum (Pothos)
Philodendron species (e.g., Sweetheart Plant)

Begonia family
Begonia semperflorens-cultorum (Wax Begonia)
Begonia tuberhybrida (Tuberous Begonia)

Bellflower family
Lobelia species (e.g., Lobelia)

Buttercup family
Delphinium species (e.g., Larkspur)
Aconitum species (e.g., Monkshood)

Carrot family
Cicuta maculata (Water Hemlock)
Conium maculatum (Poison Hemlock)

Daphne family
Daphne species (e.g., Rose Daphne)

Dogbane family
Nerium oleander (Rosebay)

Ginseng family
Hedera species (e.g., English Ivy)
Schefflera actinophylla (Umbrella Plant)

Heath family
Kalmia species (e.g., laurels)
Rhododendron species (e.g., rhododendrons, azaleas)

American Holly

Holly family
Ilex species (e.g., American Holly)

Horse Chestnut family
Aesculus hippocastanum (Horse Chestnut)

Lily family
Asparagus densiflorus (Asparagus Fern)
Convallaria majalis (Lily-of-the-Valley)
Lilium lancifolium (Tiger Lily)
Lilium longiflorum (Easter Lily)

Easter Lilies

Mistletoe family
Phoradendron serotinum (Mistletoe)

Nightshade family
Datura stramonium (Jimson Weed)
Solanum americanum (Common Nightshade)

Pea family
Abrus precatorius (Rosary Pea)

Snapdragon family
Digitalis purpurea (Foxglove)

Poinsettia

Spurge family
Euphorbia pulcherrima (Poinsettia)
Codiaeum variegatum (Croton)
Ricinus communis (Castor Bean)

Yew family
Taxus canadensis (Canada Yew)
Taxus cuspidata (Japanese Yew)

Household Poisons

If you suspect your cat has ingested a poisonous product, consult a veterinarian immediately. This chart is meant to alert you to possible signs of poisoning and to inform you of potential veterinary treatment.

Poison	Signs	Treatment
Insecticides such as flea and/or tick sprays and shampoos, especially those containing the chemical permethin, and roach and/or ant sprays	Muscle tremors, excessive drooling, vomiting, diarrhea, incoordination, breathing difficulty, convulsions. Potentially fatal.	Vet may suggest bathing the cat in body-temperature water and pet shampoo (not a flea shampoo!) before bringing him in. Make sure cat does not become chilled. Vomiting may help if insecticide is ingested.
Rodent poisons such as warfarin, brodifacoum, and other anticoagulants	Weakness, pale gums, external bleeding (from the nose, mouth, or wounds), gastrointestinal or urinary bleeding, breathing difficulty. Signs may take several days to appear. Potentially fatal.	Vomiting may help if induced within a few hours of ingestion. Treatment and antidotes administered by vet often successful if given quickly enough.
Antifreeze	Lack of coordination followed 8 or so hours later by extreme listlessness, vomiting, kidney pain or swelling, seizures, and coma. Potentially fatal; one tablespoon of standard 50:50 antifreeze mixture can kill an average-size cat.	Vomiting may help if induced within a few hours of ingestion. Once signs are evident, vomiting is of no benefit. Cat must receive appropriate treatment (including an antidote of ethanol) by veterinarian within hours of exposure to have chance of survival.
Acetaminophen (ingredient in some nonaspirin painkillers, such as Tylenol)	Gums may turn blue-brown, cat may experience breathing difficulty, and face and paws may swell; weakness, profound lethargy, and vomiting are also common. Potentially fatal.	Vomiting may help if induced within a few hours of ingestion. Treatment, including antidote (N-acetylcysteine), is most successful if cat is hospitalized within an hour or so after ingesting drug.

Poison	Signs	Treatment
Nonsteroidal anti-inflammatory drugs (NSAIDs) such as Advil and Motrin	Low dose: lack of coordination, vomiting, and abdominal pain due to gastric ulcers. High dose: kidney failure or sudden death due to respiratory and heart failure.	Vomiting may help if induced within 2 or 3 hours of ingestion. Prompt treatment at a veterinary hospital is often successful.
Lawn fertilizers	Vomiting and diarrhea. Usually not fatal.	Most cats do well as long as they receive appropriate treatment by vet to control vomiting and diarrhea and to treat resulting dehydration.
Household cleansers, detergents, disinfectants	Oral lesions, vomiting, diarrhea, lethargy, collapse, and coma. Potentially fatal.	Do not induce vomiting. Veterinary treatment involves fluid therapy and medication to soothe the stomach.
Chocolate	Small quantity: vomiting, diarrhea, excitation, or weakness; usually not fatal. Large quantity: seizure and/or heart disturbances. One ounce of baking chocolate, 4 ounces of sweet cocoa, or 10 ounces of milk chocolate can kill a 10-pound cat.	Poisoned cats are likely to have vomited already. If not, vomiting may help if induced within 2 or 3 hours of ingestion. Treatment to control dehydration, seizures, and heart disturbances may be necessary.

The Beginning and End of Life:

Times for Special Care

Much of this book is devoted to the everyday needs of growing kittens and adult cats. Because there are other important times in your cat's life, it is necessary also to consider special-care situations: mating and birth, and the senior years. It is the ASPCA's founding purpose to safeguard the health and well-being of animals. To help further that purpose, pet owners should leave breeding to qualified, reputable individuals. Choose a pet conscientiously, and remain wholeheartedly committed to meeting that pet's needs throughout her entire life.

Mating and birth are discussed here only to present a complete overview of feline life and health, not as encouragement to breed your cat. If your cat does become pregnant—or if you adopt a pregnant cat from a shelter—consult immediately with your veterinarian (and, if possible, with qualified breeders) and educate yourself on the subject by reading the books listed in the Recommended Reading appendix and any other literature that your veterinarian suggests.

In their senior years, cats require extra attention from their owners, so the end of this chapter outlines specific advice for attending to your pet's needs as she grows older. It also addresses the important choices you and your veterinarian will need to make at the end of your cat's life and some emotional issues you may face.

Kittens are incredibly cute, but owners should resist the temptation to breed their cats.

Mating, Pregnancy, and Birth

If you are interested in breeding your cat, first seriously consider all of the reasons why you shouldn't do so. The two most compelling reasons are that millions of unwanted cats are euthanized every year and that neutering your cat has significant medical and behavioral benefits outlined in detail on page 338. If after considering this information you still want to breed your cat, educate yourself about all aspects of the process—including the medical facts and the financial and time commitments required—join a local cat club to learn as much as possible about your breed and how to care for it, and promise to care for both the parents and the kittens conscientiously. Only good-tempered, healthy cats screened for hereditary disorders (such as kidney problems) are suitable for breeding. All cats that are not going to be bred should be neutered to prevent accidental pregnancies and unwanted kittens.

If you allow your cat to breed, you are responsible for the health and well-being of the kittens and the mother cat.

Feline Reproductive Cycles

Female cats are seasonally polyestrous, which means their reproductive (estrous) cycles occur during a certain part of the year—their "breeding season." Timing and frequency of the cycles (which generally last about two weeks) is determined at least in part by the season of the year, and there is much variation from cat to cat. The feline breeding season usually begins in January or February and extends through September or early October. A cat typically has three estrous cycles per breeding season. The first usually occurs between mid-January and early March, the second between April and June, and the third between July and September.

The reproductive cycle of female cats is quite complex, and consists of several phases. Estrus, also known as "heat," is the part of the estrous cycle when the female is fertile and will allow mating. On average, this phase lasts about seven days. As estrus sets in, the female cat's behavior changes dramatically: she rubs against objects, rolls about, purrs, kneads her paws, meows more than usual, and may even spray urine. As true estrus ensues, the cat adopts breeding postures meant to allow a male to mount and mate. If not mated, she may repeat this behavior in one or two weeks, or even sooner.

See page 194 for explanations and anatomical illustrations of the male and female feline reproductive systems. See page 224 for general information about feline sexual behavior.

The behavior of cats in heat may resemble that induced by catnip, with much paw-kneading and rolling about.

Reasons Not to Breed Your Cat

- Millions of unwanted cats are euthanized every year.
- Neutering your cat has significant health and behavioral benefits (see page 338).
- It's hard work that requires a great deal of energy and attention.
- It's expensive. Few breeders ever break even financially, much less make money. Be aware of the financial burden you'll be taking on.
- It's a long-term commitment, and your responsibilities literally multiply with each litter. Remember, even if you sell or give away the kittens, you are responsible for them. You must find them good homes and be prepared to take them back if the new owners are not providing for them properly or decide that they do not want them.
- It requires a rigorous education. To be a good breeder, you have to understand feline genetics, infectious diseases, and, of course, reproduction.
- Although most healthy cats do not experience complications during pregnancy and delivery, you are still putting your cat's life at unnecessary risk by allowing her to breed.

Mating

For a few hours to just minutes before mating, the female cat alternates between assuming the breeding posture (rear end elevated, tail to the side) and rolling around from side to side while calling to the male.

The male (tom) then approaches her and attempts to sniff her hindquarters. He may circle around her and make calling sounds himself.

The female may rebuff the male's initial approach by striking out at him, but sooner or later she welcomes his advances.

The male carefully approaches the female and grasps the skin of her neck with his teeth. He then straddles her. She arches her back, elevates her rear end, treads with her hindlimbs, and moves her tail to the side. When his penis enters her vagina, ovulation (release of an egg) is induced, virtually guaranteeing pregnancy. The length of time from the neck bite to actual mating can be almost ten minutes, but copulation itself is completed in just a few seconds.

After mating, the female gives a piercing wail, and if the male is not quick to retreat, she attacks him. She then proceeds to lick her genital area and roll around on the ground; the male waits nearby, and may also lick himself. He may approach her again within just a few minutes; if rejected, he will try again in another few minutes.

Cats have been known to mate as often as once an hour during a thirty-six hour period. If more than one male is present, as is typically the case with strays, several males may mate with the female, in which case littermates may have different fathers.

Pregnancy

An experienced veterinarian can usually diagnose pregnancy by gently feeling the abdomen anywhere between twenty to thirty days after mating. If necessary, an ultrasound can confirm the condition. (Owners should not attempt to determine if a cat is pregnant by probing her abdomen, as doing so could harm the fetuses.) As her pregnancy progresses, the female's abdomen swells, sometimes dramatically enough to impair her activity. Depending on the number of kittens she is carrying, she may gain between two and three pounds. About two to three weeks after mating, the female's nipples change to a rosy pink color, and they begin to enlarge at about four weeks. Gestation usually lasts an average of sixty-five days.

Pregnant cats should have constant access to food. A cat will begin to eat more almost as soon as she becomes pregnant, and toward the end of the pregnancy she will consume up to one and a half times her normal diet. There is no need to change the type of food you provide your pregnant cat as long as you are already feeding her properly (see page 234).

Resist the temptation to give your pregnant cat additional vitamins and minerals—she will receive all she needs from a proper diet, and supplementation actually may be harmful. If at all possible, avoid administering medications or vaccinations during pregnancy (consult with your vet about this). Cats that normally go outside should be kept indoors about two weeks before they are expected to deliver to keep them from giving birth in a cold or unsafe place.

Pregnant cat, three days before giving birth to seven kittens

Benefits of Spaying and Neutering

All cats that are not going to be bred should be neutered. Not only does the procedure reduce the number of accidental pregnancies and unwanted kittens, it also has health and behavioral benefits. It protects cats of both sexes against cancers of the reproductive system, and neutering also prevents a host of disruptive sexual behaviors, including howling and urine marking. Neutered males are also generally less apt to roam and fight with other males. Contrary to a common misperception, neutered cats do not lose their pep, though some may gain weight. Diet and exercise can keep weight gain to a minimum. Your veterinarian is best prepared to neuter your cat, but if the expense of the procedure is a critical consideration, you may be able to locate a low-cost spaying and neutering facility in your area by contacting your local shelter or humane society or calling 800-248-SPAY.

Nesting Box At least ten days to two weeks prior to expected delivery, provide your pregnant cat with a nesting box. It should be large enough to allow her to stretch out but not so large to permit the kittens to wiggle too far from their mother. Place the box in a warm, dry, secluded area away from drafts, and line it with something that will be easy to clean. Avoid shaggy material with loops or fringe that could entangle a tiny limb, as well as loose towels that a kitten could crawl under. Take the cat to the nesting box regularly so she becomes used to it.

If you don't provide your cat with a nesting box, she may find a place more suitable to her but less to your liking.

Birth

A day or two before a cat gives birth, her mammary glands will enlarge, filling with milk. If you have a longhaired cat, carefully clip some of the hair away from the nipples so they are more accessible to the kittens.

When delivery time is near (about twelve to twenty-four hours away), the cat will begin to exhibit nesting behavior by visiting the box frequently and scratching about to arrange the bedding to her liking. At this point, you should confine the cat to the room with the nesting box. Make sure she has easy access to food, water, and a litter box.

Anywhere from two to twenty-four hours before delivery, the cat may appear somewhat restless, refuse to eat, vomit, pace, pant, meow excessively, and/or make frequent visits to the nesting box. She will eventually settle down in her box, shift positions periodically, and lick her genital area. She may purr loudly even though she appears to be uncomfortable.

When delivery begins (sometimes preceded by the flow of an egg-white-like discharge from the cat's vulva), most cats lie on their sides while rhythmically contracting their abdominal muscles. As the contractions continue, a kitten, usually still encased in its membrane, appears at the

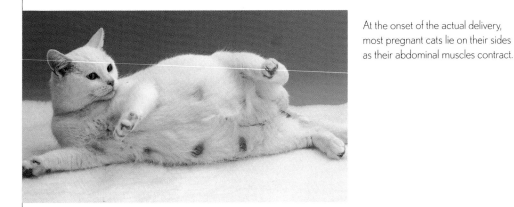

At the onset of the actual delivery, most pregnant cats lie on their sides as their abdominal muscles contract.

The kitten still encased in its membrane appears at the vulva.

vulva. The kitten is usually fully delivered within just a few minutes. Expect to see a greenish (and possibly blood-tinged) discharge with the passage of kittens.

Once a kitten has exited the birth canal (either head- or feet-first is normal), the mother cat licks away any membranes that surround him and massages and dries him with her tongue. The mother will usually deliver the placenta along with, or a few minutes after, each kitten, but sometimes two or more kittens may be delivered before their placentas pass. The mother will chew away the umbilical cord to free the kitten, and may also eat the placenta. Then, in preparation for the birth of the next kitten, the mother cleans her vaginal area. It is common for a mother to nurse the just-born kittens even while she is in labor. Half an hour to an hour usually separates the delivery of each of the kittens. However, some cats have been known to deliver one or two kittens and then wait for another day before delivering the rest of the litter, especially if some other pressing event interrupts her or if she senses too much human intervention. After all the kittens are born and the placentas passed, the contractions cease and the cat relaxes and continues to clean and nurse her kittens. Four or five kittens per litter is average.

The mother cat may eat the placenta of her newborn kittens, as shown here.

The mother cat may nurse and nuzzle her new kittens while she awaits the next delivery.

Your Role During Delivery

The owner's role during delivery is to observe closely and intervene as little as possible. Healthy cats rarely experience any problems during delivery, and an owner's best-intended efforts to help usually only complicate matters. Because of the variation in normal deliveries, however, it is often difficult for an owner to know if things are progressing as they should.

When to Call the Vet During Delivery Two signs of trouble during delivery are *excessive bleeding* (more than approximately two teaspoons—this is heavy bleeding for a

Newborn kittens huddle together for warmth.

cat) and *strong contractions persisting for more than an hour with no kitten delivered.* Call the veterinarian if you see either of these signs, and be prepared to transport your cat to the hospital or emergency clinic as quickly as possible.

When to Intervene You should also call the vet if a kitten is partially protruding from the vulva for more than several minutes despite strong contractions. However, you may not have time to get to the hospital. Your best chance at saving the kitten may be to assist in the delivery at home; if possible, confirm with your vet that you should do so before proceeding. Wash your hands, grasp whatever part of the kitten is protruding, and then pull gently on the kitten—not straight out, but backward and downward at about a 45-degree angle to the mother cat's backbone. You may find it easier to hold onto a slippery kitten if you grab it with a piece of sterile gauze. Time your pulls with the contractions. Gentleness is essential—pulling too hard can easily harm the mother or kill the kitten.

If you see that a newborn kitten is being ignored by its mother, pick it up in a warm clean towel and remove the surrounding membrane, which will still be attached to the kitten by the umbilical cord. Dry the kitten with the towel and make sure it is breathing.

If the kitten is not breathing, wipe dry the inside of its mouth with a piece of sterile gauze, and in your cupped hands hold the kitten cradled on its back with its head facing away from you. Then raise your arms and swing the kitten downward in an arc several times to force liquid from the lungs. Vigorously rub the kitten all over its body for several minutes to stimulate breathing.

If you succeed in resuscitating the kitten (or if the mother has not chewed through the cord attached to a kitten that did not need resuscitation), you will need to cut the umbilical cord. Tie a piece of thread tightly around the cord about an inch away from the kitten's body. Then, using clean scissors, cut the cord about half an inch away from the thread, farther down the cord toward the placenta. It's a good idea to dip the end of the cord in a small amount of iodine.

Mother cat with week-old kitten

Signs of Trouble After Delivery Even if the delivery has seemed uneventful, problems can develop after birthing appears to be complete. Contact your veterinarian immediately if the cat acts lethargic, has a fever, fails to eat or drink within a day or two after delivery, acts as though she is in pain, continues to strain, ignores her kittens, continues to bleed from the vulva, emits a foul-smelling discharge from the vulva, or has painful, hard, or swollen mammary glands.

Postnatal Care

It is not uncommon for a nursing cat to require up to three times the number of calories she needed before pregnancy, so it is best to allow the new mother constant access to her usual food. Of course, fresh clean water should always be available. Make sure the nest area is kept very warm and draft-free.

For the first day or two following delivery, the mother cat remains with her kittens constantly. You can place a litter box and food and water bowls nearby, but most moms won't be interested. Owners should refrain from overhandling the kittens for at least the first week; doing so will likely upset the mother. To properly socialize

kittens to humans, it's most important to handle them during the so-called "early sensitization period," from about the second week of life to the seventh. Children should not handle kittens until they're three weeks old.

Newborn kittens nurse up to three times an hour. In the rare event that the mother cat does not produce enough milk, her hungry kittens will constantly cry and fail to stay at the nipple. Unless they are hand-fed commercial feline formula or allowed to nurse from another lactating cat, the kittens will not survive. Contact your veterinarian for advice on hand-feeding kittens. If a kitten refuses to nurse, feels cold to the touch, draws away from the other kittens, or is rejected by

Mother nursing six-week-old kittens

the mother (if she fails to lick the kitten or attend to its crying), the kitten may be abnormal. Rejected kittens can be hand-fed but often do not survive.

Kittens double in weight in the first week; normal birth weight is around three and a half ounces (one hundred grams), although it varies depending on several factors, including breed and the number of kittens in the litter. A weight gain of a quarter-ounce to half an ounce (seven to fifteen grams) per day until weaning is normal. Kittens that fail to gain weight are at much greater risk of disease and death during the early days to weeks of life.

After each feeding, the mother cat meticulously grooms each kitten, paying particular attention to the face and anal region. Kittens lack the ability to urinate or defecate on their own until they are about two to three weeks of age; the mother cat's licking of the anal area stimulates these essential functions, and she ingests their urine and feces as they pass. However unsavory-sounding to humans, this arrangement is absolutely necessary to help keep the nest area clean.

The kittens' eyes and ears usually begin to open somewhere between six and fourteen days after birth. By about two weeks of age, kittens will play with objects, and by three weeks they tend to paw and bite at each other. By a month of age, they will joyfully scratch about in a litter box, vigorously batting the loose litter around. By five weeks they stalk and chase each other, and wrestling is the name of the game by seven weeks.

Mother's milk alone supplies all the nutritional needs for healthy kittens for about a month, at which time the kittens need supplemental food. When the kittens reach about three to four weeks of age, make a gruel by mixing a small amount of warm water in with the cat's food (or a specially designed "kitten food" or growth formula), and place it in a shallow dish. Allow the kittens ready access to their food several times daily. At first they will walk and run through the dish and basically make a mess of themselves—they often begin sampling food by licking it off themselves and each other—but with time the kittens will begin to eat this semisolid mixture; by five weeks they should consume it readily. At about six or seven weeks of age, kittens are able to chew dry food, so there is no longer any need to moisten the diet.

Eight-week-old kittens playing

Most kittens are fully weaned by eight weeks of age.

Weaning Kittens

Weaning is a process that begins at three to four weeks when you begin to offer the kittens food. As the kittens approach six to eight weeks of age, most mother cats finish weaning their kittens by chasing them away when they attempt to nurse and by lying in elevated areas where the kittens can't reach her. If they are more than eight weeks of age and fully weaned, the kittens can be adopted out as soon as desired, though it may be better to wait until they are ten to twelve weeks of age to be sure they are well socialized (many breeders prefer to wait until the kittens are at least four months old in order to assess their fitness for showing).

Weaned kittens should be placed in an area away from the mother cat with their own litter box, feeding and watering dishes, and scratch posts. Be sure the litter box has relatively low sides so the kittens can get in and out easily, and use a nonclumping litter until the kittens are three months of age. Very young kittens may ingest litter; if they ingest enough clumping litter, it could cause intestinal problems. Proper litter box and scratch post behavior—acquired through a combination of instinct and observation of the mother—should be well in hand by this time, but some reinforcement may be necessary. Make sure to place the scratching post in a prominent area, preferably near where the kittens sleep, as many cats like to scratch after a nap. Encourage the kittens to use the post by placing a favorite toy on top, rubbing it with catnip, by making scratching motions on the post, and/or by having a cat that uses the post around for the kittens to observe.

Be sure to take the kittens for a full veterinary exam and their first vaccinations when they are about six to eight weeks old. It is particularly important to have them vaccinated before sending them off to their new owners' homes.

Older Years

With proper care, many cats can live well into their teens, and a few into their twenties (cats of Siamese lineage purportedly tend to live the longest). Sadly, though, it seems that no beloved cat ever lives long enough. The next few pages provide guidance for taking care of your aging cat, including how to prepare yourself for the death of a pet, when to consider euthanasia, and what this humane act entails.

Extra Veterinary Attention

Many veterinarians like to schedule twice-yearly examinations for their healthy older patients, and even more frequently for those with health problems. Various laboratory tests (for example, to check thyroid, liver, or kidney function) may be suggested as part of a routine healthy geriatric cat evaluation. Also, it's especially important to have your older cat weighed regularly on an accurate scale, preferably the same one each time, as even a subtle change in weight can be significant.

Common Medical Concerns with Older Cats

The most common causes of death in geriatric cats are kidney failure, cancer, and infectious disease. Hyperthyroidism, inflammatory bowel disease, kidney disease, and diabetes mellitus are the chronic diseases that most commonly afflict older cats (see Common Feline Health Problems, beginning on page 281).

Aside from these disorders, older cats experience normal age-related deterioration of many body functions, just as people

Older cats such as this eighteen-year-old may not devote as much attention to grooming as they once did; hair mats can become a problem in longhaired cats.

do. The immune system becomes less able to stave off certain infections. Muscle tone diminishes along with bone and joint strength, as a cause and an effect of reduced activity. Obesity can become a concern, although very old cats often lose body weight. Some degree of hearing and vision impairment is inevitable, making unattended outdoor excursions more dangerous. Arthritis, though often less obvious in cats than in dogs, may cause a decrease in activity. Older cats devote even more hours to slumber. Constipation is another common problem with older cats.

Senility also afflicts cats; senile felines may act confused, wandering about the house, getting stuck in a corner, or even getting lost in the house. Lifelong faithful users of the litter box may begin making occasional "mistakes," urinating or defecating elsewhere.

Extra Help with the Litter Box

You can't always blame geriatric litter box mistakes on mental deterioration. Medical conditions such as kidney disease, hyperthyroidism, or diabetes cause cats to produce more urine, and oldsters sometimes have a hard time making it to the box on time. If you suspect that your older cat may be suffering from one of these common afflictions of the senior years, consult with your veterinarian. You can also try to make the litter box more accessible, perhaps by placing several boxes around the home, or by purchasing boxes with lower sides or even fashioning a sort of ramp up into the box(es).

Weight loss is common in older cats with impaired senses of smell and taste.

How Old Is Your Cat?

The old standard that one "cat year" equals seven "people years" is not quite accurate. Early feline development is much more accelerated than early human development; birth, puberty, and adulthood are all attained within the first year and a half to two years of a cat's life. A one-year-old cat is more like a 15-year-old person, and a two-year-old cat is more like a 24-year-old person. For each year thereafter, every "cat year" equals about four "human years." Therefore, a six-year-old cat has a phys-iological age that is roughly equivalent to that of a 40-year-old person, a 15-year-old cat compares to a 76-year-old person, and a 20-year-old cat compares to a 96-year-old person.

Exactly when is a cat is considered old? The World Health Organization classifies people from 60 to 74 years of age as "elderly," and those from 75 and older as "aged." If we apply our human age/cat age formula, an elderly cat would be about 12 to 15, and an aged cat would be about 15 and over.

Veterinarians often recommend that older cats such as this sixteen-year-old get checkups more than once a year.

Extra Grooming

Older cats spend less time grooming themselves, and matted fur may become a problem, especially in longhaired cats. Geriatric cats usually need some special attention. Not only do extra grooming sessions keep the senior cat's coat healthy, but they may also provide additional opportunities to examine your cat closely. Look for lumps, lesions, and particularly bad breath, and keep in touch with your veterinarian (see also the Mini–Physical Exam on page 268).

Special Dietary Needs

It's very important to monitor your older cat's food intake, as a decrease in appetite is often an early sign that a problem is developing or worsening. Older cats lose some sense of smell and taste, making them even more prone to appetite loss when ill. Disease in the mouth, common in older cats, can also cause a cat to lose interest in her dinner; signs of oral health problems include tooth-chattering, chewing only on one side, and dropping food. You can encourage old cats to eat by feeding them from wide, shallow, easily accessible bowls; by warming food to body temperature (warming food may also emit enticing aromas); by feeding them in a quiet environment; by providing a tasty, easily chewed canned diet; and by stroking them gently while they eat.

Cats with specific medical problems—for example, diabetes mellitus, chronic kidney failure, or inflammatory bowel disease—will benefit from diets specifically formulated for those conditions. Although there is little scientific evidence to suggest that feeding anything other than a nutritionally balanced and complete diet is beneficial for healthy cats, low-protein diets are sometimes automatically recommended once cats reach a certain age.

Older cats with kidney problems need to drink more water than healthy cats. You can encourage such cats to increase their water intake by giving them bottled water; by allowing them to drink out of the faucet; by providing several easily accessible sources of water throughout the home; or perhaps by flavoring water with ice cubes made with chicken broth.

Euthanasia

If an illness or injury is terminal and there is no hope for a cure, then euthanasia (literally "good death") is often suggested as a way of sparing a cat needless suffering. The procedure usually involves the injection of a medication that causes the cat to slip away peacefully and painlessly within seconds. While euthanasia enables owners to spare their cat the pain that may accompany natural death, it can burden the owner with a very difficult decision. For many, choosing to euthanize their cat is even more difficult than dealing with the loss itself.

To come to a decision regarding euthanasia, you might ask your veterinarian some of the following questions:

- Can you tell me if my cat is suffering?
- What kinds of treatments are available? What would the cost be?
- What might treatment accomplish? Can I expect a cure, alleviation of pain, or prolongation of life?
- What kind of care will I need to provide at home?

Even though your veterinarian will answer as many of your questions as possible, ultimately the decision rests with you. A few questions you might ask yourself:

- What is my cat's quality of life?
- Is he comfortable and happy? With treatment, will his quality of life improve or worsen?
- How much longer can I reasonably expect my cat to live?

If you decide to have your cat euthanized, discuss with your veterinarian whether you or other family members should be present. Most veterinarians will allow or even encourage the family to participate; some will perform the procedure at your home so that the cat can die in the peace of his own environment. Ask your veterinarian to explain in advance the details of the procedure so you know what to expect. As painful as it may seem, you will also need to decide how the remains should be handled.

Coping with Loss

The death of a beloved cat is never easy. Guilt, regret, anger, uncertainty, terrible sadness, and/or feelings of emptiness may accompany the loss. But remember that it is important to allow yourself time to grieve. Do not hesitate to seek professional help if you begin to feel seriously depressed or if you just need someone to talk to.

Most veterinarians can suggest professionals trained in grief counseling. An organization called the Delta Society provides a national directory of pet loss counselors, publications on pet loss, and contacts for pet loss support groups nationwide. Pet loss telephone hotlines, available from the ASPCA and many veterinary colleges, can also lend support. See the appendix Important Telephone Numbers.

When to Adopt Again

A new cat will not replace your deceased pet in your affections or your heart but can help ease the pain of the loss. The right time to adopt again is a very personal decision. Some people choose to bring home a new cat right away; others need months to mourn. Do whatever feels right to you and your family. A new cat will bring laughter and companionship into your home. When you are ready, there is a cat waiting to share his life with you.

Glossary of Cat-Related Terms

Agouti hairs Hairs marked with alternating bands of light and dark color and ending in a dark tip. In the tabby pattern, agouti hairs compose the lighter areas of the coat. *See also* Nonagouti hairs.

Awn hairs One of two hair types in the cat's topcoat. *See also* Down hairs, Guard hairs.

Backcross To breed a cat with one of its parents.

Bicolor A two-colored coat pattern composed of white and patches of another color, usually on the back, tail, and head.

Britches The longer, thicker hair found on the back of a cat's upper hindlegs.

Calico A coat pattern with patches of white and more prominent red and black or cream and blue markings.

Cat registry An organization that keeps a registry of purebred cats, such as the American Cat Fanciers' Association.

Cattery An establishment devoted to the breeding of cats.

Chinchilla A ticked coat pattern in which the hairs are light or white except for a tip of darker color at the ends.

Classic tabby A tabby coat pattern featuring large, swirling stripes on the back and legs and blotches on the flanks.

Cobby A short and heavy-boned body type.

Colorpoint A pointed coat pattern in which the points are unmarked. *See also* Pointed.

Deep color A rich coat color, such as black or red, that is seen when the coloration is evenly distributed along the hair shaft.

Dilute color A less saturated coat color, such as gray or cream, that is seen when the coloration is unevenly distributed along the hair shaft.

Domestic shorthair A common house cat, or nonpurebred cat.

Double coat A coat in which the undercoat is particularly thick and dense.

Down hairs The soft secondary hairs in the undercoat that provide additional insulation. *See also* Awn hairs, Guard hairs.

Estrous The female reproductive cycle.

Estrus The phase of the estrous cycle when a cat is fertile (commonly called "heat").

Euthanasia The use of deliberate medical means, usually lethal injection, to cause death. Used to avoid suffering in sick and aging pets, and to limit populations of cats in shelters.

Feral cat An untamed domestic cat living in the wild.

Free-choice feeding A method of feeding in which food is left out for the cat to eat at will.

Guard hairs The coarse, thick, protective hairs in the topcoat. *See also* Awn hairs, Down hairs.

Head bunting A feline head-rubbing gesture used as a scent-marking practice and also as a sign of affection.

Heat *See* Estrus.

Lynx point A pointed coat pattern in which the points have tabby stripes. *See also* Pointed.

Mackerel tabby A tabby coat pattern with fishbone stripes.

Mitted A coat pattern marked with white on the paws, chin, chest, belly, and back legs.

Neuter To render incapable of breeding by surgically removing reproductive organs—the testes in males, the ovaries and uterus in females ("spaying").

Nictitating membrane A thin protective membrane (sometimes called the "third eyelid") located at the inner corner of the eye.

Nonagouti hairs Unbanded hairs that give the cat's coat a solid pattern and that make up the dark stripes or spots in tabby coats. *See also* Agouti hairs.

Odd-eyed cat A cat with two different colored irises.

Oriental type A fine-boned, long-legged, and tubular body type.

Outcross To breed a cat with another cat of a different breed in order to strengthen the stock, refine and build features, and increase color varieties.

Patched tabby *See* Torbie.

Pedigree The line of parentage; in purebred cats, a certificate of unmixed breeding.

Piebald A coat pattern featuring a combination of white and any other color or pattern.

Pointed A coat pattern featuring a light-colored torso marked with darker shades at the body's extremities (ears, muzzle, paws, and tail).

Polydactyly Literally, "many fingers"; a genetic mutation that causes cats to have extra toes on their paws.

Purebred A cat descended from unmixed parentage within a single, recognized breed.

Ruff A collar of fur around the neck.

Shaded A ticked coat pattern in which the light bands of the hairs are even lighter and wider and the dark bands narrower.

Silver A coat in which the yellowish coloration has been suppressed in part of the hair shaft, leaving it pale or white and giving the cat a "silvery" appearance. *See also* Chinchilla, Shaded, Smoke.

Single coat A coat in which the undercoat is relatively thin.

Smoke A solid coat in which the base of the hairs are lightened or whitened.

Socialization The process by which a cat grows accustomed to the presence of humans and other animals.

Spay To sterilize a female cat by surgically removing the ovaries and most of the uterus.

Spotted tabby A tabby coat pattern with dark blotches or spots against a background of agouti hairs.

Tabby Any of a variety of common coat patterns produced by a combination of nonagouti hairs (in the characteristic stripes and blotches) and

agouti hairs (in between the stripes). The four traditional tabby patterns are mackerel, classic, spotted, and ticked.

Ticked tabby A tabby coat pattern in which the entire coat features banded agouti hairs.

Topcoat The cat's protective coat of coarse guard and awn hairs. Also called the outercoat.

Torbie A tortoiseshell coat pattern that is also marked by one of the four tabby patterns. Also known as a "patched tabby."

Tortie point A type of pointed coat pattern in which the points have a tortoiseshell pattern. *See also* Pointed.

Tortoiseshell A coat pattern typically marked by both black and red fur in deep coats or blue and cream fur in dilute coats.

Undercoat The portion of a cat's coat beneath the topcoat that consists of down hairs.

Urine marking Traces of urine left by cats to mark their territory or signal their presence in the breeding season. Occasionally used to signal stress about a problem (such as overcrowding) in the household.

Van A piebald-type coat pattern in which most of the body is white, with small patches of color mainly on the head and tail.

Important Telephone Numbers

Veterinarian _____

Animal emergency clinic _____

Boarding facility _____

Pet sitter _____

ASPCA Companion Animal Services Behavior Helpline
212-876-7700 ext. HELP (4357) Free general behavior and care information.

ASPCA National Animal Poison Control Center
888-426-4435 Consultation fee charged, payable by major credit card.
800-548-2423 Consultation fee charged, payable by major credit card.
900-680-0000 Consultation fee charged to your phone number.

Dr. Louis J. Camuti Memorial Feline Consultation and Diagnostic Service
800-KITTY-DR (800-548-8937) Consultation fee charged, payable by major credit card. This service of the Cornell Feline Health Center provides information on feline diseases and management.

Pet Loss Support Hotlines (grief counseling)
800-404-7387 PetFriends, Inc. Returns long-distance calls collect; free for southern NJ and the Philadelphia area.
602-995-5885 The Companion Animal Association of Arizona. 24-hour grief counseling, support groups, and referrals. No fee.
530-752-4200 Staffed by University of California-Davis veterinary students. No fee.
630-603-3994 Staffed by the Chicago Veterinary Medical Association. No fee.
607-253-3932 Staffed by Cornell University veterinary students. No fee.
888-478-7574 Staffed by Iowa State University veterinary students. No fee.
517-432-2696 Staffed by Michigan State University veterinary students. No fee.
614-292-1823 Staffed by Ohio State University veterinary students. No fee.
508-839-7966 Staffed by Tufts University veterinary students. No fee.

540-231-8038 Staffed by Virginia-Maryland Regional College of Veterinary Medicine students. No fee.
212-876-7700 ext. 4355 Staffed by ASPCA Counseling Services. No fee.

Spay USA
800-248-SPAY This free service will help you locate a low-cost spaying and neutering facility in your area.

Breed Registries

Breed registries or breed registering organizations are helpful on several fronts. Should you wish to get a purebred cat, they are an excellent resource for finding a reputable breeder. Registries are responsible for maintaining strict guidelines to assure the purity of all the cats they register, and sometimes specify standards used to define the breed's ideal physical attributes (i.e., coat length and color, eye shape and color, body shape). Registries also sponsor shows for both purebred and nonpurebred cats. Before you enter your cat in a show, you should attend a few as a spectator. Show schedules can be obtained from the registries themselves or from such magazines as *Cat Fancy* and *Cats* and on the Internet (http://www.fanciers.com). Following is a list of the largest and best-established breed registries in the United States, Canada, and Europe.

The American Association of Cat Enthusiasts (AACE)
P.O. Box 213
Pine Brook, NJ 07058
Tel: 973-335-6717
http://www.aaceinc.org
E-mail: info@aaceinc.org

American Cat Association
8101 Katherine Avenue
Panorama City, CA 91402
Tel: 818-781-5656

American Cat Fanciers Association (ACFA)
P.O. Box 203
Point Lookout, MO 65726
Tel: 417-334-5430
http://www.acfacat.com
E-mail: acfa@aol.com

Canadian Cat Association/ Association Féline Canadienne (CCA/AFC)
220 Advance Boulevard, Suite 101
Brampton, Ontario L6T 4J5
Canada
Tel: 905-459-1481
http://www.cca-afc.com
E-mail: office@cca-afc.com

The Cat Fanciers' Association (CFA)
P.O. Box 1005
Manasquan, NJ 08736-0805
Tel: 732-528-9797
http://www.cfainc.org
E-mail: cfa@cfainc.org

Cat Fanciers Federation (CFF)
P.O. Box 661
Gratis, OH 45330
Tel: 937-787-9009
http://www.cffinc.org
E-mail: cff@siscom.net

Cats United International
1624 Santa Clara Drive #140
Roseville, CA 95661
Tel: 916-783-7668
http://www.catsunited.com
E-mail: cats@catsunited.com

Federation Internationale Féline (FIFe)
FIFe General Secretary
Little Dene, Lenham Heath
Maidstone, Kent ME17 2BS
Great Britain
Tel: +44 1622 850913
http://start.at/fife
E-mail: penbyd@ compuserve.com

The Governing Council of the Cat Fancy (GCCF)
4-6, Penel Orlieu
Bridgwater, Somerset
TA6 3PG
Great Britain
Tel: +44 1278 427575
http://ourworld.compuserve. com/homepages/gccf_cats

The International Cat Association (TICA)
P.O. Box 2684
Harlingen, TX 78551
Tel: 210-428-8046
http://www.tica.org
E-mail: ticaeo@xanadu2.net

Italian Federation of Feline Associations (FIAF)
c/o Rag. Cesare Ghisi
Via Carlo Poma n.20
46100 Mantova
Italy
Tel: +39 376-224600
http://www.zero.it/fiaf
E-mail: fiaf@mynet.it

The Traditional Cat Association (TCA)
10340 Live Oak Lane
Penn Valley, CA 95946
http://www.tcainc.org

Recommended Reading

*Cat Behavior and Training:
Veterinary Advice for Owners*
Edited by Drs. Lowell
Ackerman, Gary Landsberg,
and Wayne Hunthausen
TFH Publishing, Inc., 1996

Cat Love
Pam Johnson
Storey Publishing, 1990

*Cat Owner's Home Veterinary
Handook*
Delbert G. Carlson, D.V.M.,
and James M. Giffin, M.D.
Howell Book House, 1995

*The Cat's Mind: Understanding
Your Cat's Behavior*
Bruce Fogle, D.V.M.,
M.R.C.V.S.
Macmillan Publishing Co.,
1992

The Cornell Book of Cats
2nd edition
Edited by Mordecai Siegal
Villard, 1997

*The Domestic Cat: The Biology
of Its Behaviour*
Edited by Dennis C. Turner
and Patrick Bateson
Cambridge University Press,
1988

The Encyclopedia of the Cat
Bruce Fogle, D.V.M.
DK Publishing, 1997

Genetics for Cat Breeders
3rd edition
Roy Robinson
Pergamon Press, Ltd., 1991

*Help! The Quick Guide to First
Aid for Your Cat*
Michelle Bamberger, D.V.M.
Howell Book House, 1995

Is Your Cat Crazy?
John Wright, Ph.D., and
Judi Wright Lashnits
Macmillan Publishing Co.,
1994

The Loss of a Pet
Wallie Sife, Ph.D.
Howell Book House, 1993

Manual of Feline Behavior
Valerie O'Farrell, Ph.D.,
and Peter Neville
British Small Animal
Veterinary Association, 1994

*Medical, Genetic & Behavioral
Aspects of Purebred Cats*
Edited by Ross Clark, D.V.M.
Forum Publications, Inc.,
1992

Pet Emergency First Aid for Cats
(video)
Apogee Entertainment,
1998

Pet First Aid: Cats and Dogs
Bobbie Mammato, D.V.M.,
M.P.H.
Mosby, 1997

Pet Loss
Herbert Nieburg, Ph.D.,
and Arlene Fischer
Harper and Row, 1982

When Your Pet Dies
Christine Adamec
Berkeley Books, 1996

Why Does My Cat. . . ?
Sarah Heath
Souvenir Press, 1993

Resources

Alley Cat Allies
A national feral cat network that lobbies for the rights and welfare of feral cats, sponsors educational programs, and provides support information for anyone interested in rescuing feral cats or maintaining feral cat colonies.
http://www.alleycat.org

The American Animal Hospital Association's "Your Link for Healthy Pets"
Up-to-date information on behavior, nutrition, and common health problems, and a nice list of recommended reading.
12575 W. Bayaud Avenue
Lakewood, CO 80228
Tel: 800-883-6301
http://www.healthypet.com
E-mail: aaha@aol.com

American Association of Feline Practitioners
2701 San Pedro NE, Suite 7
Albuquerque, NM 87110
Tel: 505-888-2424
http://www.avma.org/aafp

The American Veterinary Medical Association's "Web Page on Animal Health"
Information on feline health, buying a cat, pet loss and grief, safety issues, and much more.
1931 N. Meacham Road
Suite 100
Schaumburg, IL 60173
Tel: 800-248-2862
http://www.avma.org/care4pets

Cat Fanciers Web Site
An excellent jumping-off site for collecting information about cat registries, breeds, and a host of other topics.
http://www.fanciers.com

Cats! Wild to Mild
Produced by the Natural History Museum of Los Angeles County. One of the best cat-related sites on the Web. Includes lots of information on exotic cats.
http://www.lam.mus.ca.us/cats

Cornell Feline Health Center
Information on feline care and health issues from the world's premier center devoted exclusively to the health and welfare of cats everywhere.
Cornell University College of Veterinary Medicine
Ithaca, NY 14853-6401
Tel: 607-253-3414
http://web.vet.cornell.edu/public/fhc

The Delta Society
Publishes the Nationwide Pet Bereavement Directory with names of support groups and counselors throughout the United States. Also offers a certification program for animal-assisted therapy through Pet Partners.
289 Perimeter Road East
Renton, WA 98055-1329
Tel: 425-226-7357
http://www.deltasociety.org
E-mail: deltasociety@cis.compuserve.com

The Humane Society of the United States
An organization devoted to promoting animal welfare and to providing quality adoption services and veterinary care for unwanted animals. Offices throughout the United States. Their Web site feature "Ask the Pet Vet" provides answers to your health and pet care questions from a licensed veterinarian.
National Headquarters
2100 L Street, NW
Washington, DC 20037
Tel: 202-452-1100
http://www.hsus.org

National Association of Professional Pet Sitters (NAPPS)
Maintains a hotline for pet sitter referrals throughout the United States.
1030 15th Street, NW
Suite 870
Washington, DC 20005
Tel: 800-296-PETS
http://www.petsitters.org

NetVet Veterinary Resources and the Electronic Zoo
Veterinary and animal-related resources on the Web—a real gold mine of information.
http://www.avma.org/netvet

The American Society for the Prevention of Cruelty to Animals

Since 1866, the American Society for the Prevention of Cruelty to Animals has been committed to alleviating pain, fear, and suffering in all animals. Founded by Henry Bergh, the ASPCA is the oldest humane organization in America, and one of the largest nonprofit animal welfare groups in the world. With offices in New York, California, Illinois, and Washington, D.C., the ASPCA encourages respect for all life and offers a variety of hands-on programs designed to improve the condition of animals.

Adoptions and Animal Placement Finds suitable homes for animals that have been relinquished by their owners, rescued, or abused. The Society's policy is to spay or neuter all animals available for adoption in order to control pet overpopulation.

Bergh Memorial Animal Hospital Offers complete medical, surgical, radiographic, clinical laboratory, and biopsy services for all domestic pets. The goal is to provide excellent veterinary care at the most reasonable cost possible.

Companion Animal Services Provides training and behavior information about cats and dogs. The department offers obedience classes, operates animal behavior and counseling help lines, and provides literature and interviews on responsible pet ownership.

Consumer Products Develops positive commercial and promotional projects that help fund and create awareness for animal welfare programs.

Government Affairs Promotes and defends laws that protect the health and well-being of animals. A legislative alert program informs the public about issues affecting animals and how to contact their representatives to take appropriate action.

Humane Education Extend the Web, the ASPCA's humane education program, helps educators incorporate humane themes into the classroom through the distribution of materials, workshops, and educational forums. It is currently being applied in more than 6,000 schools.

Humane Law Enforcement Special ASPCA agents and investigators respond to more than 4,000 cases each year. Along with rescuing hundreds of abused and neglected animals, they have been responsible for crackdowns on dogfighting and cockfighting.

National Animal Poison Control Center NAPCC is the only poison control center for animals in North America. Through a 24-hour emergency telephone hotline, veterinary toxicologists provide rapid expert advice about chemicals, products, or plants toxic to animals.

National Shelter Outreach Fosters a network of communication among humane societies to address the needs of animal shelters and the local communities. The ASPCA is dedicated to promoting excellence in local shelters and assisting in the development of programs for the protection of animals at the grass-roots level.

ASPCA national headquarters are located at 424 East 92nd Street, New York, NY 10128. To learn more about these and the many other valuable programs the ASPCA provides, or how to become a member of the ASPCA, please call 212-876-7700.

Please visit us on the Web at http://www.aspca.org.

Acknowledgments

I have been blessed to spend my allotted years helping cats and the people who love them, and it has been my good fortune to be guided by many wise teachers. My mother and late father deserve my greatest appreciation, for without their encouragement and their fondness for cats, not a word of this book would have been put to paper. I owe a special debt of gratitude to my wife, Anita, the bride of my youth and the heart of my family; I am thankful for her support and for her contribution of the bulk of the book's breed entries. I also wish to acknowledge the Creator of the wonderful little creatures that have held my fascination and affection since childhood.

I extend special thanks to series editor Miriam Harris, who tirelessly guided this project to fruition. I am also grateful to project editor Lisa Leventer, a fellow cat-lover and my close partner at Chanticleer, for her enthusiasm and invaluable help.

I thank Andrew Stewart and the staff of Chanticleer Press for producing such an outstanding book. Editor-in-chief Amy Hughes provided essential guidance and encouragement. Managing editor George Scott's unfailingly sound judgment, good humor, and generous moral support were invaluable. Melanie Falick, Ann ffolliott, Anne O'Connor, Micaela Porta, Alison Rooney, and John Tarkov lent their considerable editorial expertise to reviewing, revising, and refining the text. Assistant editor Elizabeth Wright provided boundless editorial support. Virginia Beck, associate editor Michelle Bredeson, Sarah Burns, and Kate Jacobs assisted with copyediting and proofreading. Intern Morgan Topman offered research assistance. Janet Mazefsky created the index.

With photo director Zan Carter's guidance and support, photo editor Ruth Jeyaveeran sifted through thousands of photographs in her search for the engaging images that contribute so much to the guide. Photo research assistance came from Christine Heslin and Robin Sand.

Permissions manager Alyssa Sachar facilitated the acquisition of photographs and ensured the accuracy of all credits. Leslie Fink, Meg Kuhta, and Jennifer McClanaghan helped sort and traffic photographs.

Art director Drew Stevens led a team of talented designers—Kirsten Berger, Brian Boyce, Anthony Liptak, Vincent Mejia, Virginia Pope, and Bernadette Vibar—in the process of creating a guide that is both beautiful and useful. Holly Kowitt designed the icons for the breeds section. Jeanclaire Bridgers drew the cat breed body shapes. Illustrators John Yesko and Todd Zalewski created the anatomy and first aid drawings, respectively.

Director of production Alicia Mills and production manager Philip Pfeifer saw the book through the complicated production and printing processes. Interns Megan Lombardo and Morgan Topman assisted them.

Jacque Lynn Schultz, director of special projects for the animal sciences division of the ASPCA, played a vital role as project consultant, sharing her expertise and wisdom to help make this guide both informative and accessible. Judy Thomas consulted on the breed reference guide with additional help from Hilary Helmrich. Information on feline health care was reviewed and amended by both Lila Miller, D.V.M., veterinary advisor and senior director of animal sciences at the ASPCA, and Christine Ann Bellezza, D.V.M., staff veterinarian in the community practice service of Cornell University's College of Veterinary Medicine. Stephen L. Zawistowski, Ph.D., ASPCA senior vice president and science advisor, reviewed the entire manuscript. Many thanks to Roger Caras, president emeritus of the ASPCA, for the Foreword and for his work on behalf of animals everywhere.

Thanks also to Jay Schaefer, Laura Lovett, and Judith Dunham at Chronicle Books for their insightful contributions to the content and design of this volume.

Picture Credits

The credits are listed by page number from left to right, top to bottom.

71b: Jane Burton/Bruce Coleman, Inc.
71c: Jane Burton/Bruce Coleman, Inc.
72a: Chanan Photography
72b: Chanan Photography
72c: Chanan Photography
73a: Jane Burton/Bruce Coleman, Inc.
73b: Jane Burton/Bruce Coleman, Inc.
74a: Norvia Behling
74b: Chanan Photography
74c: Marc Henrie, ASC NUJ
75a: Jane Burton/Bruce Coleman, Inc.
75b: Jane Burton/Bruce Coleman, Inc.
75c: Chanan Photography
75d: Jane Burton/Bruce Coleman, Inc.
75e: Jane Burton/Bruce Coleman, Inc.
76a: Jane Burton/Bruce Coleman, Inc.
76b: Chanan Photography
76c: Tetsu Yamazaki
77a: John Daniels/Bruce Coleman, Inc.
77b: Marc Henrie, ASC NUJ
77c: Larry Allan/Landmark Stock Exchange
78a: Marc Henrie, ASC NUJ
78b: Chanan Photography
78c: Tetsu Yamazaki
79a: Jane Burton/Bruce Coleman, Inc.
79b: Pet Profiles-Isabelle Francais
80–81: Jane Burton/Bruce Coleman, Inc.
80a: Chanan Photography
80b: Marc Henrie, ASC NUJ
80c: Jeanne White/Photo Researchers, Inc.
80d: Chanan Photography
81a: Chanan Photography
81b: Marc Henrie, ASC NUJ
81c: Hans Reinhard/Bruce Coleman, Inc.
81d: Jacob Mosser III/Positive Images
83: Tetsu Yamazaki

84: Tetsu Yamazaki
85: Pet Profiles-Isabelle Francais
86: Pet Profiles-Isabelle Francais
87a: Chanan Photography
87b: Marc Henrie, ASC NUJ
88a: Chanan Photography
88b: Chanan Photography
89: Tetsu Yamazaki
90: Chanan Photography
91: Keith Kimberlin
92: Chanan Photography
93: Chanan Photography
94a: Chanan Photography
94b: Chanan Photography
95: Tetsu Yamazaki
96: Chanan Photography
97a: John Daniels/Bruce Coleman, Inc.
97b: John Daniels/Bruce Coleman, Inc.
98a: John Daniels/Bruce Coleman, Inc.
98b: Chanan Photography
99: Chanan Photography
100: Donna J. Coss
101: Tetsu Yamazaki
102–103: Chanan Photography
102a: Marc Henrie, ASC NUJ
103a: Tetsu Yamazaki
104–105: Chanan Photography
105a: Chanan Photography
106: Chanan Photography
107: Axel/Jacana/Photo Researchers, Inc.
108a: John Daniels/Bruce Coleman, Inc.
108b: John Daniels/Bruce Coleman, Inc.
109: Chanan Photography
110: Tetsu Yamazaki
111: Ron Kimball
112: Tetsu Yamazaki
113: Chanan Photography
114: Marc Henrie, ASC NUJ
115a: Ron Kimball
115b: Chanan Photography
116: Chanan Photography
117: Pet Profiles-Isabelle Francais

118–119: Chanan Photography
118a: Chanan Photography
119a: Chanan Photography
120: John Daniels/Bruce Coleman, Inc.
121: Tetsu Yamazaki
122: Tetsu Yamazaki
123: Marc Henrie, ASC NUJ
124: Chanan Photography
125a: Chanan Photography
125b: Chanan Photography
126: Chanan Photography
127: Keith Kimberlin
128: Marc Henrie, ASC NUJ
129a: Marc Henrie, ASC NUJ
129b: Marc Henrie, ASC NUJ
130–131: Chanan Photography
131b: Chanan Photography
132–133: Tetsu Yamazaki
132a: Chanan Photography
133a: Chanan Photography
134: Chanan Photography
135: Chanan Photography
136–137: Tetsu Yamazaki
136a: Tetsu Yamazaki
137a: Tetsu Yamazaki
138–139: Chanan Photography
138a: Chanan Photography
139a: Chanan Photography
140: Tetsu Yamazaki
141a: Marc Henrie, ASC NUJ
141b: Tetsu Yamazaki
142: John Daniels/Bruce Coleman, Inc.
143a: Chanan Photography
143b: Chanan Photography
144: Chanan Photography
145: Scott McKiernan/Zuma
146a: Chanan Photography
146b: Chanan Photography
147: Chanan Photography
148: Chanan Photography
149: Tetsu Yamazaki
150a: Chanan Photography
150b: Pet Profiles-Isabelle Francais
151: Chanan Photography
152a: Tetsu Yamazaki
152b: Chanan Photography
153: Chanan Photography
154–55: Tetsu Yamazaki

154a: Chanan Photography
155: Marc Henrie, ASC NUJ
156: Tetsu Yamazaki
157: Tetsu Yamazaki
158–159: Marc Henrie, ASC NUJ
158a: Chanan Photography
159a: Chanan Photography
160a: Marc Henrie, ASC NUJ
160b: Chanan Photography
161: Tetsu Yamazaki
162a: Marc Henrie, ASC NUJ
162b: Chanan Photography
163a: Keith Kimberlin
163b: Axel/Jacana/Photo Researchers, Inc.
164–165: Tetsu Yamazaki
164a: Chanan Photography
165a: Chanan Photography
166: Marc Henrie, ASC NUJ
167: Chanan Photography
168: Chanan Photography
169: Chanan Photography
170: Jane Burton/Bruce Coleman, Inc.
172–173: Erich Lessing/Art Resource
174a: D. Schwimmer/Bruce Coleman, Inc.
174b: Leonard Lee Rue, Jr./Photo Researchers, Inc.
175: Gregory G. Dimijian/Photo Researchers, Inc.
176: Erich Lessing/Art Resource
177a: A. Rodham/Unicorn Stock Photos
177b: Art Resource, NY
178a: Christie's Images
178b: Christie's Images
179a: Archive Photos
179b: Superstock
180–181: Jane Burton/Bruce Coleman, Inc.
184–185: Norvia Behling
184a: Jane Burton/Bruce Coleman, Inc.
186: Tetsu Yamazaki
187: Jacana/Photo Researchers, Inc.
188: Chanan Photography
190: Jane Burton/Bruce Coleman, Inc.

192a: Jane Burton/Bruce Coleman, Inc.
193a: Scott McKiernan/Zuma
193b: Jane Burton/Bruce Coleman, Inc.
197: Jane Burton/Bruce Coleman, Inc.
198a: Chanan Photography
198b: Chanan Photography
199: Superstock
200: Chanan Photography
201: Jane Burton/Bruce Coleman, Inc.
202: Scott McKiernan/Zuma
203a: Bonnie Nance
203b: Jane Burton/Bruce Coleman, Inc.
205: Kim Taylor/Bruce Coleman, Inc.
207: J. P. Varin/Jacana/Photo Researchers, Inc.
208–209: Chanan Photography
210a: Steve Smith/FPG International LLC
210b: Marc Henrie, ASC NUJ
211: Marc Henrie, ASC NUJ
212a: Bob Schwartz/Excalibur
212b: Norvia Behling
213a: Jane Burton/Bruce Coleman, Inc.
213b: Bonnie Nance
214: Jane Burton/Bruce Coleman, Inc.
215: Jane Latta/Photo Researchers, Inc.
216: Steven Holt/Aigrette
217a: Tim Davis/Photo Researchers, Inc.
217b: Marc Henrie, ASC NUJ
218–219: Jane Burton/Bruce Coleman, Inc.
218a: Jane Burton/Bruce Coleman, Inc.
219a: Norvia Behling
220: Steven Holt/Aigrette
221a: Marc Henrie, ASC NUJ
221b: Norvia Behling
222: Jane Burton/Bruce Coleman, Inc.
223a: Norvia Behling
223b: Jane Burton/Bruce Coleman, Inc.

224a: Jane Burton/Bruce Coleman, Inc.
224b: Jane Burton/Bruce Coleman, Inc.
225: Jane Burton/Bruce Coleman, Inc.
226–227: Jane Burton/Bruce Coleman, Inc.
226a: Pet Profiles-Isabelle Francais
227a: Larry Allan
228–229: Jane Burton/Bruce Coleman, Inc.
228: Jane Burton/Bruce Coleman, Inc.
229a: Jane Burton/Bruce Coleman, Inc.
230: Mark C. Burnett/Photo Researchers, Inc.
231: Pet Profiles-Isabelle Francais
232–233: Jane Burton/Bruce Coleman, Inc.
234: Jane Burton/Bruce Coleman, Inc.
235: Jane Burton/Bruce Coleman, Inc.
236: Jane Burton/Bruce Coleman, Inc.
237: Norvia Behling
238: Marc Henrie, ASC NUJ
239: Jane Burton/Bruce Coleman, Inc.
240: Margaret Miller/Photo Researchers, Inc.
241: Mary Bloom; supplies courtesy of Cherrybrook
242: Norvia Behling
243: Jane Burton/Bruce Coleman, Inc.
244a: Mary Bloom
244b: Jane Burton/Bruce Coleman, Inc.
245: Jane Burton/Bruce Coleman, Inc.
246: Norvia Behling
247: Jane Burton/Bruce Coleman, Inc.
248–249: Bonnie Nance
249a: Renee Lynn/Photo Researchers, Inc.
250: Superstock
251: Steven Holt/Aigrette

253: Jane Burton/Bruce Coleman, Inc.
254: Bob Schwartz/Excalibur
255a: Norvia Behling
255b: Norvia Behling
256: Jane Burton/Bruce Coleman, Inc.
257: Jane Burton/Bruce Coleman, Inc.
258: Christine Steimer/OKAPIA/Photo Researchers, Inc.
259: Jane Burton/Bruce Coleman, Inc.
260: Bob Schwartz/Excalibur
261: Bonnie Nance
262–263: Norvia Behling
266: Jane Burton/Bruce Coleman, Inc.
268a: Jane Burton/Bruce Coleman, Inc.
268b: Jane Burton/Bruce Coleman, Inc.
269a: Jane Burton/Bruce Coleman, Inc.
269b: Jane Burton/Bruce Coleman, Inc.
270: Tetsu Yamazaki
271: Norvia Behling
272: Norvia Behling
274: Norvia Behling
275: Norvia Behling
276: Norvia Behling
277: John Daniels/Bruce Coleman, Inc.
278: Jane Burton/Bruce Coleman, Inc.
280–281: Jane Burton/Bruce Coleman, Inc.
282–283: Jane Burton/Bruce Coleman, Inc.
285: Chanan Photography
286: Jane Burton/Bruce Coleman, Inc.
287: Chanan Photography
288: Chanan Photography
289: Jane Burton/Bruce Coleman, Inc.
290–291: Jane Burton/Bruce Coleman, Inc.
292: Norvia Behling
293: Biophoto Associates/Photo Researchers, Inc.

294: Chanan Photography
295: John & Maria Kaprielian/Photo Researchers, Inc.
297: Jane Burton/Bruce Coleman, Inc.
303: Pet Profiles-Isabelle Francais
305: Norvia Behling
306: Chanan Photography
307: John Daniels/Bruce Coleman, Inc.
308–309: Marc Henrie, ASC NUJ
310–311: Jane Burton/Bruce Coleman, Inc.
312a: Jane Burton/Bruce Coleman, Inc.
312b: Jane Burton/Bruce Coleman, Inc.
313: Jane Burton/Bruce Coleman, Inc.
314: Jane Burton/Bruce Coleman, Inc.
315: Jane Burton/Bruce Coleman, Inc.
316: Norvia Behling
326a: Phillip Roullard
327: Suzanne L. & Joseph T. Collins/Photo Researchers, Inc.
329a: Bruce Coleman/Bruce Coleman, Inc.
329b: Alan & Linda Detrick/Photo Researchers, Inc.
329c: Gene Ahrens/Bruce Coleman, Inc.
332–333: Jane Burton/Bruce Coleman, Inc.
334: Jane Burton/Bruce Coleman, Inc.
335: Jane Burton/Bruce Coleman, Inc.
336a: Jane Burton/Bruce Coleman, Inc.
336b: Jane Burton/Bruce Coleman, Inc.
336c: Jane Burton/Bruce Coleman, Inc.
337a: Jane Burton/Bruce Coleman, Inc.
337b: Jane Burton/Bruce Coleman, Inc.

337c: Jane Burton/Bruce Coleman, Inc.
337d: Jane Burton/Bruce Coleman, Inc.
338: Jane Burton/Bruce Coleman, Inc.
339: Jane Burton/Bruce Coleman, Inc.
340a: Jane Burton/Bruce Coleman, Inc.
340b: Jane Burton/Bruce Coleman, Inc.
341a: Jane Burton/Bruce Coleman, Inc.
341b: Jane Burton/Bruce Coleman, Inc.
342: Jane Burton/Bruce Coleman, Inc.
343a: Phillip Roullard
343b: Phillip Roullard
344: Jane Burton/Bruce Coleman, Inc.
345: Pet Profiles-Isabelle Francais
346: Jeanne White/Photo Researchers, Inc.
347: Jane Burton/Bruce Coleman, Inc.
348: Norvia Behling
354: Mary Bloom

Anatomy illustrations (182–83, 189, 190–91, 192, 194–95, 196, 197, 200, 204–05, 206): John Yesko

First aid illustrations (318, 320, 321, 323): Todd Zalewski

Breed body shape illustrations (86–169): Jeanclaire Bridgers

Icons (17, 19, 27–29, 34, 83–169): Holly Kowitt

Index

Cat breed names are in **boldface**, as are the page numbers of each breed's entry in the Reference Guide to Cat Breeds.

Prepared and produced by Chanticleer Press, Inc.

Founder: Paul Steiner
Publisher: Andrew Stewart

Staff for this book
Editor-in-Chief: Amy K. Hughes
Senior Editor: Miriam Harris
Managing Editor: George Scott
Project Editor: Lisa Leventer
Contributing Editors: Melanie Falick, Ann ffolliott,
Anne O'Connor, Micaela Porta, Alison Rooney, John Tarkov
Associate Editor: Michelle Bredeson
Assistant Editor: Elizabeth Wright
Editorial Assistant: Kate Jacobs
Art Director: Drew Stevens
Designers: Kirsten Berger, Brian Boyce,
Anthony Liptak, Vincent Mejia, Bernadette Vibar
Photo Director: Zan Carter
Photo Editor: Ruth Jeyaveeran
Associate Photo Editor: Jennifer McClanaghan
Assistant Photo Editor: Meg Kuhta
Permissions Manager: Alyssa Sachar
Photo Assistant: Leslie Fink
Director of Production: Alicia Mills
Production Manager: Philip Pfeifer
Production Interns: Megan Lombardo, Morgan Topman

Illustrations by Holly Kowitt (icons), Jeanclaire Bridgers
(cat breed body shapes), John Yesko (anatomy),
Todd Zalewski (first aid)

Book design by Virginia Pope

All editorial inquiries should be addressed to
Chanticleer Press
665 Broadway, Suite 1001
New York, NY 10012
www.eNature.com

Copies of this book are available from
Chronicle Books
85 Second Street
San Francisco, CA 94105
800-722-6657
www.chroniclebooks.com